# CURATING AS ETHICS

THINKING THEORY

*Grant Farred, Series Editor*

# Curating as Ethics

--------

JEAN-PAUL MARTINON

THINKING THEORY

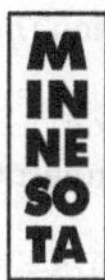

University of Minnesota Press
Minneapolis
London

The University of Minnesota Press gratefully acknowledges financial support for the publication of this series from Cornell University.



Published by the University of Minnesota Press
111 Third Avenue South, Suite 290
Minneapolis, MN 55401-2520
http://www.upress.umn.edu

The University of Minnesota is an equal-opportunity educator and employer.

---

Library of Congress Cataloging-in-Publication Data
Names: Martinon, Jean-Paul, author.
Title: Curating as ethics / Jean-Paul Martinon.
Description: Minneapolis : University of Minnesota Press, [2020] | Includes bibliographical references and index.
Identifiers: LCCN 2019017213 (print) | ISBN 978-1-5179-0864-5 (hc : alk. paper) | ISBN 978-1-5179-0865-2 (pb : alk. paper)
Subjects: LCSH: Ethics. | Curatorship.
Classification: LCC BJ1031 .M3158 2020 (print) | DDC 170—dc23
LC record available at https://lccn.loc.gov/2019017213

UMP LSI

# CONTENTS

## INTRODUCTION

# Excess and More

### Trajectories of Thought

Two distinctive trajectories of thought lead to this book. First, it stems from a long-standing reflection on the curatorial,[1] which today can only make one stark observation: curating is now a practice without any form of institutional anchoring. As is well known,[2] it has acquired this freedom with the advent of the content curator. The term *content curator* refers to anyone who selects, adds, and arranges relevant content on an Internet site. A content curator differs from a gallery or museum curator in at least two ways. First, what they curate knows no limit—basically anything tradable, shareable, or distributable. Gone is the unique artwork with a distinctive aura; in comes copyable pixels or samples in gigabyte form. This endless reproducibility frees curating from the shackles of professionalism and know-how imposed until now by art colleges and museums. This digital work is also no longer dependent on institutional frameworks but on success or profit margins. While the old-school curator selects artists or artworks following specific institutional narratives (e.g., aesthetic, historical, theoretical, political), the content curator selects images, videos, or sounds mainly to pique the interest of a target audience, and expects a quasi-immediate return (financial, viewer numbers). Gone are the art curators with an argument, and in come the aggregator curators[3] with nothing in their hands except the building of hubs around which their targeted users can access and digest their contents without having to step outside, visit a gallery, or engage with another human being. Curating has indeed lost a lot of baggage. It is free, and for good or bad, everyone now curates irrespective of any institutional anchoring.

The advent of the content curator and the surreal expansion of the activity of curating outside of the confines of museums and galleries cannot be ignored. This rapid change calls for a radically different approach to the practice itself. It needs to take into consideration a plethora of new sources, gestures, and outcomes that were previously unthinkable in the old world of curation, with its hackneyed formulations of relationality or participation. This is what leads me now to define curating not simply as the activity of exhibiting culture but also, above all, as the activity of engaging, selecting, arranging, critically evaluating, and sharing culture in general.[4] As this definition clearly emphasizes, the focus on the visual—this old ocularcentric despotic trope of Western culture—is gone. Curating today includes online curating, which is predominantly visual, but it also includes other fields less driven by the visual, like perfumery or catering. With such a wide remit, the visual, and the visual arts above all, cease to be central to the articulation of curating. The practice finally becomes detached, not only from that Enlightenment metaphysical referent ("art") but also from the artificial constraints of art discourses. Curators operate in all spheres of life, and this extraordinarily challenging diversity is precisely what needs to be thought through.

There are a number of ways this thinking can happen. If one were to focus on content curating alone, then one would need to analyze a whole range of online practices. Having no expertise in new media, I can only leave this area of work to experts addressing the radical changes that have taken place in curating since the apparition of the Internet.[5] What I can do instead is to consider this activity of engaging, selecting, arranging, critically evaluating, and sharing culture[6] in broad terms—that is, in a situation that can be applied to both the world of cultural exhibitions and to the more mundane but global activity of organizing and sharing content from around the Web on social media platforms. With such a wide remit, the activity that then needs to be thought through becomes much less driven by the trite particularities of practice, however this is understood. It becomes applicable to a limitless number of different settings, none of which can cohere into a single institutional praxis. Performance and impact indicators need to be considered alongside the old communication systems still in place in the art world, such as message, medium, code, and referent. Instant digestibility and shareability also need to be taken in consideration alongside the old model of author and viewer functions. It is this loose, protean, and uncontainable remit that the following arguments attempt to address.

But this is not just a book about curating in a new wide remit. It is above all a book about curating as ethics. As such, the focus is not about the diversification of the practice of curating but about the ethical dimensions of such a wide-ranging activity of global proportions. In this new context, the ethical issue is now this: if there is no more training or schooling to help aspiring curators navigate the muddy waters of right and wrong, if there is no more expertise or professionalism to set, represent, and protect good standards of practice, and if there are no more guilds or syndications to verify, correct, and/or defend these standards, then how can this activity remain in any way ethical? This does not mean that old-fashioned curators are ethical because they are still constrained by institutional parameters. As is well known, many museum curators are known for their unethical behaviors, and this expansion in the practice changes nothing regarding this fact. The problem is rather a much broader one, whereby anyone who curates any form of culture online and/or in noninstitutional remits is faced with making ethical choices that are equally unanchored. The freedom of a global practice inevitably comes with the freedom from any form of ethical directives.[7]

Of course, many curators today attempt to contain and direct their practices ethically. These can be broadly divided into three sorts. First, there are codes of ethics for curators. These are usually put forward by a panel of experts from the old regime (art curators, art historians, museum directors, legal advisors, etc.), and they usually focus on the fine art practice of curating in museums and galleries.[8] Then, over and beyond some social media corporations' plainly lame attempts to impose ethical limits to their platforms, there are also a vast number of tips and instructions on how to curate ethically online.[9] These are generally put forward by new media companies in the hope of vaguely controlling their users' activities. They include suggestions such as "All curators should acknowledge their sources" and "All curators should be cognizant of the Internet ecosystem in order to improve it." Finally, there are also a large number of curators putting forward their own private ethical codes. These range from simple advice on how to curate ethically to exhortations on how to lead a better life.[10] My aim in what follows is not to correct these ethical suggestions, propose new ethical codes or maxims, or question these moral tips put forward by panels of experts or curators.[11] My aim is simply to think through how such a worldwide phenomenon now practiced by millions of people around the world can be understood, outside of any institutional remit, as ethical?

This first trajectory of thought thus leads me to the first key question of this book: in a situation where a practice no longer has any institutional anchorage, can curating this now global phenomenon without expert, guild, syndication, or professionalization of any kind still be ethical, and if yes, how? This is the first of two topics that will be addressed in this book, and my hope is that the unusual structure outlined below—one provided by Martin Heidegger's fourfold—helps us articulate it. But before looking at this uncommon structure, it is necessary to address and clarify the second trajectory of thought that leads to this book: the issue of ethics.

The second path is a reflection on ethical issues. Ethics is usually defined as the process of determining, systematizing, defending, and recommending concepts of right and wrong to an individual or society at large; overall, it means "moral philosophy." This conventional definition of ethics focuses for the most part on examining, for example, the nature of our moral principles (determining which social and/or cultural conventions, norms, emotions, or habits make up a society's ethical standards, for example) and the rightness or wrongness of a society's generic (good practice, duties to follow, or the consequences of bad behavior on others, for example) or specific actions (abortion, infanticide, animal rights, environmental impacts, capital punishment, nuclear war, etc.). Overall, the aim of ethics understood as moral philosophy is to develop and cultivate some kind of rationalist self- or social legislation. The most common example of this kind of ethics with regards to curating is, as mentioned earlier, museum and curators' codes of ethics: short texts that put forward sets of supposedly rational principles that museums and/or curators should follow.

For me, however, there is always one major problem with ethics as moral philosophy. In its endless rationalizations, it never knows what to do with "what exceeds the living present," even though this "excess" plays a crucial role in all ethical predicaments. In order to make sense of this, it is necessary for me to briefly summarize my trajectory in addressing this issue. In a previous book examining how the notion of peace survives after the Rwandan genocide of 1994,[12] I put forward the premise of an ethics whereby death, this phenomenon that veers out of the living present, invisibly structures human moral encounters. In this, I followed Jean-Luc Nancy's idea that it is always finitude that guides ethics.[13] To be ethical is therefore in this context to allow the possibility of one's own demise to thwart the possibility of any violence against the other. With such an inalienable fact turned into a sentry, the hope is that we necessarily incline ourselves toward the living present; we give birth to more—that is, to furthering dialogue and not additional deaths. In this way, by retaining the importance of the finite limits of any encounter, these limits that exceed the living present; we effectively present the other with more than he or she can think, thus keeping both absolute silence and total darkness (death) and absolute light and total rationality (tyranny) at bay.

The outcome of such a vision of ethics is that as long as one is mortal, then ethics is already a given. It requires no adherence to some religious commandment or ethical imperative. It requires no specific knowledge, information, know-how, or opinion. It only requires an ability to judge that as soon as an ethical dilemma emerges, the realization of one's always impending death invariably veers the dilemma toward its resolution instead of its annihilation. Obviously, such a type of ethics could never give the "highest possible peace of mind" of having done right or truthfully. It is a type of ethics that is always ad hoc and extemporaneous to any lifelong held belief or rational maxim. While these characteristics are more or less acceptable, one thing remains problematic: how is one to always retain in our ethical dilemmas this finite horizon? How can this focus on finitude turned into sentry truly guard life over and above its destruction? The only hint I give right at the end of *After "Rwanda"* is that it would be necessary to develop a type of midwifery able to retain and exploit this sentry, thus emphasizing the birth of more—that is, the possibility of dialogue over and above absolute rationality/light-silence/darkness.

It is this midwifery that retains "what exceeds the living present" as a sentry that is developed here with regards to curating. I use the term *midwifery* as a general expression for all the gestures that allow us to point, beyond death, to a "more"—that is, to a new or other life hereto unimaginable. As the chapter "Midwifing" shows, this term is used not simply to refer to women assisting other women in childbirth, but also and above all to anyone who gives birth to more and who therefore provokes a future that defies death, exactly in the same way as when a child is begotten. In the previous sentence, I carefully use the adverb "also" to emphasize that the work and labor of women is not here undermined or sidelined but rather expanded to encompass the birth of both bodies and spirits, as well as the delivery of more: the genesis of a new dialogue or a new dawn. The second path in this trajectory of thought thus leads to another key question in this book: can there be a type of ethics that negotiates, like a midwife, the treacherous waters of the birth of the new in order to keep death and everything that stands for it at bay? Heidegger's fourfold is here again, I hope, what helps to address this issue.

So why is Heidegger's fourfold useful in articulating an ethics understood not as a set of moral principles destined to regulate a global activity but as an ethical midwifery for curators birthing the new in their arrangements of culture in general?

## Heidegger's Fourfold

As intimated in the two trajectories of thought explored above, the structure of this book is inspired by what Martin Heidegger calls *das Geviert*, "the fourfold."[14] It is what brings together and structures the twin topics addressed here: curating and ethics. I develop in the following pages my own idiosyncratic reading of Heidegger's four dimensions, at times closely reading his work (cf. "Mortals," "Gods," "Beckoning," and "Strife")[15] and at times evading it altogether (in nearly all the other chapters). My aim with this unruly approach to Heidegger's complex idea is twofold. First, and most simply, I want to evade at all cost the kind of Heideggerianism that reads the fourfold with the only aim to yet again explain it (often erroneously), judge it (unnecessarily), render us more religious (without evidence), or discard it (without understanding it) and instead to literally put it to work.[16] In doing so, there is no other choice but to betray Heidegger—not in order to annoy Heideggerians but in order to push the remarkable logic of the fourfold further. This does not mean that Heidegger's fourfold is incomplete or that it needs further explanations or extrapolations. The idea is simply to show that Heidegger's fourfold can be rethought and perhaps reactivated outside of his vocabulary in order to make it resonate differently.

Second, and more important, I want to evade the whole discourse on

Heidegger and ethics. The idea that Heidegger might have been interested in ethics is usually considered foolish. As is well known, Heidegger subordinated ethics to ontology.[17] For him, ethics basically comes afterward, once the question of being is addressed. His notions of responsibility, care, solicitude, empathy, and more generally "being-with" are primarily ontological and therefore enter the ethical register with difficulty. Furthermore, if one takes into consideration his affiliation with National Socialism, the idea that his work might have anything to do with ethics is equally senseless. The import of his work is that of a supposedly triumphant sovereign Being who has no interest in the other, the weak, or the oppressed because It is entirely absorbed in thinking Itself as the true ethos. There are already a few remarkable publications that attempt to go against these facile arguments.[18] Here I try instead to depart from Heidegger's "turning" *(Kehre)* and therefore from what I see as an ethically accentuated polylogical structure, called the fourfold, that no longer rests on either a sovereign Being or on same–other economies.[19] With this fractured and always interrelated polylogicality that is the fourfold, ethics no longer stands for the ground of Being alone; it becomes instead, as I endeavor to show in the following chapters, a midwifery—that is, an ethical practice that no longer abides in any form of epochal closure.

Free from the shackles of Heideggerianism, in this book I furthermore attempt to read Heidegger's fourfold by traversing it with seemingly unacceptable alien inputs (e.g., Spinoza, Meillassoux, Levinas). My hope with these traversal readings is that the betrayal of Heidegger's fourfold will feel less violent and more inventive, thus remaining more in tune with the actual spirit of research and investigation that characterizes so much of Heidegger's work. After all, is philosophy not an attempt to recast what appears to be already certain and acquired? Is philosophy not the task of inventing new concepts for our times not out of nowhere, but precisely from the premise of a particular lineage of thought? The difficult balance between respecting someone's ideas—in this case Heidegger's fourfold—and challenging them without altogether falsifying them is precisely what I aim to do in the following pages. Doubtless most Heideggerians will disagree with me, but I hope that some will also see that Heidegger's logic for the fourfold deserves to be pushed further in order to reveal not only its potential for philosophy but also, and above all, its power to rethink, from a completely different perspective, our own contemporary ethical predicaments.

There is no space here to present an account of the fourfold as Heidegger originally intended it. A number of well-known scholars have already done a remarkable job of analyzing it, and I can only encourage readers interested in making sense of *das Geviert* within Heidegger's corpus to read Andrew J. Mitchell's remarkably detailed book on this topic or Jean-François Mattéi and Frank Darwiche's books on Heidegger and Hölderlin.[20] Besides these key references, most of my own reading of Heidegger follows Reiner Schürmann's own insightful and path-breaking reading of the fourfold,[21] which does not focus exclusively on "things" and how they can be apprehended anew by the fourfold but rather on the way it puts forward a polylogical structure that literally defies all previous monologic takes on beings and their ethical predicaments. This specific Schürmannian reading of Heidegger's fourfold originally started in a few articles on the fourfold.[22] These articles give a more Heideggerian account of the fourfold than the one expressed here. I hope the reader—and the Heideggerian reader particularly—will forgive me for directing them to these as a way of verifying a less unruly take on the late Heidegger's work.

In the short amount of space allocated in this Introduction, the only thing I can do is to highlight the reasons why I think Heidegger's fourfold needs to be taken seriously to understand the overall question structuring this book: can there be a type of ethics for a global contemporary practice such as curating that negotiates, like a midwife, the treacherous waters of the birth of the new in order to keep death and everything that stands for it at bay? Heidegger's fourfold helps to address this overall question because it points in a polylogical way toward a type of ethics that both retains death as a sentry (mortals) and playfully remains conjectural, not unlike a midwife, of "what exceeds the living present" (gods). How so?

Out of me[23] but also with me, earth and sky—the event of being.[24] Away from but entirely dependent on this event are the gods: according to Heidegger, this "is" the fourfold. The event is that of a mortal arising with earth and sky, a "dwelling"[25] intruded on by reliant but unruly gods. The four folds (mortals, earth, sky, gods) are not proper physical, metaphysical, or religious compass points. They have no proper equivalent in the world (or in another) because they stand, however difficult this is to imagine, for the very event of time-space. The four participate in and as this event; they take part in the fact that I "am" here, mortal, with earth and sky, invariably unseated by gods.[26] There would be no being, no other,[27] and no world without this four-dimensional[28] quasi-structure that utterly defies the entire arsenal of archic and telic representations and their inevitable epochal stampings, thus also fracturing all singular points of view, exclusive vistas, and uniform narratives. We need to think of ourselves not just as one or two, but as four. The fourfold is indeed not just about mortals[29] or about things; it is also, and above all, about the event of time-space that arises out of earth, sky, and gods.[30] Out of me, as one dimension of the fourfold, and out of gods, earth, and sky, the event of time-space arises as dwelling.

But what is the point of focusing on the fourfold? The fourfold makes us aware of the conditions that make events possible, including all curatorial events. Since it constitutes the very advent of time-space, the fourfold is effectively the prerequisite for any form of happenstance. As James Edward says: "Each of the four is . . . intended to put in someone's mind the particular conditions that make possible . . . the life that brought to presence the actual thing . . . before us."[31] So for example, my existence is conditioned by a number of factors: the ground out of which humanity grew, the sky into and against which it elevates itself and allows me to breathe and work, my parents who made me mortal, and the divinities—this dimension intrinsic to mortals that, as I shall demonstrate, structure and radically disturb my living present. It would be wrong to think that this conditionality is a causality. Because the fourfold creates the event of time-space, this conditionality is relative to the always accidental occurrence of any given spatial and temporal configuration engaging mortals/gods surging with earth into and against the sky.

Three of Heidegger's four dimensions (mortals, earth, sky) are somewhat self-evident: "Earth is the serving bearer. . . . The sky is the vaulting path of the sun. . . . The mortals are the human beings."[32] I explore these first three dimensions in "Mortals," "Earths," and "Skies," albeit also transforming them in order to give them a different resonance (especially in the no doubt controversial idea of pluralizing the first two). The burning question is always the one concerning the gods. What is one to make of the last dimension of Heidegger's fourfold: the gods *(Götter)*? Although I explore this crucial dimension in "Gods," "Beckoning," and

"Obsession," in some instances closely reading Heidegger's arguments, I feel I ought to introduce it here again, this time with a non-Heideggerian vocabulary in order to avoid as much as possible what can only be inevitable misunderstandings.

## Mortals Also Happen to Be Gods

The only way to make sense of the gods outside of any theological or religious contexts is to think of them as an inescapable dimension of mortals.[33] Mortals basically also happen to be gods. To say this does not imply that mortals are somehow also immortal or that they are superhuman beings or spirits that need to be worshipped, looked up to, or adored in order to secure salvation or redemption. The nomination *gods* is used here most simply as another word for *mortals*—that is, for finite beings and nothing else. The entire book does not deviate from this inalienable finitude. The reason the word *gods* is used here interchangeably with *mortals* is simply because there is effectively something about finitude that is not quite right, and this is precisely why the juxtaposition or interchangeability works. How is one to characterize this, once again, outside of any theological or religious contexts?[34]

Let me begin by saying that the main gist of this nontheist, nondeist, nontheological, and nonreligious suggestion that mortals also happen to be gods is that the suggestion itself cannot be dissected, analyzed, approved, or disproved. This does not immediately invalidate the argument or relegate the issue to the metaphysical realm, and therefore to some nebulous or quaint transcendental philosophy that, on all accounts, has already been dumped in the dustbin of history. To say that mortals also happen to be gods is simply to recognize that, beyond their bound finitude, mortals' thought always follows a certain structure of faith, that this structure makes of them gods, and that this is not something that can easily be axed as true or false. As I hope the chapters "Mortals," "Gods," "Beckoning," and "Obsession" show, this introductory reference to thought does not relegate the issue of mortals/gods to the realm of the mind alone. Thought is here understood not as the intellect alone but rather as the heart and the demand itself. As such, thought is not something that can be quickly and efficiently identified; it is an event that takes place at the limit, marks the limit, is itself the limit. Thought is effectively a bodily event at the edge of finitude, the breaking through of the form of the sensible as sense, a breaking through that never reaches a breaking point—"a final thought," for example. Through thought, then, mortals exceed themselves beyond death throughout their lives, and this is why, as I try to show throughout this book, they also happen to be gods.

The crucial thing about this excess is therefore the never-ceasing supplementary process that always occurs in thought. Thought cannot not exceed itself. It cannot not think the maximum it is able to think. It always exceeds even the highest thought conceivable, managing in the process to exceed its own power to think. Jean-Luc Nancy talks about this excess in a quick commentary on Saint Anselm's famous text, *The Proslogion*, in *Dis-enclosure*. Focusing exclusively on thought, he writes, "Thinking . . . can think—indeed, cannot not think—that it thinks something in excess over itself. It penetrates the impenetrable, or rather is penetrated by it."[35] This has nothing to do with a banal transcendental movement, a going beyond or a prayer that no reason could attest to. As an eminently concrete thinker, Nancy is quick to highlight that his interest in Anselm's effort is only to catch the way thought takes place. Thought is not just finite; it is marked by an extraordinary unconditionality that prevents it from simply delimiting itself as a simple assemblage of inherited and repeatable ideas. This radical unconditionality that occurs in thought is again what makes mortals gods. Mortals unconditionally always open up the future while being caught up in their finite condition. They are gods precisely because of this ordeal of thought that disturbs or disrupts the shackles of mortality, even if they are the most stringent of atheists or agnostics.[36]

Inevitably, the questions now beckon: why give this ability to exceed thought the name "gods"? Why bother with a denomination that always refers to what is superior to mortals? Do we really need this old reference to characterize the an-archic or an-telic structures of thought? Should we not in our materialist, pragmatic, consumerist, and scientific world, evade a type of vocabulary that is so stained with fratricides and genocides? Should we not be able by now to grasp the excess that caries thought out of itself without automatically having recourse to the idea of god? Can we not be mortals without necessarily assuming being also gods sparking a beyond that never ceases to withdraw itself? And finally, should we not be able by now to refer to this desire beyond need without also referring to some imagined phantasm? I accumulate here the questions to emphasize that I am aware that using the word *gods* to reference this excess of thought is not just problematic but also effectively a scandal for thought—what is radically unacceptable in the face of humanity's sovereign rationality as well as of humanity's unrelenting violence, cruelty, and destructiveness. How can we be gods in this rational and violent hegemony? Yet a number of fundamental reasons impel me to insist on using the word *gods*, way beyond Heidegger's own articulations.

First, using the word *gods* to qualify mortals' ability to exceed themselves through thought is intended to simply highlight a type of nomination that, for good or bad, exceeds all concepts. After all, this is what the word *god* stands for: a nomination deliberately marked as distinct from any other nomination of concepts and as such is key to expose this excess. It is, as will be explored in the chapter "God," the name of a relation with what knows no return. Thought exceeds itself even if there is no answer coming back. As such, thought always reaches out toward the immemorial or the unhoped for (cf. "Intuiting")—that is, toward what exceeds the living present and knows no predetermined return. It is this reaching out, this excess, that indeed constitutes if not the faith that structures thought then at least its scandal. Reason cannot do without this scandal. It structures thought even if it adheres to the most stringent of formal or mathematical logic: there will always be the possibility of its absolute disruption. To think otherwise is nothing short of fascism. It is indeed to revert to the most worrisome of logics, the ones that precisely lead to inalienable truths, the imposition of the same, the rejection of the other, and so on. Using the word *gods* for "mortals" is therefore first and foremost to emphasize the importance of evading the dictatorship of concepts and the impossibility of doing away with either faith or scandal.

Second, but more important, using the word *gods* is an attempt to destabilize the monopoly held by our own two contemporary gods: the God of the Abrahamic tradition and the God of money.[37] Whether one obeys the God of monotheist religions or the God of capital, one is always obeying a tautology: God equals God or money equals money (the latter not in an equivalence among currencies, but within currencies, i.e., one dollar equals one dollar).[38] These two tautologies rule our contemporary lives because they are the only absolute values superseding and regulating all others.[39] They stand for the only language referents able to mediate and regulate all other exchanges in language. From procreation to death and from inorganic events to natural disasters,[40] God or money regulates the world with two types of return: in another life (the God of religion) or in this life (money). There are no other options, but these sovereign traffics regulating the lives of both religious and secular folk. How can one break such indomitable twofold sovereignty? By precisely bringing the referent *god* down to the level of mortals—that is, by precipitating an absolute value to the level of finitude. In doing so, the aim is to encourage mankind to think of returns other than those provided by God and/or money. This aim will not break the monopoly of the two absolute tautologies ruling our lives, but it will at least raise the question of their omnipresence. We are gods because we are the only absolute values worth considering.

Third, using the word *gods* to indicate "mortals" is also a way of rejecting any form of hierarchy, including that put forward by organized religion with god(s) above and mortals below. To qualify mortals as gods is not to determine anything to have a supernatural structure but rather to precisely disqualify the very possibility of such a structure. It is to precipitate the idea of the divine down to the level of mortals without hierarchy. In doing so, I am not elevating mortals to a special status. I am not unconsciously replicating here Psalm 82:6 and John 10:34 in which local magistrates, judges, and other people who held positions of authority were suddenly qualified of "gods." As the focus on thought above shows, I hope, no mortal is here given any authority over other human beings; no one is qualified as a demigod, demiurge, or demon, and no one is assumed to derive power and authority from God Himself. To say that mortals also happen to be gods is on the contrary to destabilize all forms of sovereignty and highlight, through the excess of thought, an absolute equality trumping all equalities of concepts. Mortals also happen to be gods, and this whomever they are.

Fourth, to say that mortals also happen to be gods is to remove from the determination "gods" any kind of moral value. Mortals are not always sinful, and gods are not necessarily exempt from sin; the bad does not reside in mortals and the good in gods. As the chapters in the last section of this book will, I hope, testify, the good is conceived precisely in the same vein as Nancy's reading of Anselm. If there is a desire to exceed thought, then this desire cannot be structured by an economic return whereby whoever thinks over and above him- or herself expects a payback or reward. This is, on the contrary, a desire for what is beyond satisfaction and as such cannot be entered into the category of need—neither as a mean nor as an end, let alone as a prayer in the conventional sense of this term. As such, if mortals recognize their godly selves, then their recognition is a desire without end; it is an excess that can only exceed itself over and beyond any form of satisfaction; it is a desire for a future in which they no longer matter (cf. "Conclusion"). In this way, free of any form of standard or right, free of the constraints of "good intentions" and "good consciences," mortals/gods expose, as we will see, the good only when they exceed themselves beyond what the value "good" stands for today: an excess, a good that is nothing other than what they themselves are.

Finally, to think mortals as gods is to bring finitude and midwifery together. Mortals are finite. They have death as their ethical sentry. But they are also gods. Godly, they are more than just mortal rational beings; they also free the possible for the future (cf. "Deeds and Ends"). As such, they operate from a double premise that allow them not only to retain in their ethical judgments the sentry that is death, but also to midwife what is immemorial or unhoped for—a time, for example, when they (and their ethical dilemmas) no longer matter. This midwifery reinforces death as sentry. As I will explore in detail in the chapters that follow, mortals also happen to be gods because they can not only regulate their world with rationality and a mortal sentry but can also do so by midwifing a time in which the "good" can still take place (cf. "Conclusion"). In other words, mortals are not just finite rational animals securing—well or badly—a better world for all. They are also, and importantly, able to playfully let their godly selves midwife what can never be secured by any form of assurance or guarantee.

These are some of the reasons for justifying the way I interpret two of the four dimensions of Heidegger's fourfold. As I said before, such polylogicality requires us to think in more than one (being, becoming, for example) or two dimensions (same/other, for example). Living beings are complex. Their ethics can no longer rest on a utilitarian accounting weighing the good and the bad and/or meting out responsibilities and exonerations for individuals understood as economic rational mortal units. We need a way of approaching the ethical dilemmas of our world that is in tune with the way we operate as fourfolding finite beings able to open up the future like the gods we are. The fourfold is indeed our new ethical constellation. It allows us—all of us, including curators and those shunning this much maligned practice—to midwife, with death as a sentry, a time in which we will no longer matter. It is by recognizing this polylogicality, this play among mortals, earths, and skies, that we can exceed, as gods, our capacity to think, thus midwifing a new world—a new fourfold hereto unimaginable.

## Curating Philosophy

This book also puts forward a specific approach to philosophy. To many, this approach will be objectionable because it does not follow the conventional structure of philosophical theses and treaties. Although long ago many past authors have brilliantly questioned and successfully disrupted these conventional structures, the conservative ideology that theses need to follow specific criteria stubbornly maintains its status quo. What will be particularly annoying to traditional *doxa* is that the authors' texts put forward in the following pages are read outside of their traditions; for example, Spinoza is read outside of Spinozism, and Heidegger is read obliquely in relation to Heideggerian studies. But this is not all. What will no doubt infuriate some readers is that philosophy is not presented as a textual analysis proving past or contemporary authors right or wrong. Instead, I use it in order to push the argument in a completely new direction. For example, the most antitranscendentalist philosopher imaginable, Quentin Meillassoux, is placed in dialogue with the least materialist thinker conceivable, Emmanuel Levinas. The aim of such seemingly unacceptable juxtapositions is not to provoke readers gratuitously or deliberately misread authors. The aim is simply to give birth to a different thought all in the belief that philosophy would go much further if it stopped its endless game of textual buggery[41] and embraced its varied richness together.

This is what leads me to think up what I call here curating philosophy. Again, the idea of such juxtaposition will doubtless send shivers down the spine of a number of readers. If curating is an indeterminable activity with diverse disciplinary heritages and little scholarly import, then philosophy must stay well clear of it. Inversely, philosophy is too dry, textual, and abstract for curating, so it must therefore remain confined to what curators know best: the visual and this last meaningless refuge of the philistine, "practice." I have little time for such reactionary pseudo- or postdisciplinary distinctions. What matters above all for me is to come up with a way of addressing the issues that is adequate to the topic explored, a way whereby form and content somehow match each other, if this is possible. Because curating now permeates the lives of many people around the world, curating thus needs a new mode of thinking adequate to its vast undertaking. This is what curating philosophy aims to achieve. However, the aim was not to patch together two distinct fields (art history and philosophy, for example) and hope for the best, but to think them through one another. Curating here helps philosophy, and vice versa. The outcome of such a double activity is a type of thought that hopes to continue the long work of disrupting institutional and disciplinary structures and apparatuses, these ideological falsities that ruin everything, including thought itself, and to begin thinking again.

The main aspect of this new type of thought is that it takes both curating and philosophy at its task. On the one hand it takes the textual fabric of philosophy and its context seriously, not as theorizations of art, curating, or visual culture but for its potential to articulate life overall and contemporary experience more specifically. On the other hand, it takes the cultural elements explored here equally seriously, not as illustrations for philosophical arguments but for their intrinsic cultural characteristics (as demonstrated, for example, in "Images"). The outcome of such a twofold attempt is a type of thought that is characterized by an essential incompletion. This is taken not in a negative sense (e.g., as a thesis that lacks something or fails to achieve something substantial) but rather in a way that positively matches what happens in life. As such, this sense of incompletion is taken in the way Friedrich and August Schlegel think of the fragment. As Philippe Lacoue-Labarthe and Jean-Luc Nancy say in a commentary on their work, "the [Schlegel] fragment designates a presentation that does not pretend to be exhaustive and that corresponds to the no doubt properly modern idea that the incomplete can, and even must, be published (or to the idea that what is published is never complete)."[42] The following chapters adhere to this idea that incompletion is not a call for completion but instead is proof of the essential characteristic of both life and thought.

This, however, does not mean that because it is incomplete it is necessarily formless. Curating is famous for an ordered appearance that on quick inspection is always flawed. Exhibitions always give the impression of cohesion when in fact what is exhibited is often the result of many compromises, concessions, and trade-offs between institutions, funders, lenders, contexts, and/or artists. The "ordered clutter" of curating (cf. "Skies") is thus often criticized or dismissed as the typical outcome of a hotchpotch discipline. I'm not disputing this. However, I also think that there is some potential for this much-maligned flawed order that is curating. What presents itself as ordered but in fact hides an essential disorder should be, when successful, perceived as a reflection on the way life always presents itself. Life does not appear as utter chaos but rather appears under certain guises that make sense today. To present these guises truthfully is to try and reveal the essential incompleteness of what presents itself. Lacoue-Labarthe and Nancy help us to see this again with the Schlegel brothers' fragments: "The . . . task is not to dissipate or reabsorb disorder, but to construct it or to make a Work from disorganization."[43] This does not excuse or justify shambolic exhibitions or philosophical work. On the contrary, this is a call to see curating philosophy—understood together or separately—as the work of exposing a single and comprehensible life caught up in the throes of utter disorder. The outcome will be not yet another comprehensive system but the characterization of a feeling for the disorder outside of all systems, like mankind's feeling for something beyond mankind.

The formal guises in which the disorder called *Curating as Ethics* presents itself here and now are as follows: the book is simply made of three parts of ten short chapters. The three parts draw up the structure of the ethics. First is the ontic-ontological[44] structure of the ethics ("Gods and Mortals"). I have to start somewhere, so I begin with a few definitions about key terms that will be used throughout this book: how everything stems from dark matter, how everything is constituted by matter, how mortals deal with God, how mortals apprehend interhuman relationships, and so on. This structure proceeds carefully from more or less nothing (cf. "Dark Matter") to more or less everything (cf. "The Absolute") without, of course, assuming any form of exhaustiveness. This first part—abstract and on all accounts seemingly alien to curating—prepares for the (inevitably always loose) boundaries of this ethics.

The second part ("Earths and Skies") establishes some of the parameters of this ethics—the stuff that makes up, in what concerns us here, *Curating as Ethics*: the textual and visual evidence, the digital medium, the materiality of the (art) object curated, the play of imperatives, the game of knowledge, and so on. This exploration of the ethics' boundaries proceeds, again, carefully from an ontic-ontological description of the event that is the curatorial (cf. "Earths") all the way to the manner in which the protagonists involve themselves in this event (cf. "Names"). This second part—less abstract and a little more in tune with the everyday practices of curating—lays the groundwork for understanding anew the actions of curators.

The third and final part ("Deeds and Ends") indeed focuses on the ethical issues associated with the activity of curating understood broadly: preparing, caring, fraternizing, dispensing. This last part deals with some key actions of curators, whether these take place in museological or extramuseological contexts or online. They are exemplary inasmuch as they touch upon specific ethical predicaments. These are obviously not exhaustive of all ethical predicaments incurred by curators; there are no tips here, for example, on how much it is ethically fair to pay artists or how curators should respond to the #MeToo movement. The actions explored in this final part only expose general but salient ethical curatorial predicaments and not immediate ethical problems and/or how to address them.

Inside these three parts, each short chapter addresses a specific topic and how this topic imbricates itself in the overall structure of the ethics. Strangely, perhaps, the chapters are not necessarily linked one after the other in order to form a continuous line of argumentation within each part. This will be the most rebarbative aspect of this thesis for traditional philosophers, but perhaps the most coherent for curators in general. The idea behind this lack of continuity is to deliberately exploit shifts in registers in order—again, to evade the logic of conventional academic theses. But these shifts in register within each part are not gratuitous. They carefully adhere to the logic of a curated exhibition whereby each individual chapter stands for one argument in the overall exposition of the thesis, not unlike works on display in a show. The table of contents is therefore like an exhibition map, and the cross-references in the text (signaled with a cf.) are signposts along the way. This does not undermine the distinctness of each chapter or its self-contained character. The chapters can be read independently of the whole or the parts. The shifts in register should therefore be read as curated segments of reflections in the exposition of the ethics. The overall trajectory, as for any exhibition, can never, of course, constitute a comprehensible all-encompassing system; it simply catches here a set of flights of thought in their necessary incompleteness.

# GODS AND MORTALS

# Dark Matter

**Dark matter is not antimatter. • It is matter without light. • It is an effect of hyper-chaos. • Dark matter is an effect without evidence. • As such, it can only be a hypothesis. • It has some energy in order to matter. • Dark matter generously impresses. • It is a generous stupidity. • It requires us to remain dumb. • Mind and dark matter are siblings. • No economy can deal with it. • Yet it is not nothing. • It is what gives rise to matter as it expresses and reexpresses itself. • As such, it is also what gives rise to the strife between earths and skies.**

Dark matter is everything that is not on this page. It is not the title or text, the font or paper. It is not even the shine of the print or the space between or around the letters. Dark matter is not even the glue that binds the pages together or the electricity that powers the electronic device that holds this book. And it is certainly not the air around it, in close proximity to it, or a great distance away from it. Frustratingly, dark matter is not even the new or inherited ideas and concepts that make up this book. Dark matter is an elusive thing because it has no weight (calculable in scientific, intellectual, or artistic terms), yet it is not the reverse of weight either; it is not absolute lightness, or total lack of density or thickness. To make things worse, dark matter is not even the opposite of matter. It is not antimatter. It is not made of antiparticles or anything hidden and supposedly making up the matter of this book or of any other in any library (digital or otherwise) on earth or anywhere else. If dark matter were antimatter, it would instantly be recognized by science as the antiparticles of the matter making up, for example, the hands holding this book or device.

No, dark matter is just matter, only without light. This is a rather difficult thing to conceive because everything everywhere is continually scrutinized by science under ever-more light. If *matter* is a general term for what makes up all observable physical objects in the universe that we can cast light onto, then dark matter is everything that refuses to be observed, emitting no light, enlightening no one. No collider can bring light to it. This does not mean that dark matter is simply dark atoms. It is on the contrary that which gives the slip to light, what always excludes itself, even when all eyes are turned toward it. Part of the reason it is so elusive is because dark matter refuses the structure inside/outside or same/other that characterizes all matter, whether it is squeezed, bumped into, measured, analyzed, or simply touched. There is no "inside" the darkness of dark matter in contrast to the "outside" of visible matter. Dark matter is not the "same as" or the "other to" this or that. Dark matter permeates and surrounds everything that matters, including subatomic particles made up of nucleuses of protons and neutrons with clouds of orbiting electrons.

Although it enlightens no one, dark matter is nonetheless an effect of hyper-chaos (cf. "The Absolute"). This does not mean, however, that it is a physical phenomenon that can be discerned as a reaction, a repercussion, or even a reverberation of this very chaos. Nothing comes out of or transpires from, and nothing enters or passes into, hyper-chaos. If it did, not only would hyper-chaos be identifiable in relation to dark matter, it would also be a recordable event, the measurable comings and goings of dark matter, the joy of scientists, philosophers, and artists alike. Dark matter is an unrecordable effect of hyper-chaos without the latter being an identifiable cause or origin strictly speaking. It is an effect in the sense that it impresses on matter. Dark matter impresses that something else is effectively taking place as part of matter. It is the impression that results in no form of recording, not even any form of conceptualization properly speaking, including this one. This impression does not mean that it is therefore a ghost, spirit, breath, or mysterious force within or without hyper-chaos or matter. Dark matter is simply an effect without evidence, the impression that things are not what they seem, that something else is at stake here.

As such, dark matter can only be a hypothesis—not only in astronomy and cosmology (the stuff that accounts for a large part of the mass that appears to be missing from the universe) but also in art and philosophy. It is a hypothesis in science because dark matter neither emits nor reflects enough electromagnetic radiation to be observed directly and because its presence can only be inferred from gravitational effects on visible matter. As such, it is never there where one expects it. Dark matter also remains a hypothesis in art and philosophy because it is not the intangible, the elusive, or the ethereal—quick denominations heavy with metaphysical insights and artistic visions. If one discards all these easy denominations, then dark matter can only be a hypothesis because it cannot even be understood as what escapes rationale. It is a type of irrationality beyond all logic, a madness beyond all discourse. Because it evades the scrutiny of science, philosophy, and art, dark matter can only therefore be a hypothesis that something indeed impresses all matter, even what does not matter at all, what we discard with liberal abandon.

Although it is only a hypothesis, one thing remains curiously constant: dark matter is definitely not energy as such (bright or dark). If it were, it would oppose itself to gravity, and we would all be bouncing in space like astronauts in zero gravity. Dark matter is not energy as such simply because it has some energy. Without this tiny amount of energy, there would be no impression on matter; nothing would carry momentum or be of importance, "this dark matter matters," for example. Again, frustratingly, dark matter's modest energy can never be observed, let alone calculated because it is a type of energy that no instrument can detect or vocabulary can articulate. Having some energy means that dark matter is never radically insubstantial or insignificant. The meager level of energy it possesses is simply enough to let itself be suspected, thus encouraging researchers (again, scientists, philosophers, artists) all over the world to continually consume themselves with conjectures, opinions, feelings, and ideas, generating more and more hypotheses. Unlike these consummate researchers, this is an energy that does not let itself be consumed. Dark matter burns a little, but not enough to be noticeable and therefore potentially exploited and traded.

Etymologically, if I discard the false equation "matter equals substance," matter comes from the Latin *mater*, "parent," "plant," "mother." In the 1550s, the word acquired the much broader meaning of something from which something else develops or takes form. Standing for what has no light and cannot be seen, dark matter, this effect of hyperchaos is thus the impression from which matter forms itself without again constituting an origin as such. Once more, there is no chain reaction here between the effect of hyper-chaos, impressing dark matter and matter. Darkness here simply impresses on matter to express and reexpress itself (cf. "Matter"), an uncontrollable and undeterminable effect of hyper-chaos. After all, was the early universe not opaque to light, a darkness that impressed the big bang, this questionable origin to express and carry on reexpressing itself? Dark matter generously impresses. There is never an end to this somber pressing prodigality. It is what impresses all subject matter as something to be dealt with. It is what makes objects, words, images, and names resonate with significance, including the words contained in this book. We would not be able to communicate (or curate) if it were not for the elusive liberality of dark matter.

In addition to being the impression from which matter originates (dark matter), this hypothesis is also injudicious. It is that which on all accounts leaves reason stumped by the guided or misguided aspect of all this impressed matter. What reply can indeed be given to the hackneyed question, why is there matter instead of nothing? Because there is no possible answer, dark matter—this impression from which matter originates—can only therefore be an administration without administrator or administrative power, an effect stemming from a perplexing judgment. Dark matter just gives. It is most simply a generous abstruse stupidity,[1] an overwhelmingly liberal donation that remains mute in its intentions and yet still manages to give matter for reflection—a foolish expenditure that no judgment (a priori or otherwise) can make sense of. This is a prodigality that comes, injudiciously, as if from nowhere, for no reason, and, inconveniently, for no one.

So dark matter—this hypothesis, this effect of hyper-chaos—gives itself over to the imagination. Unobservable, it is that which we imagine hovering around matter, penetrating it, impressing more dreams and fantasies, thus frustrating this world that always wants hard evidence, something to pin down with measures and graphs—a rather annoying matter. Nobody wants stuff that evades all forms of scrutiny and certainty and that is left stranded in the imaginary. This imaginary—on top of everything—does not come easy. It requires an emptying of all concepts in order for it to focus on what precisely evades all concepts. In order to imagine dark matter, it is necessary to let go of all preconceptions. As philosopher Jean-François Lyotard says about most matter in general, such an attempt requires "a mindless state of mind . . . *so that there be* some something."[2] Dumb and inarticulate, dark matter requires of us in turn to remain equally dumb and inarticulate, to let the imagination play without constraints. It is a play of dumb and dumber that rebels against all forms of articulations and calls for a type of imaginary that is not pure fantasy but ever renewed hypothetical impressions that defy all odds as well as all phantasms, illusions, or delusions.

Curiously, because it calls so clearly for the imagination, dark matter is also, paradoxically and perhaps a little secretly, related to mortals' mind. This does not mean it is the same as the human mind (cf. "Matter"). Because it requires a mindless state so that there indeed can be some something for the imagination, mind and dark matter are effectively related. In the same way that it is impossible to make sense of mind, it is impossible to make sense of dark matter. The two are intrinsically tied by their evasiveness. Lyotard, once again, says with regards to most matter in general: "The mind of Man is also part of the 'matter' it intends to master. . . . The relationship between mind and matter is no longer one between an intelligent subject with a will of his own and an inert object. They are now cousins.'"[3] Cousins or siblings, mind and dark matter have therefore this common characteristic of always dissolving themselves as soon as they are apprehended, evading all forms of capture, reasoned or otherwise. They always die the same death, darkness fading further into darkness, mind into blissful oblivion.

In this way, dark matter, like the mind that imagines it, rebels against the Cartesian program of mastering and possessing nature. It signs off this program that ruthlessly imposes its will by diverting everything into what supposedly is here and real, and above all matters. Dark matter is precisely what suffers none of this diabolical mastery diversion. Nothing can divert dark matter to light. It takes place without ever becoming real, without ever being here or there, and therefore without ever forming an event such as a strife, for example (cf. "Strife"). As such, it is an immaterial (in a Lyotardian sense) that forfeits all will to power, all economic reduction, all programmable diversion. Dark matter, the impression on all matter that expresses and reexpresses itself, is the ruin of all these efforts, something that hardly sits well with . . . well . . . everyone: believers and unbelievers, priests and philosophers, artists and laypersons. Perpetually giving the slip to humans is not something that provokes excitement, only frustration, which is nothing other than a fabulous relief, an immense breath of fresh air that mastery, reason, and prayers no longer need to have a role to play.

This does not mean, in the end, that dark matter is the equivalent of absolute nothingness—the radical opposite of all matter—which would again, of course, matter. As many have seen before, Emmanuel

Levinas being one of them, nothingness is already a content; it is already something to be observed, dissected, analyzed, stored, and/or ignored.[4] Dark matter, however, is that which does not even manage to constitute itself into nothingness, including atmospheres or densities of void; it is that which has no content or form. As previously noted with regards to the evasion of outside/inside and same/other, dark matter cannot enter into any dialectical relations, not even with an absolute negation of all and everything. Inevitably, and perhaps ironically, dark matter can never therefore be the fodder of negative or positive theologies, endlessly negating or positing it as this or that in the vague hope of becoming something or other. Dark matter playfully mocks these by both evading and confirming them at the same time. Beyond, below, beneath, or even inside presence and absence, thingness and nothingness, dark matter is thus without compare. Only dreams or hallucinations—and also perhaps laughter or tears—can accommodate its exasperating slipperiness.

Dark matter impresses and gives, but gives what exactly? I said matter. But what does that mean? As we will see (cf. "Strife"), by impressing, dark matter gives rise to matter in at least two ways. On the one hand it gives rise to the brute opacity of earths (cf. "Earths")—that is, to what unconditionally self-secludes itself. If there were no dark matter, there would be nothing to bathe with light, nothing to demand more light, however much this demand is often blindingly pointless. On the other hand dark matter also gives rise to matter understood as the limpid clarity of skies (cf. "Skies"), in which light makes itself and everything else manifest and visible. If there were no dark matter, then there would be no enlightenment and no hiding from the harsh scrutiny of light. If there were no dark matter, then there would also be no refuge in reason or unreason, concepts or prayers. Our life of enlightened things, objects, and ideas would be nothing without this darkness that knows no contrast or polarity. By impressing, dark matter gives everything that occurs in the strife of earths and skies, including the print on this page, the whiteness of the page or screen, and, of course, the hands holding this book or device.

# Matter

**Matter takes place as dawning. • This dawning is violence. • This violent dawning matter is everywhere the same. • Matter is both mind and body. • As such, matter is expressivity itself. • It expresses itself absolutely. • It is always already in-finite. • It is without support, exit, or exterior. • An expression, it is also a reexpression. • With reexpression comes understanding. • It indicates an understanding always to come. • It is equalizing and never achievable.**

Out of dark matter, matter dawns. This dawning is not quite an event yet (cf. "Strife"). Matter does not slowly or suddenly emerge at sunrise and then progressively or instantly disappears at sunset, for example. This dawning is not an event because matter can be identified neither as being finally in full light (under a midday or Platonic sun,[1] for example) nor as being in complete darkness (in the dead of night or in the darkness of Levinas's "there is,"[2] for example). Matter always takes place as this dawning, notwithstanding the time of day, night, or any other kinds of bright or dark events. As such, matter effectively takes place as a dawning that never becomes anything else but dawning matter. It is what always already exposes itself without ever reaching a final exposure as such. Like for dark matter (cf. "Dark Matter"), this does not imply the logic of an inside and an outside. The two take place at the indecision of the one and the other, albeit with dark matter prodigally giving out matter and matter remaining always on the side of light, a light never light enough. In this way, even the sun dawns on its own because it is matter exposing itself to itself. The same could be said of pitch blackness. It can only be so if at least some light identifies it as pitch blackness, this dawning matter.

This dawning is violence, the violence of matter tearing itself away from dark matter, ceaselessly edging an eruption without pause. This violence is not a physical force intended to hurt, damage, kill, or destroy someone or something, and it is not a strength or a natural creative or destructive force. If it were, matter would then oppose itself to inertness, death, or peace, the supposed tranquility of dark matter, for example. The dawning of matter is violence because that is the only way matter takes place. Matter does not have violence at its disposal. It is violence doing; it is its basic trait.[3] In this way, the dawning of matter is violence even if it is utterly peaceful; the peace and quiet of the herbaceous borders is matter at its most violent, for example. Volcanoes erupting, a baby sleeping, the stench of a landfill, pulsars, rabbits hopping on a field, electrons orbiting positively charged nuclei of atoms, the aroma of freshly baked bread—all indicate the violence of matter dawning, turning itself out without pause or outside.

This matter dawning is everywhere the same. Benedict de Spinoza says something similar in his own take on this complex issue: "Matter is everywhere the same, and there are no distinct parts in it except insofar as we conceive matter as modified in various ways. Then its parts are distinct, not really but only modally."[4] In other words, even if—and especially when—we conceive of matter as having distinctive parts, it is still paradoxically everywhere the same because these distinctive parts are only different "modalities"—to use here Spinoza's vocabulary—of matter as such. Spinoza gives a good example to explain the possibility of thinking matter without distinct parts. He suggests that we usually conceive of water with separate parts insofar as it is water ($H_2O$), but not insofar as it is matter. In this latter respect, water is not capable of separation or division.[5] Matter thus remains dawning matter—here, there, gushing or trickling, immobile or erratic, resilient or evanescent, dead or alive, violently everywhere on earth and (one can only assume from the poor vantage point of this speck of dust) in the whole universe.

Dawning matter is everywhere the same, but it is also, paradoxically, multifocal, multicolored, multivocal, multilingual, multifarious, polychromatic, polymorphic, and so on. There is no end to the multiple aspects of dawning matter. This does not mean there are specific attributes and/or modalities—some identifiable, some not—to the singularity of dawning matter, as in Spinoza's vocabulary. The multivocal aspect of matter—to take just one example—should be understood in a purely qualitative way. Dawning matter has many vocal qualities, a situation for which the term *many* applies inadequately—not because it is infinite but because it is never achieved. On earth, for example, matter violently dawns itself vocally in many ways: a cat's meow; Maria Callas's vibrato; the grunts of a bodybuilder; the chirps, squeaks, and clicks of beluga whales; the put-downs of Nicki Minaj. What is at stake here is not the diversity but rather the fact that each of these events is made up of a vocal trajectory that is never quite achieved and always calls for more. The futural dimension of matter is indeed what prevents it from being axed as this or that voice, and this even if it is recorded for posterity. To the great annoyance of mortals, these reluctant gods (cf. "Introduction"), there will always be more to dawning matter.

Furthermore, when it comes to dawning matter with its multiple qualities, there cannot be a distinction between matter and mind, matter and soul, matter and heavens. There is no split here between physical matter and what would supposedly be ethereal or superlunary. Matter concerns both the brute materiality of stones, for example, as well as the immateriality of mind, to name again dark matter's distant cousin (cf. "Dark Matter"). Matter is mind and vice versa. This does not imply interchangeability, only the impossibility, when considering matter as such, of distinguishing between the two strictly speaking. This also does not imply that everything is mind, including stones, but only that mind, taken individually (if this is at all possible), is still matter dawning—that is, matter violently enlightening itself with thought, ideas, ways of altering itself, matter minding matter. In this way, everything is matter, including angels and spirits, mindfulness and absentmindedness, nominal God and Its utter absence (cf. "God"), as well as all these messages from unruly but dependent gods (cf. "Gods").

Curiously—and however paradoxically, considering the use above of ontological statements such as "matter is . . ."—matter cannot, in the end, be a noun. It can only be a verbal-adjective. Let's take the verbal form first. Matter matters not in the sense of importance but in the sense of expressing something, even if this something is nothing at all. If dark matter impresses, matter expresses. The etymology of the verb *to express* helps make sense of this strange expressivity; it is from the Latin *pressare*, "keep pressing," and *ex-*, "outwardly." To express is therefore to keep pressing out of or away from dark matter. It is matter stubbornly expressing itself as dawning matter. This expression does not mean that at the same time something else embodies existence. There is no chasm here between expression and existence.[6] Expression is all there is. Existence is only a figment of our imagination, the delusion of thinking the persistence of being as what is identifiable as expressed—that is, a supposedly perduring state of expression called *y* or *z*. Matter expresses itself; that is, it simply presses out, in brute opacity and/or limpid clarity, in the strife of earths and skies (cf. "Strife," "Earths," and "Skies"). Matter matters; that is, it violently distinguishes itself from dark matter.

As it dawns, matter expresses itself absolutely. The "absolutely" does not refer to the absolute as such (cf. "The Absolute"). "Matter expresses itself absolutely" simply means that matter has the property of what is absolute, and hence its second aspect: its adjectival form. To have the property of being absolute does not make it proper, real, genuine, actual, or true. It simply emphasizes the fact that in dawning, matter expresses itself without restriction or limitation. Nothing reins in matter. Nothing, not even dusk, opposes itself to its taking place. Like there is no soul, spirit, force, or power besides or against matter, there is also no other or radically Other[7] alongside, within, or outside of matter. Matter expresses itself absolutely, and it does so without help or countercurrent. This does not posit matter as the cause of all things and all thinking—a kind of Spinozist monism of act and thought, for example. If this were the case, then there would still be something to give rise to matter: God or Nature, for example (cf. "God"). Just as dark matter stupidly gives (cf. "Dark Matter"), matter violently expresses itself absolutely because nothing impedes, guides, or controls it.

In this way, the "absolutely" in the expression "matter expresses itself absolutely" makes no reference to anything remotely resembling the infinite. The two cannot be confused. The "absolutely" refers to the way matter expresses itself. There is no way of ascribing a determination such as "infinite" or "finite" to matter. Matter is neither finite nor infinite strictly speaking; it is always already in-finite, a strange split word that accepts neither one of the two terms (finite/infinite) nor both together (infinite).[8] If matter's absolute expressivity was infinite, then it would be either a positive plenitude or a negative absence, what is unthinkable, inexpressible, beyond logos—again, the joy of positive or negative theologians, for example. Conversely or inversely, if matter's absolute expressivity was finite, it would oppose itself to something called the infinite and we would start again the merry-go-round of dialectical thought and/or of apophatic and cataphatic games. Matter is simply the absolute breaking out of matter from dark matter, an indefinite violent dawning that always has a hard time deciding, so to speak, whether it is finite or infinite.

Inevitably, this absolute expression expressing itself always infinite-ly cannot be proved by an operation performed by an understanding because to do so would be to exit matter and show the odd process encapsulated in this verbal-adjective as if from outside (objectively, for example) or from inside (instinctively, for example). The problem is indeed that no form of understanding (spiritual or computational, for example) can surpass the dawning of matter and contemplate it as if from within or without. Expression violently expressing itself simply takes place as matter dawns, and in dawning gives forms of understanding the opportunity to reflect without in turn ever being able to freeze-frame the so-called process. Understanding always arrives too late. There is thus no interior or exterior point of view to matter. There is only matter dawning, including the eyes scanning or reading this page, the mind assessing or judging it. As such, there can be no external governing tautology (e.g., "God") structuring matter from above or within. There is only an unfolding of matter mattering away from dark matter, an unfolding without original fold. Matter lacks nothing and needs nothing. It simply dawns, expressing itself for or on behalf of no one.

Yet there is no denying that in order for matter to express itself, matter needs to be able to reexpress itself. This second degree—if it is one as such—shows, as Gilles Deleuze tells us in his incontrovertible reading of expressionism in Spinoza's work, that in order to express itself, matter needs to reexpress itself in order to take place. This reexpression is effectively what produces the dawning of matter—not only what is visible, palpable, discernible, and so on, but also what offers itself to understanding. As he says, "Expression has within it the sufficient reason of a re-expression."[9] This reexpression is obviously not a repetition or succession. If this were the case, then everything would be seamless, identical copies of the same, everywhere. Reexpression is not death. Reexpression gives us, on the contrary, the way in which matter performs time-space,[10] and in doing so, gives itself over for scrutiny and consideration. There would be no event, strife, earths, skies, mortals, or gods (cf. "Mortals," "Gods," "Strife," "Earths," and "Skies"), if there were no reexpression—a sufficient reason that curiously, as we will see in the next chapter (cf. "Law"), defies all forms of expressionisms.

Inevitably, but perhaps also surprisingly, as matter expresses and reexpresses itself, matter also understands itself. In other words, matter understands itself insofar as it reexpresses itself. This does not mean that matter makes progress in understanding (well or badly). This simply means that there cannot be a reexpression without, in its slow or speedy, successful or unsuccessful accrual, some kind of understanding. However, what is understood is never achieved. Understanding indeed never manages to progressively introduce a counterpower to matter, intelligibility at last conquering physical substance, for example. There is, on the contrary, an adequation here between matter, reexpression, and understanding. In reexpressing itself, matter understands itself in and as an object of understanding—that is, in and as matter itself. Again, this does not mean there is a time lag between expression and understanding, "thought always follows on from matter," for example. The two come together, not side by side, but as one through reexpression. With reexpression comes understanding, and this even if there is no comprehension whatsoever. "No one has yet determined what the body can do."[11]

Never achievable, understanding thus takes place indiscriminately among mortals—in the brutal gestures of a murderer, the lofty meditations of monks, the turgidity of doctoral theses, the babbling of babies. Understanding takes place in each and every one of these events. There is no hierarchy between some more or less intelligent matter. Matter expresses itself and through reexpression understands itself indiscriminately in whatever language, code, script, sound, or noise. This is the downside of always being on the edge of dark matter, at the cusp of light, on the dawning rim of in-finity. Matter's understanding is always violently to come without one understanding (philosophy, for example) being ever able to trump the other (anthropology, for example) (cf. "Midwifing"). The ontic sciences weirdly fall for this false competition as if their aspirations to surpass one another make them equal to gods (cf. "Beckoning") when in fact the gods themselves, these mortals, these events of dawning matter, always thwart all efforts with unexpected odd messages always disrupting all forms of understanding, all disciplinary confinements. Dawning matter equalizes all understanding in its ever renewed, violent, and multiple dawning process.

# Law

**The reexpression of matter implies some law. • What is this law? • It is not the law of contingency. • Contingency is basically confused knowledge. • Contingency is not just confused knowledge but rather an illusion because it is unanchored in the present. • The law of contingency is thus always stained with a false value. • The law that governs reexpression can only therefore be its own absolute heterogeneity. • It is the law that unsettles all assurances of the same.**

In the dawning of light—at both daybreak and dusk, right under the fierce midday sun, and at the darkest hour—matter expresses itself everywhere and in everything. Matter expresses itself unflinchingly, without a care for nonexpression, always seeking reexpression. In turn (a turn that is not one, strictly speaking), reexpression always undermines the very possibility of a final expression as such, the end of matter, for example. There is a certain pigheadedness to this insistence that there should always be a reexpression, that expression should perversely never settle. Although no one who is part of it can make sense of it (cf. "Matter"), it nonetheless reveals some law—not a rule or command, not a principle or axiom, but a law as inextricable as a fact, as terrible or gracious as any fact: if there is so much obstinate reexpression, then a law must surely be governing it, provoking expression to reexpress itself. In other words, there would be no expression or reexpression without some kind of law making it turn imperceptibly or seamlessly from one to the other. What is this law at the heart of matter?

In order to answer this difficult question, it is necessary, and perhaps paradoxically, to turn again to Gilles Deleuze. Deleuze indeed evasively points to this law in a remark on Spinoza's all-encompassing monism. For Deleuze, this law takes place right when expression becomes reexpression or, to use his vocabulary, when composition becomes decomposition.[1] He writes:

> When Spinoza says that the *facies* remains the same while changing in infinite ways, he is alluding not only to the composition of relations, but also to their destruction and decomposition. These decompositions do not however (any more than compositions) affect the eternal truth of the relations involved. A relation is composed when it begins to subsume its parts; it decomposes when it ceases to be realized in them. Decomposition, destruction amount then only to this: when two relations do not directly combine, the parts subsumed in one determine the parts of the other to enter *(according to some law)* into some new relation that can be combined with the first.[2]

According to some law: the evasiveness is fabulous. What law could indeed sustain this relation of composition and decomposition, or, to use our vocabulary, of expression and reexpression? What law could sustain this willful insistence? Deleuze does not say, cannot say, for to say it would be to fall for transcendence, to admit defeat: not everything takes place on a plane of immanence. In order to have the *facies*[3] remain the same while changing in infinite ways, in order to have the movement of one part be subsumed by another, in order to have expression and reexpression, there must indeed be a law allowing the change, sparking and sustaining the movement of matter.[4] Again, what is this law?

This law is not the contingent, the random, or the fortuitous. It is not even the law of chance or *le hasard*, to use the poet Stéphane Mallarmé famous characterization of this law.[5] If one follows Deleuze's version of Spinoza, then the contingent or the fortuitous are only the result of bodies not knowing the way the *facies* works—that is, the way the universe takes place. In this, Deleuze adheres to the letter to the strictest Spinozism, one that allows nothing so mistaken and misguided as "the contingent" to play a part in this work. We are either confused or simply ignorant of the way things work. As Spinoza says in *The Ethics*: "I say expressly, that the mind has not an adequate but only a confused knowledge of itself, its own body, and of external bodies, whenever it perceives things after the common order of nature."[6] Chance, contingency, fortuitousness, *le hasard*, or randomness are therefore only confused knowledge because we do not yet embody the full necessity of expression and reexpression. In this way, however much it looks like a random event determining reexpression or decomposition, the law is still part of immanence. So this law cannot be a law of contingency as such. To say the opposite would simply be to misunderstand absolute immanence.

But Deleuze does not stop there. He also says that to assume that this law is contingency is simply to fall for an illusion. As he sternly remarks, echoing Spinoza's own admonition: "The categories of possible and contingent are illusions."[7] Why an illusion specifically? Because to characterize this law as the law of contingency is to assume an illusory temporal perspective: a contingency already past or yet to come. In other words, to opt for contingency at the heart of reexpression or decomposition is to fall for an illusion because such a contingency can only be unanchored in the present. I can only witness a past contingency or predict a future one; I can never pin one down as occurring now. Matter necessarily expresses and reexpresses itself both in its intrinsic relations (expression/reexpression, composition/decomposition, etc.) and in its extrinsic determinations (birth, death, affections, etc.). The law operates there, in this present necessity allergic to all kinds of perspectives unanchored in the present. In this way, the law that we try to pin down can only really be understood as part of matter, as part of expression, because there is ultimately nothing contingent in such unyielding reexpressivity, in such mulish insistence. Nothing that matters (cf. "Matter") takes place because of a law imposed by some atemporal perspective standing or sitting inside or outside of matter.

But this is not all. Matter simply imbricates itself with itself and this without ever forming a formal calculative chain of causality. To make sense of this, let's take Deleuze's Spinozist example of poison, again with decomposition in mind. He writes: "Everything in nature is just composition. When poison decomposes the blood, it does so simply according to a law that determines the parts of the blood to enter into a new relation that can be combined with that of the poison. Decomposition is only the other side of composition."[8] Again, a mysterious law is announced. This law is clearly neither causal nor mechanical; no hematology could detect it precisely. This law is effectively incalculable; it is a law that no science could indeed pin down for it changes every second of time in this or that blood, in this or that matter. Matter is therefore ruled by some ever-changing law that can never rest long enough to be qualified and calculated as causal, properly speaking. If we are to take this law seriously, we must therefore never forget that the law governing reexpression or decomposition is resistant to all forms of calculations, including the calculative causal adjudications of scientists.

Yet can one be satisfied with such a characterization: incalculable? Deleuze explains that to end up thinking this law as incalculable is still to imbue it with an artificial transcendental value that in fact stands for no value as such. In other words, we perceive it as incalculable because we attribute to it a false transcendental value. He writes, trying to make sense of the difference between things (composition and decomposition, for example): "It is no longer a question of specific or generic characteristics by which one establishes external differences between beings, but of a concept of Being or concepts coextensive with Being, to which one grants a transcendental value and which one counter-poses to nothingness (being/non-being, unity/plurality, true/false, good/evil, order/disorder, beauty/ugliness, perfection/imperfection)."[9] The words could not be clearer: to make sense of the difference between things over time, one always grants a transcendental value (i.e., it is incalculable) that in fact stands for nothing at all. To qualify this law of incalculable is therefore to erroneously attribute it with a value that stands for nothing.

One could object and say that this law, no matter what, is ultimately exposed at death, right at the end of the ceaseless process of reexpression, right when there can be no more reexpression at the heart of expression, right when decomposition fails to take place coextensively with composition, right at the big crunch. Eventually, matter must meet its end, surely. Unfortunately, death, even complete annihilation or total apocalypse, can only fail to interrupt reexpression or the coextensive occurrence of decomposition because such an event can never be placed in symmetry to its supposed opposite: origin, birth, genesis, or flourishment, for example. So long as there is expression, so long as there is matter, there is only a lived transition, a passage from expression to reexpression, composition to decomposition and back again to composition. Matter's insistence is just a relentless variation of the existing power of expression. Death therefore neither heralds something other (an afterlife, for example) nor interrupts anything whatsoever. Death is therefore not the law. Reexpression is indeed neither finite nor infinite properly speaking; it always rides, as we have seen, in-finitely (cf. "Matter"), brushing aside death or complete annihilation as yet another confused knowledge or illusion.

But can we be truly satisfied with such a radical view? Even if we accept that this law is only a misunderstanding, a confused knowledge, an erroneous value that we mistakenly attribute to the difference between things, can reexpression or decomposition really take place at all on such an odd basis? Does this in-finite gliding of expression and reexpression truly know nothing but the despotism of its mulish insistence? Can this law still not be understood without automatically afflicting it with the stench of transcendence? Raising these questions does not imply reintroducing the transcendental through the back door. It is intended, on the contrary, as a way of alleviating the immanental despotic hold of the process by which matter expresses and reexpresses itself. The law is there—Deleuze would not have placed it between parentheses if this were not the case—so something cannot just be reduced to some misunderstanding, confused knowledge, or false value that not even death can embody; something must nonetheless make matter glide at the cusp of in-finity.

What perhaps might help here is to look at the main property of this relentless reexpression. As the above has shown, it always defies all rules, regulations, patterns, structures, and ultimately all scientific veracity and universality. Such an extraordinary defiance reveals this stubborn reexpression as being utterly uncontainable and incommensurable—in a word, heterogeneous. Matter's relentless reexpressivity or decomposition is in fact an "absolute heterogeneity."[10] The property of reexpression or decomposition is thus a law that I would call of absolute heterogeneity. This law does not refer to the incalculable causal (or acausal) relation between expression and reexpression, composition and decomposition, good or poisoned blood, for example. This law is the mark of a heterogeneity right at the heart, as it were, of all matter. It is a heterogeneity that simply unsettles all assurances of the same, destabilizes the smoothness of an in-finite reexpression. There is only matter here and on Mars. There is only matter here under my skin and on this unknown planet in galaxy MACS0647-JD, this young cluster, a fraction of the size of our own Milky Way, 13.3 billion light-years from earth. Yet this ubiquitous seamlessness would not take place without this law of absolute heterogeneity that challenges the very idea of seamlessness, rendering it necessarily questionable and thus prey to reexpression.

Fear not—there are no whiffs of transcendence here. Even with such an absolute heterogeneity, there is still no abyss or elsewhere, not even one encapsulated in the adjective *absolute.* There is still only matter. Immanence still knows no punctual interruptions or disruptions spread along any axis (temporal or spatial). This does not mean that the two can be confused, that matter and this law of absolute heterogeneity are interchangeable. Matter is matter. It spreads out and hiccups at the dusk of writing *(écriture),* that is, at first light, in the shadow of its very taking place. The relation among matter, reexpression, and this law can never be autonomous, that is, recognizable and synchronized as such.[11] It simply stands for "the falling out of phase with itself *[le déphasage de l'instant],*" to use Emmanuel Levinas's wise words,[12] for which immanence or the *facies* never settles. If the indecision of dark matter and matter takes place at all, then it can only be so because of this heterogeneity that knows no other, this falling out of phase that never calms down. Matter is structured by this law that escapes even death itself. I would not be able to write this sentence if this was not the case.

# Mortals

**What distinguishes us amid the in-finite expressivity of matter is our finitude. • This finitude is a sting, the un/certainty of death. • This sting does not demarcate us from animals. • Fleeing the sting is how we become mortal. • This fleeing is not a task but a situation that indecides itself. • The situation is one of presencing-absencing (hold). • It gathers us together (pour). • The hold is an outpouring. • The outpouring is a gift to gods, without whom there would be no mortals.**

Everyone dies someday. The banality of this confused statement is staggering. It symbolically unifies all mortals: the "everyone" is radical, universal; there is no escaping it. We will all eventually kick the bucket. Yet this statement also divides all mortals: "one" is not "everyone." One dies uniquely. One only has one death. The divisive aspect of this statement therefore highlights a primordial condition that says: "I alone will die, and this solely defines me." Death defines me, and therefore—a "therefore" that would require lengthy analysis—everyone else does too. The one thinker who gives this its most profound analysis is Martin Heidegger, who puts it thus: "Insofar as I am, I am *moribundus*. The *moribundus* first gives the *sum* its sense."[1] In other words, "I am dying" not only comes before "I am," but it also defines it. Mortality not only takes precedence over being, but it also gives it its unbreachable dignity, its emblematic seal. This is what is at stake underneath the banality of this statement. This is what defines and distinguishes mortals amid this in-finite matter that expresses and reexpresses itself absolutely (cf. "Matter"). Everyone dies someday, even though nothing truly interrupts the pigheadedness of reexpression.

Someday. The uncertainty of this "someday" is equally staggering. While "everyone dies" is absolute certainty, the "someday" puts this certainty into jeopardy. Mortals are certain that they are going to kick the bucket, yet there is no verifiable certainty when the kicking will take place. Someday can be tomorrow, in a year, in twenty. Again, Heidegger talks about this "certain-uncertainty" with great precision: "[Death] can come at any moment. This in no way weakens the certainty of its coming, but rather gives it its sting and the character of an utmost and constant possibility."[2] A sting. Mortals are wounded by the sting of the uncertainty of their certain death. Mortals are hurt, upset, annoyed by the fact that they know they have to die, but not when this will happen. Mortals carry this injurious sting throughout their lives. Heidegger goes as far as to say that mortals not only carry this injurious sting but they also flee it every day. They busy themselves with work and other things in order to avoid the sting, the impossibility of ascertaining the date of the inevitable. Someday mortals will be relieved of the sting.

Everyone. Let's briefly return to this vague term. It is clear that "everyone" here refers to every person, and every person necessarily denotes human beings. Inevitably the question that arises here is this: when we speak of mortals, do we then only speak of human beings? Or are animals also included in this "everyone"? If one follows Heidegger, then the demarcation between the mortality of human beings and that of animals is clear-cut: "The mortals are human beings. They are called mortals because they can die. To die means to be capable of death as death. Only man dies. The animal perishes. It has death neither ahead of itself nor behind it."[3] Animals are thereby deprived of that unique human characteristic: they cannot die. Mortals are therefore the only ones who are capable of death as death. The lesson has been learned. However, there is also this other lesson from this other great thinker of finitude, Jacques Derrida, who tells us that there cannot be a clear-cut demarcation between the two: essences no longer dictate the way we understand humans and animals.[4] It is thereby impossible to clearly distinguish between humans and animals when it comes to this "everyone." There can be no distinction between being capable of death as death and simply perishing. All mortals perish and die, somehow.

The question is therefore not one of distinguishing between who or what is and is not mortal exactly, but of the relationship that one (human and possibly animal) has to this certain uncertainty. How do mortals relate to the uncertainty of their certain death? This relation with death is not a task that can be planned and/or programmed. It is a way of accepting and receiving, consciously or unconsciously, with eyes wide open or shut, this future "someday." How does one indeed accept and live with this sting, this inevitable and unforgiven fact? Heidegger replies that "living beings must first *become* mortals."[5] The crucial word is here highlighted: become. Although one is born already dying, one must learn to accept and live with this fact that one day we will be taken down, stricken without exact forewarning. This is the only way one can address the sting that wounds us every second of time and this, having heard Derrida on this point, whether one is human or, if this is knowable, animal. Everyone indeed dies someday, which means nothing other than everyone must first become mortal.

To become mortal is strange. Technically, and contrary to what some may think, "to become mortal" does not convey a single trajectory. To become mortal is both a pull away and a push toward death. This is what the verb *to become* in this specific case means. To put it more concisely, to become mortal stands, as Reiner Schürmann says in one of the most careful readings of the late Heidegger, for a "situation," a situation whereby total absence is at once addressed (and therefore kept at bay: "I'm still alive") and out of reach (and therefore vexatious: "I'm not there yet"). He writes: "Mortals indicate the impossibility of total disclosure. Death is the pull toward absencing in every situation. In that sense, it *is* situation."[6] I cannot *not* disclose that I'm not dead yet, yet I'm dying. To become mortal is therefore to bring together both the pull and the push, to live out a situation beyond any form of control or resolution. The sting that we turn into becoming mortal is a situation that unfortunately can never be undermined or overcome. Becoming mortal is assuredly a curious state of affairs because it shows that mortals can avoid neither the pull away nor the push toward death with every breath.

As such, mortals carry with them at all time, whether they like it or not, the locus of both presence and absence. They keep in their hearts, notwithstanding all their efforts contrariwise, what has no place (yet): both absolute fullness or utter void. Again, as Schürmann says, "The 'mortals' are so named because for them it has never been full presence that is originary. . . . They are the locus of absence. They 'belong and do not belong' to what is present."[7] Mortals are thereby deprived of full presence and absence, yet they are both somewhat present and absent at once. They come into presence without reaching full presence, and they withdraw from presence without absenting themselves entirely. They thus err as situations, slowly or furiously, lazily or determinedly becoming mortal. Ultimately, because they are unable to indicate total disclosure as presence or absence, they are most simply stung situations of presencing-absencing.

But this is not all, of course. Mortals also "do" something else besides being mere stung situations. They engage themselves with the living present; that is, they face every day with ideas, business, and projects. In doing so, as we have seen, they flee the sting of not knowing when death will present itself. Fleeing, mortals involve themselves in logos (cf. "Introduction"). Derived from *logos*, the Greek verb *legien* means "gathering together," which means nothing other than to "hear," "deliberate," "consider." This is what mortals do. This is how they flee the sting. This does not mean that besides being the locus of presence and absence, they are automatically rational beings with logos at their disposal. The ambiguity of the verb *legien* means at once hearing, deliberating, and considering, thus indicating an activity that does not necessarily come with reason (cf. "Deeds and Ends"). In other words, mortals do one thing, rationally or not. They gather together; they hear, deliberate, consider. That is, they flee the sting. This gathering and involvement in logos has therefore nothing systemic about it; it does not depend on any form of socioeconomic, political, or technological representation (idiom, social context, culture, politics, etc.). Mortals simply gather together; they involve themselves in logos. This is what they do, even if they are alone and what they do makes no sense at all.

As such, when one considers both their "situations" and their "gathering," mortals are not too dissimilar to that famous jug. In Heidegger's much-quoted text, "The Thing," the reader is given an existential analysis of the "thinging" of a jug. In other words, how the jug "jugs" (instead of just being a jug, for example). The jugging of the jug is twofold: it holds and pours. To hold is to contain. To pour is to give. Mortals are the same.[8] They hold in themselves the locus of presence and absence ("situation"), and they pour this very locus as they live out their lives in logos—that is, as they hear, deliberate, consider ("gathering"). As Heidegger writes:

> Holding needs the void as that which holds. The nature of the holding void is gathered in the giving. But giving is richer than a mere pouring out. The giving, whereby the jug is a jug, gathers in the twofold holding—in the outpouring. We call the gathering of the twofold holding into the outpouring, which, as a being together, first constitutes the full presence of giving: the poured gift.[9]

The metaphor of the jug is thereby not gratuitous. It indeed stands for mortals and how they hold the "situation" of absence/presence while "gathering" in the outpouring, in the giving. Mortals gather together; they hear, deliberate, consider, which means nothing other than holding out the outpouring—and this whether they sing, deal, pray, steal, draw, kill, or love. It is a strange status that involves both ontological (situations) and indeed ontic considerations (gathering) that could also be called "being-together as separation."[10]

What is clear in the above is that it is no longer possible to think of mortals as single units. They neither unify as subject nor extend themselves as durational ventures. They are annoyingly more than these simplifications. In order to make sense of this unusual approach to the idea of being mortal, it is therefore necessary to abandon all forms of ontological or ontic ossifications as well as all types of protean projections and embrace a rather rebarbative type of thinking that takes mortals in the double movement of their taking place—namely holding and pouring at the same time, that is, in a simultaneity that is not one strictly speaking. This type of thinking is rebarbative because it goes against all forms of economy—the hallmark of logos. However convenient it is for trade, mortals are not just there as beings, and they do not just become. They are here and yet not here; they contain and yet they give; they are a gathering that never congeals into something or other. These are no mere paradoxes. They stand for a different—richer and more complex—way of thinking mortals: neither dead nor alive but holding a locus of presence-absence in their very outpouring—a rather tall order, especially for psychology.

But to whom are mortals giving? To whom are they "a poured gift," this giving that evades all forms of economy, all expectancies of return? To whom do they gather as separation? In "Building, Dwelling, Thinking," Heidegger tells us in no uncertain terms: mortals give to the gods (cf. "Gods"). This creates a really annoying situation that prevents us from rounding off on mortals and completing the analysis in a satisfactory way. Mortals cannot be understood sui generis, as if independent entities unrelated to the darkness that brought them to light (cf. "Earths") or the light in which they bathe in half-tones (cf. "Skies"). And mortals cannot be understood without these gods to whom they are an outpouring/poured gift (cf. "Gods"). Being mortal implies relationships to earths and skies as well as to these gods. This is a frustrating situation that forces us to think mortals and gods between darkness and light, earths and skies, all at once. It is a difficult task in a situation that always calls for easily recognizable single linguistic units (Being, Dasein, becoming, *esse*, the mind, the soul, for example) that reduce ad absurdum situations of presencing-absencing and gatherings into false or imaginary entities, devices, or cyphers.

How is one to accomplish such an unusual task? How is one to think mortals without reducing them to singular self-governing entities? How is one to think of mortals and gods at once together and apart amid earths and skies? (cf. "Gods," "Beckoning," and "Obsession").

# God

**Amid events of matter, God expresses omnipotence. • This omnipotence knows no bounds. • It exposes itself as it expresses itself. • We express and understand God as God expresses and understands Himself. • As such, God is both thinking and existing. • Thus it is a nominal event. • Yet it is a name that indicates nothing in language. • It is only a relation. • This relation is with what is now lost. • This loss annoyingly and paradoxically always disrupts God's omnipotence. • God self-effaces Himself as He maintains His hold.**

Amid the in-finite event of matter reexpressing itself absolutely, one thing is sure: God[1] is not impotent. On the contrary, He[2] is obviously omnipotent; He is more than potent. *Potent* is a strange adjective. It can only be defined with the use of the word *power* (from the Latin *potent*, "being powerful," for example), yet it has nothing to do with power as such.[3] Potent refers instead to an ability (being able to have an erection and ejaculating makes a man potent, for example). As an ability, potent therefore refers to what can be held for a certain length of time (the time of having sex, for example). Being potent therefore means "to hold" or "to keep up." When it comes to God, the fact that He is, in most cases, omnipotent therefore indicates that He has been holding "it" together for a very long time—so long, in fact, that no one can identify an origin or an end, and that His "hold" is supposedly perceivable everywhere in the universe. God has been omnipotent—that is, He has been holding "it" together all over, forever. No impotence here—just a firm and constant grip that nothing can escape.

In his *Ethics*, Spinoza defines God by referring to this firm universal hold. He succinctly but famously writes: "God's power is His very essence."[4] In other words, the essence of God is power, this universal hold. Now, Spinoza does not use the Latin *potesta* for power; he uses the word *potentia*. I give here the Latin version for reasons that will become clear further down: “Dei potentia est ipsa ipsius essentia.”[5] Spinoza does not stop there. Further down in the *Ethics*, he extends this potentia to everything that follows from Him. He writes: “In God there is necessarily the idea both of His essence and of everything that necessarily follows from His essence.”[6] In Latin, this gives: “In Deo datur necessario idea tam eius essentiae, quam omnium, quae ex ipsius essentia necessario sequuntur.”[7] The double move is here clear: on the one hand God is potentia; this is His essence, and whatever follows from this essence is equally potentia. Again, there is no questioning God’s potency. God has a hold, and this hold is what characterizes Him and everything that follows.

Spinoza further explains this allusion to God as potentia by comparing this potentia, this hold, to that of a mortal sovereign. He writes, somewhat dismissively, “By God’s power *[potentiam]* the common people understand free-will and God’s right over all things that are. . . . Furthermore, they frequently compare God’s power *[potentiam]* with that of kings. But this doctrine we have refuted. . . . We proved that God acts by the same necessity whereby he understands himself.”[8] I leave aside for now the issue of understanding to focus only on Spinoza’s comparison of God with sovereign kings. To make sense of such a comparison, it is necessary to turn to one of Spinoza’s most diligent readers: Gilles Deleuze. Deleuze explains Spinoza’s dismissive rejection of the God of common people in favor of a God as potentia in the following way: “One of the basic points of the *Ethics* consists in denying that God has any power *(potestas)* analogous to that of a tyrant, or even an enlightened prince. [God’s] will is only a mode according to which all consequences follow from his essence or from that which he comprehends. So, he has no *potestas* but only a *potentia* identical to his essence.”[9] Potentia thus goes a long way. It is precisely what distinguishes Him from all forms of finite secular sovereignty. He holds it together while sovereigns, who still follow from Him, only cling on to delusory *potesta*.

But this is not all. Deleuze then emphasizes the dual aspect of Spinoza’s potentia for God. Spinoza indeed goes against the common people’s idea that God first thinks through and then acts *(potesta)*, because for him, God both thinks and acts at the same time (potentia). Deleuze explains: “Divine power is really twofold: an absolute power of existing, which entails a power of producing all things [and] an absolute power of thinking, hence of self-comprehension, which entails the power of comprehending all that is produced. The two powers are like two halves of the Absolute."[10] We therefore have two mutually supporting powers: in thinking, we have God thinking Himself and in existing, we have God realizing Himself. This is further confirmed in Spinoza's own text, in which he shows the paradoxical equality between *to think* and *to exist*. "The power of Thought to think about or to comprehend things, is not greater than the power of Nature to exist and to act. This is a clear and true axiom."[11] In other words, thought cannot be greater than action. We have here an undecidable explanation of the dual nature of God's potentia: in act and thought, existence and thinking.

However, as is well known, the problem is that Spinoza's axiom hinges on the fact that it is effectively in part demonstrable. As Deleuze says, "The equality of powers is all the better demonstrable if one begins with an already existing God."[12] To start from thought alone is impossible because a thought would obviously be unable to demonstrate, let alone activate, God's existence. Exit Descartes.[13] The axiom of the dual nature of God as both act and thought, existence and thinking, therefore relies on an assumption that there is such a thing as God to begin with. In other words, however much at the beginning was the Word, that Word needs a mind to conceive It as taking place, even if the two are later said to be indistinguishable ("the Word was with God, and the Word was God"; John 1:1). Still, for there to be thought and existence, something must have triggered these in the first place, however much, again, the two come as One. In this way, Spinoza needs to start from an already existing God. The logic of the demonstration cannot overcome the limitations of logos, for which thought and act are necessarily distinguished. The *Ethics* (or the Bible) cannot overcome the limitations of its own language. How is one to circumvent—if this is at all possible—this old, nay antediluvian problem of priority?

This is where it is necessary to change course, and in order to change course, it is essential, at least at the level of the thought of God, to focus on the *name* God. This naming is indeed crucial: there would be no God without it. Spinoza would not be able to say "Deus" as he does in the sentences in Latin quoted earlier without first and foremost thinking Him as a proper name in his thought. Deleuze tells us that Spinoza obviously resolved the issue of priority by making names into attributes of God.[14] Names are attributes that are a part of the power of God in thought. The crucial thing here is inevitably that attributes are dynamic and active forms. He writes: "The attribute refers his essence to an immanent

God who is the principle and the result of a metaphysical necessity. Attributes are thus truly *words* in Spinoza, with expressive values: they are dynamic, no longer attributed to varying substances, but attributing something to a unique essence."[15] The name of God, including each individual letter, is then an expressive value of potentia as thought. Naming and thinking are just two different aspects of the same omnipotence in act. The priority is thus resolved inasmuch as naming is a part of thought.

Something, however, is still puzzling. If we can only start a posteriori—because we can only begin, as we have seen, with an already existing God—does the name *God* then not hide something utterly unfathomable that no other phoneme can express? Does the duality of the endeavor of thinking and acting not automatically retain God as an empty tautology? Even taken as a dynamic attribute, why should this particular word stand out for all it embodies? Worse still, does the proper name *God* not point to what does not, in the end, belong to potentia, an empty vehicle for what escapes His absolute grip? Finally, could this very naming (i.e., this very posteriority) be—God forbid!—a weakening in God's omnipotent hold? All these questions reveal again the necessary limitations of language to think the logic of Spinoza's perfect equality. However much God is both act and thought, Spinoza's nomination can only point to what exceeds Him, His act and thought. Logos still wins with this trump card named *God*. In other words, the thought of God "in act" runs effectively empty because it does not know what it stands for. To make sense of this, it is necessary to turn to another Talmudic reader: Emmanuel Levinas.

Levinas indeed reminds us that God is always a proper name at the edge of language. He writes: "The first point is that the Hebrew terms of the Old Testament that we are led to translate by God, or *Deus*, or *Theos*, are proper names according to the wishes of the Talmud. The name of God is always said to be a proper name in the Scriptures. The word God would be absent from the Hebrew language! A fine consequence of monotheism in which there exists neither a divine species nor a generic word to designate it."[16] As a proper name, the appellation *God* therefore never indicates anything in language, expresses nothing that would make sense in Hebrew, Latin, Greek, or English. In fact, this time going against Levinas, God means so little that it could be replaced by the generic or improper word *Name*, as Maimonides in the twelfth century famously remarks: "The foundation of the foundation and the pillar of wisdom consists in knowing that the Name exists and that it is the first being."[17] The generic or improper word *Name* can thus also designate God. God is the word *Name*, a word that again jars in comparison with other words with more stable referents, such as *triangle*[18] or *Nature*, precisely because it curiously but necessarily falls out of language.[19]

Spinoza's unique attribute is therefore of something that has no referent. Even rendered undecidable with Nature,[20] the nomination still expresses what cannot be expressed. As such, it names what cannot be an essence in thought. In the end, Spinoza's Deus can only be referred to as a relation. Again, as Levinas says: "To say '*Dieu*' [God] as we say it in French, or *Gott* like the Germans, or *Bog* like the Russians . . . evokes above all separation (like our word 'absolute'). The term thus names—and this is quite remarkable—a mode of being or a beyond of being rather than a quiddity."[21] Relations and not quiddity. There would be no potentia, no hold without this nominal relation to what curiously knows no hold and perversely destabilizes from behind, as it were, God's omnipotence. This makes no assumptions about what is being related; this only highlights the impossibility of using a word, such as *God*, without automatically projecting a going beyond thought. Even as an attribute, even as an expression, *God* names a relation other to potentia, a going beyond all attributions, and this without even assuming any form of actual transcendence.

This is indeed the flaw of all monotheisms: reliance on a single word whose history points not so much to an elsewhere as such but rather to a forgotten elsewhere. This is Levinas's most remarkable lesson, the one in which he shifts God's relationality from space to time, and specifically to an immemorial Past:[22] "Monotheistic humanity is a humanity of the Book. Scriptural tradition provides the trace of a beyond of this very tradition. Monotheistic humanity, despite its philosophical claim to be posited at the very origin of self and nonself, recognizes in the Written the trace of a past that precedes all historical pasts capable of being remembered."[23] In other words, every time we use the word *God*—as inherited from the Abrahamic tradition—we use a referent whose origin is necessarily lost. In the case of Spinoza, the consequence of such an extraordinary loss is clear: however powerful and immanent, however potent and transfixed by a single hold, God also effaces Himself behind His very nomination. As He creates, He also erases Himself from the memory of all those whom He has created. He couldn't do otherwise. Ignoring this forgetfulness is misinterpreting God's omnipotence. This memory loss is the condition of His absolute hold. It accompanies Him in the very dynamism of His thought and act. His universal hold would not otherwise make sense.

This memory loss does not revert us back to God as creator or sovereign king, as the common folk believe. Instead, it allows God to be not only active thought and existence but also a relation with what disappears in the night of forgetfulness. This does not reinstate yet again a dialectical sublation or resolve the difference between negative and positive theologies. Right when thought and action reexpress themselves and thereby manifest themselves in all their most unconditioned occurrence, forgetfulness teases us, letting us hear not the other of thought or existence, not impotence or powerlessness, but what is necessarily at odds with omnipotence: God's very own name. In that name, forgetfulness teases not in the sense of making omnipresence appear amnesiac or senile but in a sense whereby with time, the referent behind the "holy One, blessed be He," inevitably always effaces Himself from history. This forgetfulness—a radical nonquiddity that knows no essence or referent—is a teasing from a Past no longer omnipresent, which is also, as we will see (cf. "Beckoning," "Obsession," and "Intuiting"), a teasing from a Future[24] not yet predictable, a relation beyond all economies and all philosophies. God might not be that omnipresent after all.

# Gods

**The gods are mortals. • They have an excess of immortality and go without feeling. • As such, they are not separate entities. They simply are an intrinsic part of the event of being mortal. • If mortals are fallible and imperfect, then the gods are infallible and perfect. • But their excess of immortality and their lack of feeling are what makes mortals be and feel. • This intrinsic interrelatedness in the event of being mortal is not a negativity or a dialectic. It is a tension. • This tension knows no rest. • It is what constitutes the strife alongside earths and skies—language as love/war.**

Amid the in-finite event of matter reexpressing itself absolutely, mortals give; they are a poured gift without return to the gods (cf. "Mortals").[1] But who are the gods? The gods are not the opposite of mortals but are mortals themselves. They are at once the recipients of mortals' outpouring and the unknown into which mortals pour. The terms *recipient* and *unknown* are preliminary at this stage. They only aim to indicate the receptivity and radicality of what is hinted at here—a hint and not a statement of fact, for the gods do not exactly reveal themselves in the light of day. The gods operate in half-hues and half-hours, in places that are not necessarily evident and at times that are not necessarily timely. How is one to make sense of these gods who are never present as such? I already hinted at these gods in the Introduction. Let me present them again, hopefully, in the most secular manner possible. In order to do so, I will turn to the one person who exposed this curious aspect of mortals' lives, Martin Heidegger. Amid the various texts dedicated to this topic, I will focus on his reading of the German Romantic poet Friedrich Hölderlin, and specifically his reading of strophe 8 of the poem "The Rhine."[2] The reason it is necessary to turn to this particular strophe is because it is there that Heidegger exposes, in the most concise and clear manner, what he understands by mortals/gods.

Here is strophe 8 of Hölderlin's poem "The Rhine":

> Yet of their own
> Immortality the gods have enough, and if one thing
> The Heavenly require
> Then heroes and humans it is
> And otherwise mortals. For since
> The most blessed feel nothing of themselves,
> There must presumably, if to say such a thing
> Is allowed, in the name of the gods
> Another participate in feeling,
> Him they need; yet their own ordinance
> Is that he his own house
> Shatter and his most beloved
> Chide like the enemy and bury his father
> And Child beneath the ruins,
> If someone wants to be like them and not
> Tolerate unequals, the impassioned one.[3]

And here is an earlier draft of Hölderlin's poem:

> For unerringly, looking straight ahead they go
> From the very beginning to the preordained end
> And always victorious and in any case the same
> Is deed and will for them.
> Thus the blessed ones feel it not themselves,
> But their joy is
> The saying and the talk of humans.
> Born restlessly, these soothe
> Their hearts, intimating afar, by the happiness of those on high.
> This the gods love; yet their ordinance . . .[4]

What does this mean? First, there are a few facts worth noting: the gods are not immortals themselves; they simply have too much of their immortality. This is a first fact that does not establish a state of being but rather a condition: overflowing with immortality. This is not an easy thought. To make it easier, it is probably worth thinking the opposite: mortals lack immortality. The converse should therefore now be easier to imagine. Second, the gods feel nothing for themselves, so they are without feeling. This lack of feeling means that they not so much require mortals as depend on them, because only mortals have feelings. Finally, however much they depend on mortals, the gods are also able to cause havoc, taking lives at will—and most especially when these mortals have the audacity of wanting to become gods. This ability does not mean they have a capricious attitude toward mortals. They are not almighty detached tyrants. I will come back to this (cf. "Beckoning"). In the meantime, let's just say that their dependence on mortals simply spoils mortals' time on earth; it ruins their always short lives. This is what their dependence inflicts on mortals—a strange and seemingly unfair situation.

Mortals indeed appear here at a disadvantage. But this is not quite the case. In his own interpretation of this poem, Heidegger highlights what is at stake overall when it comes to the gods: the event of being mortal. What must always be remembered is that the gods are not self-contained entities living alongside mortals, as if shadowy presences lurking about. The gods are an intrinsic part of the event of being mortal. There would be no mortals outpouring without gods to whom they are the poured gift. The interrelatedness between an excess and lack of immortality, the rapport between those with feelings and those without, the relation between those giving and those needing and between those aspiring and those taking away are all unbreakable to the point of being fused. All the facts expounded from the poem therefore cohere even though, by all appearances and for obvious reasons, they lack formal logic (i.e., ontological certainty): "this here is a mortal, and that there is a god," for example. Let's excavate further how this event of being mortal exposes itself as the tension mortals/gods.

Reading the draft, Heidegger remarks that the gods are what is always blessed. There is no superiority here. There is only a description of what a counterpoint to mortals could be: if mortals are unblessed because fallible and imperfect, then the gods can only be the opposite, namely infallible and perfect and therefore blessed. As Heidegger says, "Gods are blessedness. . . . Blessed means unerring, always victorious and the same."[5] To be always right, victorious, and the same is not something that mortals can boast about, but that does not mean it is not also a characteristic of the event of being mortal as such. The important thing to remember here is that this blessedness is always already concealed (cf. "Introduction"). In other words, there is no evidence for this blessedness (while there is plenty of evidence of mortals' wretchedness). The counterpoint to mortals, the gods, are therefore necessarily, but mysteriously, blessed. Hence the fact that Hölderlin never "describes" this blessedness or any other aspect of this event. As Heidegger explains: "Such [an event] is not described. . . . It is concealed and, in this concealment and closedness, the lack of need on the part of the blessed ones that prevails in essence within itself comes to light."[6]

Heidegger's sentence is crucial in the way it explains the tight interrelatedness mortals/gods: the gods need nothing, but this lack of need is what comes to light for mortals. How is one to make sense of this odd state of affairs? Focusing on feelings, after having focused on blessedness, should perhaps clarify matters. The gods do not feel a thing. This lack of feeling is precisely what makes them rely on mortals, who alone feel. Let's hear Heidegger: "The final version says rigorously and essentially: 'they feel nothing of themselves.' Excessive fullness even closes them off from beings. Yet this supreme self-contentment and this closedness on account of excessive fullness is the ground for the fact that they require an Other."[7] The interrelatedness of mortals and gods thereby takes place not between fullness and lack but between a closedness and its disclosure. The gods, these blessed ones, are so in harmony with their feelings that they themselves no longer feel a thing. This excess of harmony is precisely what in turn makes mortals feel. Mortals would not have any feelings without the gods' lack of feelings; they would not cry or laugh without the gods feeling nothing.

So this is what the gods are all about. Everything revolves around a question of lack of need (cf. "Introduction") and its exposure. The gods have more than enough, yet this excess is what comes out in the light of day as dependency on mortals. In other words, the burden of having no need reveals itself as a dependency on mortals. Let's unpack this. The gods are the counterpoint to mortals, for they have it all and need nothing while mortals have very little and desire the most. Yet the gods' absolute wealth shows that no matter what, they are still dependent on mortals. This is not a grotesque contradiction (an absolute fullness that is not quite absolute after all). This is, on the contrary, the mark that what appears to have it all (i.e., [a] god) can only be so if they are dependent on mortals who have little. Inversely, there would be no mortals without the lack of need of the gods. Using another vocabulary, this also means that mortals die, yet their death would mean nothing if gods did not exude an excess of immortality. Gods are the intractable counterpoint to mortals without, as we will see, forming a couple as such.

Their mutual interdependence is therefore total. The issue is thus not one of negativity but rather of tension between mortals and gods, between nonfeeling gods and feeling mortals. This tension does not create a dialectic between the same (mortals) and the other (gods) either. The tension is what matters over and beyond all negativities and dialectics. Hence Heidegger's insistence that it is not a "but" that structures the relationship between gods and mortals but a "for because"—that is, a logical correspondence. The draft indeed says, "But their joy is / The saying and the talk of humans." Heidegger comments: "It is not a merely descriptive 'But' that leads over to humans, but a 'For because' that furnishes the grounds."[8] This logical correspondence, this "for because," only says one thing: logical correspondence (logos) governs the relationship mortals/gods. It is what seals their mutual interdependence between feeling and not feeling, mortality and immortality, blessedness and wretchedness. The tension at stake in this event of being mortal cannot be weakened, unknotted, or broken. There would be no mortals/gods "leading over," to use Heidegger's words, without it.

In that tension, as we have seen, mortals give; they are a poured gift to the gods. They are the ones who always outpour, who give—even sometimes with their lives. This outpouring is effectively a refusal to admit a limit, a desire to make the gods, who have everything, their equal. This poured gift is a longing to overcome the limit, a yearning to bring the gods down. Mortals obsess over gods (cf. "Obsession"); they never cease to emulate them, always pretending to be like them. The higher they go, the harder they fall because the gods can only shatter such presumptuousness, such obsessive aspirations, ravaging bodies with cancer or waging wars between siblings.[9] Their dependency prevents the very possibility of absolute plenitude, an easing of the tension, of any form of unity. Mortals aspire to equality; they use language to appease tensions. Yet the gods must prevent such aspirations, thereby shattering language's delusory claim to any form of godliness. The gods have no choice in this. Their blessedness and absolute lack of need smash those who always desire the most (cf. "Beckoning"). As Heidegger says, "The gods themselves must smash those whom they [depend on]."[10]

The tension that constitutes the event of mortals/gods knows no rest as long as it remains an event.

This tension mortals/gods is ultimately what constitutes language as war or lovemaking—that is, a strife: the greatest enmity that is nothing other than the greatest intimacy (cf. "Strife"). As Heidegger concludes:

> Thus, in the greatest severity of saying, *strife* is shifted into the ground of [the event] itself. Yet this originary enmity is the truest intimacy which we are admittedly unable—and above all, not permitted—to assess by the standards of human feelings. For this origin of what has purely sprung forth is the mystery, pure and simple. This mystery remains, even where that which has purely sprung forth contents itself and makes do with its having sprung forth.[11]

The tension mortals/gods, this tension that constitutes the very event of their happenstance, is a strife, and this strife, this originary enmity that is also the truest of intimacy, is a mystery not because it is beyond reason or human experience but because it cannot explain itself. It can only be tense. This strife cannot express its own eventness; it can only pull the event apart and together. It is the strife between earths and skies (cf. "Earths" and "Skies"), this war- or lovemaking, that brings together and pulls apart mortality and immortality, mortals and gods. There is therefore, notwithstanding their radical differences, no proper distinction between mortals and gods. The two expose the tension of the event of being mortal.

Overall, the difficulty here is to never reduce either one of them absolutely, but to think them together, in or more precisely, as separation amid the strife (cf. "Introduction," "Mortals," "Strife," "Earths," and "Skies"). Torn in that tension, mortals, these gods, hold themselves into the outpouring, a poured gift never "one," never "there," never properly mortal or immortal, present or absent. Recognizing this tension, one that again literally prohibits any other value, enduring entity, or cypher trumping, superseding, or regulating it as if from above (an overarching ontological, subjective, or other being, for example), forces a reconfiguration of what matters above all in such an event (not only ethically but also socially, culturally, politically, etc.). There are not just mortal economic units exploiting the earth, breathing and polluting the air above and playing at being gods while the going is good. There is only an intractable tension of four in which not one dominates the other, however much everything now points to the contrary. The event of being mortal is this tension in which, amid the strife, mortals/gods beckon each other (cf. "Beckoning"); that is, they open up the possible for themselves.

When writing about this, I am therefore no longer writing to another fellow mortal who simply knows that he or she will eventually die, who unambiguously negotiates the world exploiting the earth's resources, who quietly or clamorously abuses others, often without even realizing it. I'm writing this to someone who can never disclose himself or herself properly, who gathers together without ever becoming "one" "here" or "there" reading and judging this (i.e., some "one" already thematizable as such), however great the temptation. To be more precise, I'm writing this to "what" is effectively no longer and not yet some "one" because he or she is also earths and skies, strife ceaselessly overreaching itself as strife. Torn in the tension with earths and skies, this reader, this fellow mortal/god, opens this unhoped-for Future from a Past so immemorial that it does not even bear a name. You are, reader, an outpouring/poured gift, self-secluding yourself amid immeasurable earths and skies, a god who also happens to be mortal.

# Beckoning

**How do gods shatter all mortals' aspirations to equality? • They stand for "my death." • This is not an external event affecting mortals. • It is the possibility of the impossible for mortals. • Why? Because the gods suffer no comparison or repetition. • They free the possible for the future, even if it is no future at all, even if it is impossibility itself. • Futural, they thus beckon. • "My death" beckons. Gods beckon. • They sting every second of time. • Trying to hear the gods' beckoning is as futile as divining the time of my death.**

In the previous chapter, I tried to show that the gods are at once a recipient and an unknown and also that they are able to shatter mortals' presumptuousness, their pretensions to equality. While being a recipient and an unknown is somewhat self-evident inasmuch as mortals are understood as an outpouring/poured gift, the fact that they are also able to shatter all aspirations to greatness, blessedness, and equality is perhaps a little strange because this implies the dramatic power of inflicting death, a way of drastically cutting down mortals' longings and dreams forever. As such, the gods give the impression of standing for death. They are death coming to mortals. However, because we are addressing here the event of being mortal, an event that can be neither self-enclosed nor utterly open to what does not belong to it, the gods are obviously not the harbingers of death, as if they were some entirely separate king-like creatures lording over mortals and able to kill them at will and without impunity. As stated earlier, the gods are always already an intrinsic part of mortals' very own happenstance. As such, in the same way that there can be no gods without mortals, there can be no mortals without gods; their mortality implies the overflowing immortality of the gods. But how is one to make sense of this shattering at the heart of the event of being mortal?

The injurious sting of death mentioned earlier (cf. "Mortals") is again what is at stake here. Mortals do not just feel the sting of death every day; they live with it since birth, with every sigh and wrinkle as if an injurious mark. Mortals die insofar as they exist. But what has this injurious sting got to do with gods? Previously (cf. "Introduction") we have seen that the gods free the possible for the future. They trigger what can no longer take refuge in the immemorial or what can no longer refuse to remain unhoped for (cf. "Obsession" and "Intuiting"). As such, the gods open up the future to mortals; they provoke mortals to think more than they can; they trigger unhealthy obsessions to the point of passion. But this is not all. In addition to freeing the possible for the future, the gods also free the possibility of the impossible, namely death. The gods therefore play a part in this injurious sting inasmuch as they themselves are also the possibility of the impossible for mortals. They play a part in becoming mortal by being that which shatters their becoming.

Inevitably, to think about the possibility of the impossible in this way is to stick to a classic Heideggerian scheme, albeit here formulated with gods in mind. The well-known scheme is as such: "The closest closeness which one may have in Being toward death as a possibility is as far as possible from anything actual. The more unveiledly this possibility gets understood, the more purely does the understanding penetrate into it as the possibility of the impossibility of any existence at all."[1] First, it is clear here that this sting (this possibility of the impossible) is not something that can be recognized and represented. Although at times it feels as if it were a birthmark carried throughout life, it is not something identifiable on the body or anywhere else. It is on the contrary something so close that it can hardly be seen, heard, or felt. Second, and paradoxically, there is also the fact that this possibility of the impossible (this sting) is an unveiling. In the end, death is not something utterly indiscernible. It is something taking place here and now as unveiling. With these two seemingly contradictory points alone, one highlighting a quasi-absolute lack of perceptibility and the other a progressive unveiling, gods' role in the becoming of mortals becomes clearer. The gods are indeed as far as possible from anything actual (they are never recognizable), yet being the closest closeness, they sting every second of time (they are mortals' unveiling). In this preliminary way, the gods stand not for death in general but rather, more precisely, for "my death,"[2] this death that takes place every second of time and is uniquely mine. This is the role they play as this injurious sting, this freeing of the possibility of the impossible.

But why call the possibility of the impossible, this sting, *gods*? Simply because death is unique, and only that which is unique can be called mortals or gods. Death is one god—that is, one unique possibility that cannot stand for any other sort of possibility whatsoever. This should be understood at three levels. First, it is a kind of possibility that suffers no comparison; no other event can compare with "my death," for example. All gods are unique. Second, this uniqueness has to be as shattering as an earthquake, as cutting as a knife, as insidious as a cancer; it therefore has to be an event that cannot be repeated. I cannot die again. A god cannot take place twice. The gods are the possibility of the impossible because they, like mortals, are unique. Third, this uniqueness does not mean, in turn, that they are a generic "one" god, attributable to all and affecting all. If this were the case, then we would return to death understood as a nonproprietary external event. Neither death nor the gods are "one" (cf. "Gods"). The gods, "my death," are always and most obviously, like mortals, multiple, a scattering of uniqueness in matter's absolute reexpressivity (cf. "Matter" and "Mortals"). This explains not only why the possibility of the impossible can be called *gods* but also why the gods can only be understood, in the plural, as these unique possibilities of the impossible (cf. "Obsession").

Inevitably, if one uses an expression such as "the gods are the possibility of the impossible for mortals," then one touches on not only a uniqueness (the gods, "my death"), but also, once again, a futurity that cannot be made present, turned into an event. The gods, "my death" are obviously always necessarily futural. The exchangeability between "my death," the gods, and the Future cannot be emphasized enough. However, the Future at stake here is not, as intimated earlier (cf. "God"), an ordinary "future-present"—that is, something that is foreseeable or predictable. If the certainty of what comes (the gods, "my death") were only one category of the possible, then there would still be other possibilities, other futures understood from out of the many horizons of awaiting—"these gods that I can always forecast as coming," for example. The gods or "my death" would then be something representable, a concept, an image, a thing. It would be something comparable and repeatable, and ultimately tradable: an economic product. No, the Future at stake with the gods, "my death" is always radical; it stands for that which cannot be anticipated in advance. The freeing of possibility (future or impossible) needs to come from an elsewhere never elsewhere enough (immemorial or unhoped for).

Inevitably, in the same way that the gods cannot be an ordinary "future-present," they cannot be, in reverse, "the impossible," a solid entity definable and identifiable as such. An impossible that would be utterly impossible (always nonpossible), an impossible surely and certainly guaranteed, accessible in advance, would be a poor impossible—an impossible already set aside, so to speak, life assured—"this, we all know, will never happen," for example. Furthermore, if it were really "the impossible," it would then be a program, something that one could plan to confront. It would be part of a causality or development: next stop, "the impossible." It would be a process with an already known outcome and therefore without event.[3] But this cannot be the case for the gods because they are always already part of the event of being. The gods, "my death" can only therefore be an impossible as an absolute excess of chronological time either by inflicting death (bringing calculable time to an end) or by opening possibilities (extending calculable time further). The gods are impossible in always being impossible to determine as this or that, including radical impossibility itself.

All this can be said differently using another vocabulary. For example, one could say that the gods sting by their absence, but this absence is not nothing; it is a radical no-longer (immemorial) or a not-yet (unhoped for), the two utterly undecided. Whether no-longer or not-yet, this absence is effectively a veiled "fullness" revealing itself (cf. "gods' blessedness" in "Gods")—that is, a presencing. As Heidegger says: "The default of . . . divinities is absence. But absence is not nothing; rather it is precisely the presence . . . of the hidden fullness and wealth of what has been and what, thus gathered, is presencing. . . . This no-longer is in itself a not-yet of the veiled arrival of its inexhaustible nature."[4] It is precisely in this always veiled arrival either no-longer (an immemorial past without anchor in the present) or not-yet (an unimaginable future without life assurance) that the presencing of the gods take place (cf. "Obsession" and "Intuiting").

As such, these gods can only therefore be "beckoning messengers."[5] What else could they be as this possibility of the impossible? What else could they be as this veiled arrival that comes from either the immemorial or the unhoped for? What else could a sting stand for if not what falls out of strife and yet is already here as part of strife itself? In order to make sense of this odd Heideggerian expression, "beckoning messengers," let us return to his reading of *Hölderlin's Hymns*. He explains:

> Whoever beckons does not draw attention to himself—for instance, to the fact that he is standing at such and such a place and can be reached there. Rather, beckoning—for example, when departing—is the retaining of a proximity as the distance increases, and conversely, when arriving, is a making manifest the distance that still prevails in this felicitous proximity. The gods simply beckon, however, insofar as they *are*.[6]

Beckoning thus means signaling that a proximity or distance is at stake. But this proximity or distance is, once more, not understood in any measurable sense. Beckoning can involve no calculation (measuring the closeness or distance, for example). Beckoning simply highlights the way the possibility of the impossible exposes itself or how an immemorial Past or an unhoped-for Future comes: it signals a distance or proximity without guaranteeing that this distance will be shortened or this proximity will become felicitous. This is how the sting occurs—as a sign that something is here and yet not exactly here. Beckoning highlights how the gods, "my death" unveil themselves without ever being fully unveiled.

"My death" thus beckons me that it is near and yet I am still alive. The gods beckon me from the Past that there is still Future, and yet I have no idea what shape it will have. In either case, whether as gods or "my death," a signaling is taking place; a message keeps stinging me every second of time, beckoning me and reminding me that my time is up and still to come. There is no letting go of it. It takes place at all times, whether flagging, orgasming, walking, cheering, or sleeping. These beckoning messages do not indeed take place in exceptional circumstances or in the mundanity of the everyday but at all times, disorientating me with always uncertain messages, unclear approximations of distance or closeness. I can never be prepared for death or the unexpected; I can never be prepared for gods' messages. Each time, every time, leaving me stranded between distance and proximity, between what can never be remembered and what can never be anticipated, until a time when the messages suddenly no longer are in play, when they no longer arrive, the strife is over even if its reexpression never ceases properly speaking (cf. "Matter").

Unfortunately, however much mortals would like it otherwise, these gods, like "my death," cannot be approached or apprehended by either cunning or scientific acumen. Trying to hear gods' messages is as futile as trying to divine the moment of my death: a supreme and empty delirium, a useless divagation. It suffices simply to acknowledge what these beckoning messengers point to: this immemorial Past or unhoped-for Future that is precisely utterly absent and yet (paradoxically) always stingingly present. This is what Heidegger points to when he writes: "It is within our being transported to that which has been, and in such transport alone, that something un-suspected is possible."[7] The vocabulary is clear: "what has been" provides us with "what is unexpected." Once again, the interchangeability between the immemorial Past and the radical Future gives us not only our destinal trajectory but also the shifting boundaries of the event that we are dealing with (the gods, "my death"). Neither of them can be precisely identified or scientifically measured. This is not a failure of thought but a constant invitation to rethink our lives structured by and as mortals/gods and this, with every breath, each time, our last breath.

In the end, and in answer to our original question, the shattering at the heart of the event of being thus takes place simply because there cannot be a symbiosis of times; the immemorial and the unhoped for or distance and proximity can never come together in the delirium of presence, a final happy coincidence. The event of being mortal simply prohibits it, leaving us always stranded in a situation in which death can occur at any time and yet is already here. We are thus clearly dependent on these gods that retain this horrendous ability to potentially spoil our time on earth. Realizing the intractability of these messaging gods frees us of many uncertainties, anxieties, and fears. For it is mortals who in the end always send these messages, who shatter themselves (cf. "Obsession"). "My death" is mine even if an asteroid puts an end to it. I beckon and sting even if an insidious illness curtails my life. The gods are mortals. The mortals are gods. The beckoning never ceases so long as the time-space of mortals, these gods, remains in play, so long as the event continues its dwelling.

But this is not just a double play of forces, of course; this is the event of being mortal. The gods or "my death" take place between distance and proximity amid the strife earths and skies (cf. "Strife," "Earths," and "Skies"). There would be no messaging gods, there would be no "my death," were it not for self-secluding earths and immeasurable skies providing the ground and air, so to speak, in which presencing occurs, in which the sting of death wounds, in which the freeing of the possible and the freeing of the possibility of the impossible relentlessly express themselves. But why recalibrate or expand the event of being mortal with the fourfold? Because, as intimated before, it is only by taking into consideration this constellation that we can finally move on from reductive epochal perceptions of being and death (cf. "Introduction"). The gods' beckoning messages do not take place in a vacuum, in the supremacy of an alienated being facing its demise every second of time. They need to signal or be heard—if at all—amid the half-light of the surge of matter (cf. "Matter"), this half-light structured by the law of absolute heterogeneity (cf. "Law").

# Obsession

**What justifies the plural for *gods*? • Mortals' thoughts overflow their limit. • They overflow their incomparability or unsubstitutability. • They overflow the invisibility of their face. • Each constitutes an obsession. • We obsess over mortals/gods because they beckon. • They beckon because they trump all thematization. • They do so to the point of passion. • This passion is without content. • The plural *gods* is therefore no hominization of some idea of God and it is no incarnation. • It simply reminds mortals that god is always one, not because He is unique but because they themselves are incomparable and unsubstitutable.**

What else is truly unique? If "my death" is one god (cf. "Beckoning"), then what other unique mortal god is there? What justifies the plural over and beyond the event of being? These questions are difficult because in order to truly make sense of the plurality used in the word *gods*, it is necessary to think of something that is as unique as "my death," something incomparable, unrepeatable, unlike anything else. It would also have to be something that can beckon from an immemorial Past—that is, from an unhoped-for Future (cf. "Intuiting"), times that strangely know no temporality properly speaking and yet can still somehow be identified as such. This kind of uniqueness is not easy. God cannot be one of a kind, one god amid many others, for example. God has to be truly unlike anything else, not in the sense of an exception but rather in the sense of an irreplaceability or unsubstitutability. Because "my death" is unlike any other's, then what is equally unique? The plurality must be thought out in order to escape the—at times claustrophobic—confines of the event of being mortal and of this one god, "my death."

In philosophy, Emmanuel Levinas teaches us the only way to go about identifying (another) god. He writes in "Subjectivity as An-archy": "The non-onto-theo-logical approach to the idea of god goes by way of the analysis of the inter-human relationships that do not enter into the framework of intentionality, which, always having a content, would always think in proportion to itself."[1] Levinas is careful. He does not write of the non-onto-theo-logical approach to god but rather to the idea of god. He already knows that there cannot be a supposedly direct approach to god; it is always mediated, always an idea. His aim is indeed to explore how god comes to mind and not god as such (cf. "God"). The only way to let god come to mind is therefore to focus on interhuman relationships, and specifically to pay attention to how humans—these mortals—relate to each other outside of all intentionality. In other words, the only way to let god come to mind is to pay attention to these mortal thoughts that allow us to break through to the idea of god. This is the only non-onto-theo-logical approach to the idea of god possible.

But these mortal thoughts are not simply opinions produced by thinking. If this were the case, then these thoughts would simply be repeatable and tradable products that can be spun one way or another. As such, they would simply be concepts totally unrelated to how god comes to mind. In order to approach the idea of god, the thought taking place amid interhuman relationships needs to surpass itself (cf. "Introduction"). As Levinas writes: "Thoughts overflowing their limit, like desire, searching, questioning, hoping—these are thoughts that think more than they can think, more than thought can contain.... Therein lies a breaking-away, a defeat, a defection from the unity of transcendental apperception, just as there is here a defeat of the originary intentionality in every act. It is as though there was here something before the beginning: *an an-archy*."[2] The message is clear: in order for god to come to mind, the interhuman thought needs to break away from all identifiable beginnings, all concepts of origin, departures, or arrivals. It needs to defect from what is already language, what language identifies as the placeholder of an outside. This idea of god does not come therefore from a concept but from an overflow of mortal thought in interhuman relationships, a surpassing of all intentionality, an-archy itself.

Because we are focusing here on interhuman relationships, the question inevitably is not "what kinds of thoughts make us think more than we can?" (because identifying them would necessarily lead back to thought as economy), but "who can possibly make us think more than we can?" "who can defeat the originary intentionality in every act?" God can only come to mind if there is indeed a shift from *what* to *who*, from a search for an essence to the other. So who? Levinas answers quickly:

"The other person." He writes: "The other person *[Autrui]* is not beyond measure but incomparable; that is, he does not hold within a theme and cannot appear to a consciousness."[3] The incomparable aspect of this other is what is crucial here. The other person can never appear as if yet another object of thought; the other person can never be reduced to a theme but is simply other: incomparable (cf. "Beckoning"). This incomparability is precisely what allows this other person to provoke this overflow of thought beyond all concepts, all intentional reductions. If this were not the case, we would sadly all think alike. The idea of god thus comes to mind in this overflow of thought stemming from what is effectively incomparable: the other person. But how is this evident?

Levinas continues in the same essay: "[The other] is a face, and there is a sort of invisibility to the face that becomes obsession, an invisibility that stems not from the insignificance of what is approached but from a way of signifying that is wholly other than manifestation, monstration, and consequently vision."[4] First, the lack of visibility is here, alongside being incomparable, again crucial. Over and beyond outwardly visible signifying economies, the other always signifies above all in a way that cannot be seen, in a way that escapes all monstration that can easily be thematized or conceptualized. As is well known, for Levinas, this odd signification occurs through the face. Even though the face is in full light, it is in its expressivity invisible, never ascertainable as such, never reducible to a mask, for example. It is this strange invisibility that precisely signifies—a signification that, as Levinas never tires of repeating, is not a thematization or manifestation. The other person thus signifies, brings god to mind, through their face, what is other to all forms of visibility. In other words, the invisibility of the face signifies the idea of god as what defies and defects all reductive conceptualizations.

But Levinas does not stop there. This invisibility creates not so much a fascination but an obsession: we look up to the other, we grow up, we long to be united with them, we work and play with them, we celebrate their births, we fight them in wars, we kill them, we mourn their passing. In each case, we obsess because of their invisibility, because they are always more than simple manifestations, monstrations, bodies. We obsess over them because they give us more than we can think even if we have already judged and sentenced them to death. We obsess over them because they shatter all intentionality. In turn, the other person cannot properly thematize their signification; they cannot reduce themselves to a concept, a neat package, not even when they die, not even with a biography, and this is what also obsesses us to the point of either admiration, adulation, and idolization or frustration, anger, and, again, murder. So we never give up. We can never give up. We obsesses over them because of this odd invisibility in their face.

The reason we obsess over them is not just because of this mysterious invisibility in their face or because they signify in a way that is wholly other than manifestation, but also and above all because they are always at odds with our time—in one word, anachronistic. This anachronism renders them unsubstitutable to each other. As with death, you occupy a time I cannot take over, a time that is uniquely yours. This unsubstitutability is what prevents any form of absolute synchronicity between us, a total fusion in times, a total coherence of times. You always jar in relation to my time. The odd anachronism in question here is precisely what signifies but annoyingly can never be fathomed, let alone made into an equalized relation. It is exactly what makes us think more than we can, what defeats all intentionality and all language. This anachronism amid all economic exchanges, amid all these seemingly synchronized events is, again, what obsesses us. It is "a disequilibrium, a delirium overtaking the origin, rising earlier than the origin . . . being produced before any glimmer of consciousness."[5] Beyond the given, beyond the tyranny of language, mortals thus relate to each other through this anachronistic overflow.

The other person is therefore an anachrony who is always for the other "late . . . and incapable of covering up that lateness."[6] This means that if one tries to look for god in other people, if one tries to stare in their faces in order to fathom god "there," one can only fail, because one can only arrive too late (cf. "Beckoning"). There can be no coincidence even when there is a revelation, apparition, or epiphany, or when there is passionate love. And even if there was a coincidence, it would be a doubtful occurrence, a suspicious event that pitifully calls on faith to justify this unexpected and unruly promptness. So other people remain an anachrony who can only upset all orders, taxonomies, hegemonies. They defy language, calling from what is immemorial or unhoped for, temporal dimensions that again obsess us precisely because they can be somewhat identified and yet suffer from a total lack of visibility. The idea of god comes to mind through this strange anachrony that never settles and leaves us, all of us, always at odds with one another.

Hence passion. Obsession always turns to passion. The obsession for the other person always ends up with passion. This passion is not simply a strong and barely controllable emotion, an intense sexual impulse, or a strong desire for something. It is also not an account of a suffering. The obsession turned passion that mortals address one another focuses on an intrigue that knows no plot. This intrigue is that provoked by this invisibility in the face of the other that can never be synthetized or established once and for all. In other words, the other, this fellow mortal, obsesses me to the point of passion because I can never render visible that which precisely defies all language. Passion arises there, in this anachronism. If one pays attention to this passion, then one must be warned: this is not for the fainthearted. It is an extreme passion in which "consciousness is struck or wounded despite itself; in [which] consciousness is seized without any a priori (the other is always encountered in an unexpected fashion—he is the 'first to come')."[7] Is this precisely not how passion occurs, in the perilous enthusiasm of an encounter before judgment and objectification takes place?

This passion has of course nothing to do with lust—that is, with a form of desire that seeks a return (i.e., a need). In order for the idea of god to manifest itself in the anachrony of the face of the other, consciousness needs to be touched by something that evades all economies. As Levinas writes sternly: "With this passion, consciousness is touched by the *nondesirable*... there is no libido in the relationship with the other; it is the anti-erotic relationship *par excellence*."[8] Our obsession is therefore with something that is always already not wanted—not because it is harmful, objectionable, or unpleasant but because it cannot provide for any form of economy. The anachrony cannot be wanted, desired, lusted after. Again, if it were, it would be a delusion, a fantasy, the promise of redemption, salvation, ecstasy, absolute knowledge. This is a passion without object and without investment, catechism, *ḥifẓ*, or dharma. Nothing is to be gained from this passion precisely because it hinges on signifying without content, origin, or end, properly speaking.

So this is how the other allows us to break away, defeat, and defect from the unity of our transcendental apperceptions. Other people, in this uniqueness, this irreplaceability, allow this defeat not in the sense that they mysteriously hold in themselves god as an idea, but in the way they overflow and surpass thought, thus breaching language and all origins. If I push Levinas's argument further, then this means that these fellow mortals are effectively gods inasmuch as they make me think more than I can; they allow for this breaking away from all identifiable beginnings, all points of origin, departures or arrivals; they allow for this defection away from language. They are gods also because they are indeed unique, incomparable. I cannot die in their place. Their "my death" is as incomparable as mine. Still extending this trajectory, one could also say that ultimately our interhuman relation is therefore that of gods inasmuch as it expresses these overflowing thoughts. Our relation is godly inasmuch as it is always an-archic, never identifiable as original or final, never properly in language. After all, if I am allowed this other unruly shortcut, is the image of Elohim not precisely found in all mortals, even though Israel is always called upon as sunrise and sundown to hear that God is one *(Adonaï Ehad)*?

Mortals are gods in the way they break the form of the sensible; they make each other think more than they can; they foster obsessions, passions. There is no hominization of God in this obsession that turns into passion. No mortal has been given here a godly character. There is also no incarnation, the kind of incarnation that would call for fervor, devotion, prayer. If this were the case, then there would still be something otherworldly at stake in this obsession, this passion. Mortals would be, in one way or another, representatives of some God or other on earth or elsewhere. They would be exchangeable symbols for an elsewhere, prone to worship, fetishism, and iconographic renditions. But here is all there is. The anachrony takes place in lofty spaces as well as in squalor, in the face of hardened criminals as well as pious saints. Obsession-passion is simply mortals coming together as gods. Mortals and gods come together; they contaminate each other, create communities and collectivities; they create worlds without netherworlds or heavens, unique, incomparable, unrepeatable. This is what justifies the plural to the word *god*: mortals playfully reminding each other that god is always one, not because He is unique but because they themselves are incomparable, irreplaceable, unsubstitutable, stubborn breakers of all forms of thematization.

# Strife

**Matter reexpresses itself. In doing so, it sunders. • This sundering creates an event. • This event is that between earths and skies. • Earths and skies self-assert themselves, and this is what causes an event. • There is no negativity here. This double self-assertion knows no outside. • It takes place at the cusp of in-finity. • But what maintains the strife as strife? • Work is what produces a change, what turns earths into skies. • This includes work as struggle. • Together, they make history.**

Matter matters. In mattering, matter, as we have seen (cf. "Matter"), expresses and reexpresses itself thanks to the law of absolute heterogeneity (cf. "Law"). This reexpression, which is not yet an event, takes place in both lightness and darkness, opacity and transparency, the unfathomable and the utterly self-evident. It matters little, for it takes place as dawning everywhere. The crucial thing, for now, is that with reexpression, time-space[1] also sunders, not in a way whereby space would sunder from time but in a way whereby both sunder from each other; time temporizes itself as space spaces itself. This time-space sundering turns reexpression into an event. This sundering renders manifest matter as event expressing and reexpressing itself, here, there, everywhere, an event that always occurs without "why" or "for whom": a baby girl is born, a parasite finds a host, a man burps, lightning breaks a rock apart—to take only earthly examples. As we will see, there would be no history if it were not for this sundering time-space not as a condition for matter's existence but as the only way matter matters at all, that is, as the only way it can be recognized as an event.

The event of matter is therefore a sundering, a temporizing-spacing. Heidegger talks of "time-space *[Zeit-Raum]*—the *site of the moment* of the sundering."[2] This is not conventional physics. Time-space refers here not to calculable time-space but to the event of matter, this making present that occurs, here, now, everywhere. Hence Heidegger's strange expression: "The site of the moment." The expression combines both space and time, gives space (site) to time (moment) and time to space, each sundering from each other, each setting off an event, something new or unexpected.[3] But why *sundering*? Heidegger explains that all events constitute a sundering, which is not a splitting apart, severance, or disunion between two entities (time and space) but rather an eruption of the new: time-space, an event. The site of the moment, this sundering of time-space is not just about what is here or there. It is also about what happens, what occurs here, now, speedily or at a glacial pace.

But all this does not happen in beautiful imaginary abstractions. The event of matter, this sundering, has, as hinted earlier with our meager earthly examples, a concrete reality that indeed submits itself to the ontic sciences as observable and verifiable (scientific evidence, for example) and to religion as "gifts from God" or unfathomable mystery. This concrete reality is the event of matter, what concretely can be seen as giving and bathing in half-light: a growing child, a parasite settling inside a host, a man with digestive problems, rocks rolling down a hill. This event always occurs in half-light because, as we have seen (cf. "Mortals" and "Gods"), it can never enlighten entirely and it can never be fully comprehended or entirely verified, always giving the slip to all forms of careful examinations. There is always something amiss, missing, or awry that stubbornly refuses observation, verification, or unquestionable faith. Half-light is the only way events of matter—this sundering—can be understood as a concrete reality that needs to be dealt with.

Hence Heidegger's concrete and straightforward expression: earths and skies.[4] Time-space sunders as earths and skies. As we will see (cf. "Earths"), earths do not refer to land surfaces as distinct from skies or seas or to the present abode of humankind as distinct from heaven or hell. And earths do not even refer to the third planet from the sun in the solar system. Earths, in the plural, refer to whatever gives itself over for enlightening scientific scrutiny, whatever shows itself in and against the light of skies. Similarly, as we will see (cf. "Skies"), skies do not refer to the region of the atmosphere and outer space seen from planet earth or to the heavens in general. Skies, in the plural, refer to whatever sheds light to self-secluding earths, whatever enlightens what presents itself as earths. We will come back to these two quasi-indistinguishable events. For the moment, the event of matter, this sundering, takes place as earths and skies in half-light, what overall gives itself over to the always puzzled ontic sciences and the always mystified religions.

When it comes to earths and skies, when it comes to this incontestable concrete event of matter, we are faced with a strife. I have already hinted at this strife when exploring the tension between mortals and gods (cf. "Mortals" and "Gods"). But what exactly is a strife? We said that the strife is language—a language that cannot express its own eventness. But how are we to make sense of this, irrespective of mortals and gods? The dimensions of earths and skies are here to help. A strife is a type of friction, but not one that resembles a feud or war against two opposing parties. Not unlike the sundering of time-space, a strife is a friction because it is a double self-assertion. Earths and skies self-assert themselves, and this is what causes a strife. As Heidegger writes: "The opposition of [sky][5] and earth is a strife. But we would surely all too easily falsify its nature if we were to confound strife with discord and destruction. In essential strife, rather, the opponents raise each other into the self-assertion of their natures."[6] The strife of earths and skies stands for the way each manifests their own nature: the earths for their self-seclusion, their darkness, and the skies for their self-openness, their light. But this strife is not just some kind of spacing event. It is also a temporizing event. Time-space constitutes the strife, this mattering event of earths/skies that never reaches an elsewhere, only the resumption back into strife.[7]

Why this resumption? As we have seen (cf. "Gods"), neither the sundering of time-space nor the strife earths/skies is obviously a negativity. Again, that would be too easy. There is no othering in the strife. Nothing (and no one) is expecting the strife. The strife is simply the outbursting or upflaring movement that maintains itself as strife; it is what allows the differentiated to hold sway in its difference.[8] To use another vocabulary, we could say that the strife is *différance*, the only difference being that what differs/defers here is specifically earths/skies, what gives and bathes in half-light. This strange focus shows that unlike *différance*, the strife does not open itself to an other always already other—that is, to a radical Other—but rather to each other. The strife is a movement of happenstance that knows neither origin nor destination and whose misstep never announces or reaches a (temporal) beyond. It is a strife for which each self-asserts itself without outside—the earths in their self-seclusion, the skies in their openness: birthing, parasitizing, burping, resting.[9]

Without origin or destination and without Other, the strife therefore only knows itself. The earths are earths only as the earths of skies; the skies are skies only insofar as they act on earths. Earths and skies belong together in an in-finite relation. As Heidegger says, "Earth and heaven belong in-finitely to one another in the relation which 'thoroughly' holds them together from its center. The center, so called because it centers, that is, mediates, is neither earth nor heaven, God nor man."[10] Again, the in-finite of earths and skies is not a vulgar infinity, an infinity of accountant. It is not an infinite that has a calculable or incalculable end. Opened with a hyphen, the in-finite in question here is necessarily undecided; it is at the cusp of finitude and infinity (cf. "Matter"). The strife earths/skies in-finitely plays each other in order to maintain itself as strife. Now, there is a center. . . . Annoyingly, this center is not the point that is equally distant from every point on the circumference of a circle or sphere—the core of planet earth, for example. The center is a mediation; it is "between" earths and skies without ever constituting a middle, nucleus, heart, core, hub, kernel, or interior (cf. "Gods"). The center simply mediates the in-finite relation, the self-assertion earths/skies: strife.

The strife maintains itself as strife, but what maintains it as such? What participates in the maintenance of the strife? Can there be something specific, something easily recognizable by all? Heidegger clearly says that what maintains the strife as strife—that is, what maintains the self-assertions of earths and skies—is work. He writes: "In setting up a [sky] and setting forth the earth, the work is an instigating of this strife. This does not happen so that the work should at the same time settle and put an end to the conflict in an insipid agreement, but so that the strife may remain a strife. Setting up a [sky] and setting forth the earth, the work accomplishes this strife."[11] Work does not necessarily mean an activity that involves mental or physical efforts to achieve a result. Work should be understood here in its broadest sense and not with an exclusive utilitarian aim in sight. Work is simply what in that center—which is not one, strictly speaking—produces a change, what turns earths into and against skies. This means both "what is in the works" and "what is not in the works"—the spanner that prevents the work being carried out, for example. Without origin or end in sight, the work of strife is to simply maintain itself as strife, even though, by all outward appearances, everything tends to give the impression (look out of the window wherever you are) of development, progress, and goals achieved by nature and humankind.

No progress, then, just strife overreaching itself as strife. This places economy, understood broadly, under a different light. There is indeed no need to struggle to achieve profits because the struggle only accentuates itself as struggle. The struggle of work is the strife of earths and skies, and because the strife only overreaches itself as strife, the work can only do the same: struggle overreaching itself as struggle. Is there no rest to the struggle? Is there no pause to this economy that knows not where it is going, except repeating itself as struggle? Heidegger answers this question simply: "The repose of the work that rests in itself has its presencing in the intimacy of strife."[12] The answer is clearly no. All temporary cessation of work is part of the strife. All attempt to exit the economy is still strife. This is not a defeatist or fascistic idea or ideology.[13] On the contrary, it is the realization that earths and skies are engaged in an enmity/intimacy that can neither break apart nor fuse altogether, and that all work, profitable and nonprofitable, participates in it.

As such, the strife is also, necessarily, history, not in the sense of a series of identifiable or nonidentifiable chronological events connected to a particular person, group, or thing but as the "playing out of the strife *[Bestreitung des Streites]* between earth and [sky]."[14] The strife happens, events take place, history becomes recordable. The overreaching of the strife as strife leaves a (historical) mark that is nothing less than strife. This does not reduce everything under the homogeneous denomination *strife*. This simply exposes both the process and the exposure of that process. The same can be said of work and struggle. Struggle happens, work or nonwork takes place, history is made. This work or struggle leaves a mark that is nothing less than struggle, further work, further struggle. Again, there is neither circularity nor autism, and there is neither causality nor teleology, only matter mattering as event, without "why" or "for whom": an elderly lady passing away, a parasite expelled, a man on a diet, rocks made smooth and round by the action of water. To realize this is the first step toward abandoning the delusions of progress. It is to embrace the enmity/intimacy of the strife, to play out the strife between earths and skies, struggling, as mortals, as gods.

# The Absolute

**None of the above would take place if it were not for hyper-chaos. • It is not a chaos that would derive from necessity or chance. • It is rather a chaos so chaotic that no reason or law can pin it down. • This chaos is basically capable of impeccable order and frenetic disorder. • It is something philosophically and scientifically unthinkable. • It is ruled by no law, not even that of disorder. • It is the very happenstance of the universe. • It is the truth of things. • It is the absolute and thinkable property of that which is.**

All of the above (cf. "Dark Matter," "Matter," "Law," "Mortals," "God," "Gods," "Beckoning," "Obsession," and "Strife") would not take place if it were not dis-organized by hyper-chaos. This does not mean that hyper-chaos organizes or disorganizes any of the above. If this were the case, then one would have a kind of superior being lording over and organizing or not all of this. To dis-organize is to give the possibility of an underlining organization as well as its radical undermining. The verb is open with a hyphen, and therefore again necessarily undecided. Hyper-chaos dis-organizes all in the way it allows dark matter to give out matter, lets matter express and reexpress itself, grants absolute heterogeneity to break apart and constitute matter, enables mortals to gather in their outpouring, entitles God's name to point to an elsewhere, and authorizes unruly gods to be blessed so that mortals may obsess over their inequality. Hyper-chaos dis-organizes all of this amid this event or strife parting away the unfathomable and the clarity of day, earths, and skies. Hyper-chaos knows no bounds even the limits of bounds themselves.

But what does hyper-chaos actually mean? In order to make sense of it, it is necessary to distinguish between different kinds of chaos. Quentin Meillassoux helps us make the right distinctions. He writes: "We traditionally conceive of two different kinds of chaos: On the one hand there is a *necessary* chaos, which we identify as composed of a series of necessary processes that exist but are ultimately devoid of any purposive ends—i.e. a kind of physical chaos of deterministic sort, but otherwise lacking any design capable of being rendered to sensibility. And on the other hand the concept of chaos can also denote a *random* chaos, in so far as its processes are governed by chance encounters between independent particles or causal series."[1] There are two types of chaos, then, one that derives from necessary processes and another that derives from chance. Neither of these two chaoses is at stake here because the former implies a principle of reason (otherwise the necessity would not make sense) and the latter implies a constancy of laws ensuring that chance still remains comprehensible (probabilities, for example). In both cases, these chaoses are appended to thinkable disorders or confusions and are thus dependent on particular spatial and temporal perspectives (human, for example).

Having discarded what is usually understood by chaos, Meillassoux then proceeds to explain what he understands by a chaos that would be appended to neither principles of reason nor laws. He writes: "The chaos of which I'm thinking here is capable of altering or even reconstituting the laws of nature themselves. I label this extreme kind of chaos—which is neither deterministic nor random—a hyper-chaos . . . [which] is independent of thought, in so far as it's capable of ushering in both thought's emergence and annihilation."[2] The difficulty here is to think a chaos so chaotic that no reason and no law (not even those ruled by necessity or probability) could pin down. Hence the Greek prefix *hyper-*, which denotes a chaos over and beyond conventional understandings of chaos. This chaos is hyper- in the sense that it defies understanding yet paradoxically, as will be succinctly shown here, can be thought out.

Meillassoux draws attention to the fact that a hyper-chaos cannot be understood as an intensification of either or both a necessary and random chaos. In a footnote, he modestly admits having made a mistake in the past:

> At one time, I used for myself the term "*sur-chaos*," because ["hyper-chaos"] seemed to me to give the false impression that I had tried to think a chaos more disordered, more absurdly frenetic than those that had preceded it in various philosophical systems (the prefix "hyper-" having acquired, wrongly, an intensificatory connotation in current language). Now, the chaos that I envisage is just as capable

> of producing an impeccable order as a frenetic disorder—whence the idea of sur-chaos, which refers to the ancient metaphysical order and the ancient chaotic disorder alike. But I resolved to commit a barbarism by mixing a Latin prefix [sur-] to a Greek noun [chaos]—whence the return to "hyper-chaos" whose meaning, I believe, can be posited clearly enough to avoid any equivocity.[3]

No barbarism here, then. A hyper-chaos, with its still-problematic anchoring in Greek thought,[4] therefore refers to a type of chaos that is capable of both necessary and random chaos and their utter arbitrary destruction.

How is one to make sense of this hyper-chaos that dis-organizes all of the preceding explorations? A hyper-chaos "simply denotes that everything either *could* or *could not* change without reason; it could remain in perpetual flux or could remain in the same state for an indefinite duration (as it appears to be the case, for instance, with the 'universal' laws of physics). In fact, it is entirely conceivable that hyper-chaos might just as well result in a world wholly comprised of fixed objects, without any becoming whatsoever."[5] The use of the modal verbs *could* and *might* clearly indicates that Meillassoux is thinking here of an unbridled possibility that can give either (or both) perpetual flux or (and) absolute invariability. Further still, it indicates an unrestraint possibility that can even be, if one pushes his logic all the way, impossible, "without becoming," as he says (cf. "Beckoning"). Scientists would inevitably balk at the idea of something that does not obey some kind of universally acceptable law. Such a wild idea is effectively scientifically and philosophically inadmissible, a true disgrace. So how can Meillassoux dare to think this unthinkable hyper-chaos that even refuses the idea of a theoretical possibility, the likelihood of things?

Inevitably, Meillassoux can only think of hyper-chaos as a form of time. As he says, "hyper-chaos denotes a Time whereby everything could be abolished just as readily as everything could persist in an eternal becoming. From the vantage of hyper-chaos, everything is contingent—even disorder and becoming themselves."[6] Now this time is not any other kind of time. This is a special time. In order to put forward this special time, he needs to discard commonplace understandings of time-space, which he rightly lumps together under the denomination "ontic time-spaces,"[7] that is, time-spaces understood by modern sciences (the time of the physicist, history, or psychology, for example). He writes: "There are time-spaces within our world, bound to determinate laws—physical or otherwise. But all these time-spaces are ontic—that is to say they are contingent beings, that emerge for no reason and can perish likewise."[8] Meillassoux is thinking of a time that would obey no known laws, physical or otherwise. He calls this time free of ontic time-spaces: hyper-chaos Time with a capital T. "Hyper-chaos is this capacity of (capitalized) Time to destroy or create, for no reason, all ontic time-spaces."[9]

Hyper-chaos is therefore a special kind of Time that has the capacity to create or destroy all other kinds of time-spaces, including those constituting dark matter, matter, the structuring law of heterogeneity, and the sundering events of strife, mortals, gods, earths, and skies. This is a type of Time that can create or destroy the very event of time-space, that of strife, that of the fourfold (cf. "Introduction" and "Strife"). This is the kind of Time for which one can only exclaim "Wow!" because, as he says, this is a Time that "can bring forth any non-contradictory set of possibilities . . . bring forth new laws which were not 'potentially' contained in some fixed set of possibles."[10] Hyper-chaos Time is therefore a Time able to create new realities, new universes, new laws, and new principles, and able to destroy them at will and for no reason. The crucial thing here is that this Time creates new temporal situations without at the same time existing eternally as a shadowy figure behind all these ontic time-spaces. Again, hyper-chaos Time is not a God creating and destroying time-spaces at will but an absolutely random Time that does not even obey the rationale of creation and/or destruction. As he says, "I would like to suggest thinking a Time that would be ruled by no law, not even the law of disorder or that of a future always to-come."[11]

Meillassoux's hyper-chaos Time is therefore free of all archaeological and teleological constraints, liberated from all physical laws and metaphysical principles because it is capable of "destroying every determinate entity, even a god, even God."[12] Nothing restricts hyper-chaos Time. It stands for the very happenstance of the entire universe, a happenstance that cannot be limited to our little blue planet, its inhabitants, or anything remotely close by, alive or dead, long forgotten, or *in potentia*. Meillassoux describes this hyper-chaos in the most dazzling way:

> [This is a] *hyper-chaos*, for which nothing is or would seem to be impossible, not even the unthinkable. . . . What we see there is a rather menacing power—something insensible, and capable of destroying both things and worlds, of bringing forth monstrous absurdities, yet also of never doing anything, of realizing every dream, but also every nightmare, of engendering random and frenetic transformations, or conversely, of producing a universe that remains motionless down to its ultimate recesses, like a cloud bearing the fiercest storms, then the eeriest bright spells, if only for an interval of disquieting calm.[13]

Hyper-chaos is therefore a type of chaos that would be so chaotic that it could even be capable of order, the most desperate consistency, the most joyous immortality.

Inevitably, to think such an extraordinary Time is to think something that no reason can make sense of. Hyper-chaos Time is effectively without reason. Meillassoux is aware of this when he says, for example, "Unreason . . . is an extremely powerful and chaotic property of Time . . . capable of radically becoming otherwise, but now according to a process that is without law, without reason, wholly inaccessible and ever unknown."[14] Hyper-chaos Time is therefore a temporality that is devoid of all reason, and therefore also capable of any and all reason, however contradictory this sounds. If it were not utterly unreasoned, it would still obey some law or principle. Contrary to what one might expect, this unreasoned Time is not the sign of our incapacity to think Time, but rather is the very truth of things. The truth of everything on earth and in the universe can only indeed be unreasoned. As he says, "When we stumble upon the irrationality of all things, we do not come up against a limit to our knowledge, rather we come up against the absoluteness of our knowledge: the eternal property of things themselves consists in the fact that they can without reason become other than they are."[15] This clearly marks hyper-chaos Time as the fundamental—without fundament per se, of course—characteristic of all things everywhere: without reason.

However, this does not mean, of course, that everything is unreasonable or absurd. Meillassoux is aware that, from our limited perspective, some universal laws persist over time, some reasonable ontic principles still hold together for a while amid hyper-chaotic Time. There are indeed, from where we stand, some constants in this hyper-chaos;

otherwise there would be no fourfold and therefore no event such as earths and skies, mortals and gods, and science would never be able to impose itself as holding some kinds of temporary truths. He describes these meager perspectival scientific constants as if forming the eye of a hurricane amid hyper-chaos: “The phenomenal constancy of the world is the eye of a hurricane without beginning or end—a hurricane that I call [hyper-]chaos . . .—nestled in the heart of the manifest irrationality of all things.”[16] So it is not all utter nonsense, complete havoc, foolish farce. There are local constants that allow us to articulate our eventness for a little while, but these only remain thus without intrinsic necessity, without particular reason. In this way, the events of earths and skies, mortals and gods, for example, just happen, the fortuitous occurrence of a set of reasoned short-lived and parochial laws.

Of course, in the end, or maybe at the start, hyper-chaos Time is only a principle. Meillassoux says it in *After Finitude*. As such, hyper-chaos Time is not directly available to experience.[17] Mere mortals, mere gods, we can only make sense of our event, the phenomenal circumstances that weds us to our biological mortality, our divine limitations, our earths and skies. Again, this does not signal a failure of thought. On the contrary, this signals the contents of this truth: “The absolute and thinkable property of that which is.”[18] Hyper-chaos Time is thinkable not because it is dependent on thought, but precisely because it is free of thought, the most unreasoned but not unreasonable of thoughts, the truth of its taking place. Meillassoux highlights this characteristic of hyper-chaos Time in the most blunt way: “That which we took for a lacuna *is actually knowledge*; and so facticity (more specifically understood as arch-facticity) is transmuted into hyper-chaotic contingency.”[19] If there were anything more concrete and more true in the world today, it is precisely this hyper-chaos Time that evades all scientific and philosophical scrutiny and yet constitutes the very core and periphery of all that there is, including dark matter, matter, and law, as well as the event of strife holding itself together apart.

# EARTHS AND SKIES

# Earths

**Earths: whatever gives itself over to light and scrutiny. • Skies: whatever allows itself to be scrutinized in and by light. • Taken on their own (if this is possible), earths shatter all attempts at penetration. • They withdraw from every disclosure and keep themselves closed up. • The self-seclusion of earths is what allows the rising into light. • But what modes and shapes do earths take? • *A Poet in New York*. • New York shows the skies' murder as well as the earths' self-seclusion. • Mortals' work participates in this self-seclusion. • Curators' work participates too.**

From the failure of thought—that is, from what can only call for imagination, conjecture, and hypothesis because no science can shine light to it (cf. "Dark Matter")—comes the matter of earths. It is not just matter as such (cf. "Matter"), but the event of matter called earths. As noted earlier (cf. "Strife"), earths do not refer to the surface of the world as distinct from sky or sea, the present abode of humankind as distinct from heaven or hell, or the third planet from the sun in the solar system. However much the temptation is great to reduce everything to an easily comprehensible determination (a surface, an abode, a rock) that opposes itself to another facile and plain-speaking assertion (an expanse, a vault, a cosmos), there is more to this event than that. The word is here conceived in the plural: earths. There is not just one earth but many earths. The plural allows one to think of earth not as a unique entity lost in space on which humans build their dreams and nightmares and over which some hypothetical divinities position themselves haughty and proud, but as whatever gives itself over to light and scientific scrutiny. Again, there is not one event called earth, but many mattering events called earths.

Earths then are a much more complex affair. This complexity is further enhanced when earths are measured in relation to skies, but not, as we will see, in a logical or dialectical rapport (cf. "Skies"). Not unlike the fact that earths do not respond to a singularized facile determination, skies are equally rebellious to easily comprehensible categorizations. The skies are not just the region of the atmosphere and outer space seen from the earth or the heavens. Pluralized, the skies are whatever allows itself to be scrutinized in and by light. The measure of the relationship earths/skies is therefore not one of logical contrasts (darkness/light, solid/air, for example) or opposing forces (material versus immaterial, for example), but paradoxically of complementarity and incompatibility, both of which constitute the mattering events called earths and skies: strife (cf. "Strife"). The events earths and skies trouble science and, amusingly or annoyingly, constitute supreme fodder for skeptics precisely because neither of them is distinguishable with scientific precision. When earths are taken in consideration, then, it is not long before skies also need to be taken care of. Their bond/discord or strife between them knows no rest, easy axing, or healing.

But what do earths mean? What does it mean for the earths to give themselves over to light for scrutiny? One of the first characteristics of earths is that they are self-secluding. In order to make sense of this, it is necessary to turn to a simple example given by Heidegger: the stone.[1] He writes:

> A stone presses downward and manifests its heaviness. But while this heaviness exerts an opposing pressure upon us it denies us any penetration into it. If we attempt such a penetration by breaking open the rock, it still does not display in its fragments anything inward that has been disclosed. The stone has instantly withdrawn again into the same dull pressure and bulk of its fragments. If we try to lay hold of the stone's heaviness in another way, by placing the stone on a balance, we merely bring the heaviness into the form of a calculated weight. This perhaps very precise determination of the stone remains a number, but the weight's burden has escaped us.... Earth thus shatters every attempt to penetrate into it.[2]

With the example of the stone, Heidegger gives us the clue as to why the earths self-seclude themselves—that is, why they refuse, whether as a whole or as fragments, the possibility of their very exposure. No matter how much they are scrutinized, the earths always wreck every attempt at revelation. Light is what the earths seclude themselves from.

Darkness is therefore the first characteristic of the mattering event of earths, and this whatever their state, one or multiple.

But these earths are not just *the* self-secluding. If they were, they would be comparable to matter before becoming an event, dark matter refusing to be scrutinized (cf. "Dark Matter"). Unlike dark matter, earths are also—second characteristic—paradoxically what rises up as self-secluding. Heidegger says, "The earth is not simply the Closed but rather that which rises up as self-closing."[3] This rising up is not the converse movement of self-seclusion but the only way self-seclusion actually manifests itself. The undisclosable knows only one way to self-seclude itself: by rising up, by manifesting itself, by giving out the possibility for scrutiny to take place. Heidegger again: "Earth is the serving bearer, blossoming and fruiting, spreading out in rock and water, rising up into plant and animal."[4] Or: "Earth is the building bearer, nourishing with its fruits, tending water and rock, plant and animal."[5] The self-seclusion of earths is therefore what permits the rising of mountains, the blossoming and fruiting of trees, the rushing of water, the grazing of animals, and to be all inclusive, the taking place of planet earth itself. Without the self-seclusion of earths, nothing that matters would rise up as an event worth scrutinizing with ever more light.

However, let's not fall for an easy bucolic spirit. To rise up as the self-secluding does not necessarily mean that the earths stand again for a ground, vegetable, or animal life under a cloudy, stormy, or blue yonder. The plurality of earths prevents such easy reduction. As we have seen (cf. "Strife"), the issue here is that in order that there be earths, there needs to be a work. The self-seclusion takes place because of the work of strife between earths and skies. This work must not be understood as an exclusively natural process but also as a willed determination to keeping self-seclusion rising up as such. Heidegger explains this by referencing mankind: "Earth, self-dependent, is effortless and untiring. Upon the earth and in it, historical man grounds his dwelling in the world. In setting up a world, the work sets forth the earth. This setting forth must be thought here in the strict sense of the word. The work moves the earth itself into the Open of a world and keeps it there. The work lets the earth be an earth."[6] One among many in the self-seclusion of earths, mankind works, and this work sets forth the earths in their self-seclusion as they themselves rise up into and against the skies. In other words, mankind's endeavors participate in earths' self-seclusion through their rising up.

The work of strife between earths and skies clearly knows no distinction among plants, bodies, or buildings; all is work rising as self-seclusion.

But what among man's work can be seen to represent in the clearest possible way the rising self-seclusion of earths? The self-seclusion of earths cannot be a generic and uniform "staying under cover" applicable to all material things. It necessarily unfolds itself in an inexhaustible variety of simple modes and shapes.[7] Otherwise the plurality would not be justifiable. So what are these modes and shapes? One could take many examples in Heidegger's work to show these many modes and shapes: bridges, sculpture, painting, poetry. I would like to give a different tone and set of references to this rising self-seclusion. As stated in the Introduction, the aim is indeed to never adhere strictly to particular corpuses but rather to open up a philosopher's vocabulary in order to expose a different angle or perspective. In this case, the aim is to show with a different example what Heidegger understands by this "setting forth the self-seclusion of earths." In order to show this, I need to turn to another horizon totally unfamiliar to Heidegger's corpus. This other horizon is the work of a contemporary of Heidegger, a poet who also wrote about earths, albeit with a different vocabulary and aim in sight.

This poet is Federico García Lorca, and the work that reveals in the clearest possible way the rising self-seclusion of earths is *Poet in New York*. This collection of poems has been analyzed in a number of ways, including as an expression of the poet's own emotional crises at the time: his homosexuality, his feeling of alienation, and his inability to be a father. It has also been analyzed as a response to the severe criticism that Surrealists addressed to his previous work, with many poems taking on Surrealist tones in order to demonstrate that he was not just a gypsy lyrical poet unable to create anything but clichés and stereotypes to please flamenco drama enthusiasts. Finally, *Poet in New York* has also been analyzed as a desperate condemnation of urban civilization and of the spiritual emptiness of the modern world, New York in particular. These analyses are usually coupled with Lorca's elevation of black culture (the Harlem Renaissance) as the only surviving counterpoint to modernity's metaphysical vacuum. While all these approaches (and many others less popular alongside them) are all equally valid, I would like to show how some aspects of *Poet in New York* also express the rising self-seclusion of earths.

The first line of the first poem in *Poet in New York* already gives us much to reflect on when it comes to self-seclusion. Lorca writes in the poem "After a Walk": "Cut down by the sky *[Asesinado por el cielo]*."[8] The Spanish literally reads not "cut down" but "killed," or more precisely "murdered," by the sky. The poet's first walk in the city reveals how the sky oppresses the earth to the point of murder, or to put it differently (namely in our vocabulary), how the earths shield away from the murdering sky. In the next poem, Lorca emphasizes, but this time in a reverse order, that New York is a city that no longer bathes in light: "The light is buried under chains and noises / in an impudent challenge to rootless science."[9] In other words, New York, with its noises and mechanization, kills and buries light, thus challenging science—this discipline that always needs more light—to make sense of it. In both poems, the important thing here is the double movement implied: on the one hand an elevation into and against light that ends in murder, and on the other an impossibility of having any light in all this self-seclusion. Self-secluding earths meet here the always unsatisfied light of skies.

Obviously the main evidence of Lorca's murderous sky is the New York skyline. He writes in a lecture reflecting on his trip to New York that "the sharp-edged buildings rise to the sky with no desire for either clouds or glory. The angles and edges of Gothic architecture surge from the hearts of the dead and buried, but these climb coldly skyward with a beauty that has no roots and reveals no longing."[10] Or again, later on, when the poet leaves New York for Havana, he notes that from a distance, "No longer does tower battle cloud, no longer do swarms of windows devour more than half the night. . . . The sky has conquered the skyscrapers."[11] The particular fight cannot be clearer: the industrial and mechanical world of skyscrapers, with its sharp-edged angles, elevates itself skyward without any other purpose than to obliterate the sky, even if this very same sky remains always victorious from a distance. This particular fight clearly highlights the unsparing strife between self-secluding earths and skies. The sheer brutality of New York constitutes the most evidential proof of earths' darkest elevation and the skies' ceaseless thwarting of all these efforts.

But the New York skyline is not the only evidence of the skies' victory or of the earths' relentless self-secluding elevation. Through their work, mortals also participate in it. In his denunciation of the lack of metaphysical and spiritual dimensions among New Yorkers, Lorca qualifies Wall Street workers as being "herds of men who cannot count past three, herds more who cannot get past six, scorn for pure science and demoniacal respect for the present. And the terrible thing is that the crowd that fills this street believes that the world will always be the same, and that it is their duty to keep that huge machine running, day and night, forever."[12] This criticism is not just a bland form of antimaterialism or anticapitalism. It is also a way of highlighting what constitutes the earths: mortals busily helping through their work the rising up of the self-seclusion of earths. As he says in the poem "New York": "You yourself are the earth as you drift in office numbers."[13] Again, this is not entirely negative. It also shows the importance of the work of mortals in helping the surge of earths into and against the skies (cf. "Strife"). As Lorca says elsewhere, "The real people of New York, the salt of the earth."[14]

Through its dark elevations and through mortals' work, New York thus stands as an example of this rising up of self-secluding earths. The skyscrapers rise into and against the skies, and mortals participate in this process through their work. However, let us not be too reductive. Saying this does not indeed reduce the earths and therefore all human endeavors to some kind of urban jutting out into and against the skies. This reveals, on the contrary, the movement of earths, however this movement is understood: the laugh of a child, a volcanic eruption, the death rattle of the dying, the digestion of a deep-sea anglerfish, the gossip by the well, the stench of sewage, the incense of temples, the growth of algae in the Atacama Desert, the tremors of financial markets or that of space stations. In this way, any work whatsoever takes part in earths' rising self-seclusion, not just the visible work of mortals. Everything that is therefore perceivable, everything that offers itself to the ever-dissatisfied light of skies, stands as a testament to earths' self-seclusion. In this way, no skyline can solely define, encapsulate, or emblematize such a movement that never ceases to self-seclude itself. The many different manifestations of earths simply know no limits.

In this way, all work participates in this sheltering manifestation, including, in what concerns us here specifically, the work of curators in whatever medium they choose. An exhibition or a project, whatever its nature or location, whatever its size or scale, consists of earths self-secluding themselves in their reaching out into and against the skies. No curatorial works—not even mundane Instagram or Pinterest curatorial endeavors—are exempt from this. Anything that offers itself to curating (spaces, artworks, images, sounds, smells, information, etc.) is indeed made of earths, not because it uses arte povera materials but because it participates in this giving over to the scrutiny of light, this light that never ceases to thwart all giving over. Even the most immaterial exposure—I'm thinking here of American artist Robert Barry's *Inert Gas Series* (*Helium, Neon, Argon, Krypton, Xenon/From a Measured Volume to Indefinite Expansion*, 1969)—stands for earths' self-seclusion, not by its ephemeral and evanescent qualities but because it offers itself to light even if no light is able to perceive it rising up and against the skies: "In [all] things that arise, earth is present as the sheltering agent."[15] Overall, the beauty of curating, even if an exhibition is a total failure, is that it always exposes the work of earths as self-seclusion. The curatorial, as an event, could not take place without this exposing self-secluding elevation.[16]

# Skies

**The skies refer to whatever allows itself to be scrutinized in and by light. • As such, they are intrinsically related to mortals. • With skies, mortals measure themselves in relation to what has no measure. • Inversely, what has no measure (the skies) is the measure of mortals. • This immeasurable comes across in the sight and appearance of things. • It also comes across as mortals' destinal trajectories. • Balzac's *The Wild Ass's Skin* addresses skies as mortals' destinal trajectory. • The uncurated shop reveals skies as the immeasurable that measures. • The hero loses himself in the measuring, which is nothing other than his destinal trajectory.**

From what disappoints thought—and prompts many conjectures and hypotheses because no science is able to make sense of it (cf. "Dark Matter")—comes the matter of skies (for the plural, cf. "Earths"), once again not just matter as such (cf. "Matter") but the event of matter called skies. As we have seen, the skies do not refer to the region of the atmosphere and outer space seen from the earth or the heavens. Skies, in the plural, refer to whatever allows itself to be scrutinized in and by light. This is a strange definition that can never extricate itself entirely from the earths: the "whatever allows itself" intimately refers to the earths understood as that which rises up as self-secluding. This intimacy between earths and skies is also an enmity (cf. "Strife") inasmuch as they mutually complement and antagonize each other. As previously stated, the bond/discord between earths and skies knows no rest, easy axing (as this or that), or healing. Nothing can reabsorb or transcend this intimacy/enmity, even if (or when) there is no longer a planet called earth and mortals are dispersed across the Milky Way. The event of matter called skies depends on earths but not because it is something observable on the third rock from the sun.

How is one to make sense of this strange definition of skies—whatever allows itself to be scrutinized in and by light? The role of light in this definition of skies gives a clue: light is the natural agent that stimulates sight and makes things visible (the light of the sun or streetlamps, for example). Because it primarily concerns sight, the skies are thus intrinsically, but not exclusively, related to mortals (cf. "Mortals"). Skies give mortals not only the possibility of seeing but also all the material they see. In other words, the light of skies gives mortals the possibility of seeing both themselves and their world. Unlike earths that rise up as the self-secluding, the skies bathe and give meaning to all of what has arisen in light. Without skies, there would be nothing to see; all would be self-secluding, without any retinas capturing light reflecting on the surface of what has arisen. This does not mean that the skies are for mortals with two eyes only. The skies are for whomever or whatever senses light—a coral reef's response to light in warm water, for example.

With skies, there is therefore a particular kind of measuring taking place. Retinas, for example, have the ability to measure (well or badly, it matters little) what bathes in the light of day or goes out like a light, what lights up or plunges into darkness. The skies allow the retinas to measure what has arisen from the earths; they allow them to evaluate, compare, analyze, and/or discard whatever needs measuring or whatever has not (yet) lived up to a measurement. The problem with the skies' endless allowance to measure is that there appears to be no definite limits to what can be measured, not even the electromagnetic radiation whose wavelength falls within the range to which a human retina, for example, responds (i.e., between about 390 nanometers for violet light and 740 nanometers for red). The reason there appear to be no limits is because the skies equally never cease to challenge mortals' limitations, including their fragile retinas. For the skies, nothing can be given enough light; everything can be made clearer, more enlightened, more discernible with ever-more sophisticated extensions to the human eye. The challenge of the skies' bountiful allowance will go on for as long as there are skies and for as long as the earths do not engulf everything in darkness.

The work of retinas and of these machines that push further the work of retinas thus knows no end. It is as if mortals can never stop measuring (and measuring themselves up) in and against something identifiable (the skies) that in turn knows no limit as such. Put differently, it is as if mortals can never cease to measure in and against that which knows no beginning or end—that is, no measure: the limitless skies. In the end, if there is indeed an end, however much a measure always appears to be taken, and however much this measure is often considered reliable and scientifically verifiable, mortals and their retinas always lose—killed by the skies, as Lorca intimated in one of his New York poems (cf. "Earths"). The retinas are therefore engaged in an impossible task: to squint hard so as to always capture something beyond the blue yonder, weather patterns, atmospheric domes, and constellations—that is, something beyond themselves. There is no end to their scrutinizing creations and idealizations; there is no end to the endeavors of philosophers, artists, and poets musing over the heavens; there is no end to the work of retinas and of their alternative prosthetics.

In order to make sense of this unusual situation where a limit appears to be drawn and yet there is no limit, it is first necessary to read a short commentary by Heidegger on a small passage of Hölderlin's poem "In Lovely Blue":

> Is God unknown?
> Is he manifest like the sky? I'd sooner
> Believe the latter. It's the measure of man.[1]

Let's not scare ourselves off unnecessarily. This is not about "God in heaven." This is about the unknown that God represents. Hölderlin believes that this unknown manifests itself like the sky—that is, it stands for what has no limit, and this limitlessness is precisely the measure of man. As such, God is here not the measure; rather, the unknown is the measure. As Heidegger comments: "The unknown god appears as the unknown by way of the sky's manifestness. This appearance is the measure against which man measures himself."[2] In this way, the unknown is not what is otherworldly or superhuman, but rather something limitless yet familiar—as familiar as the sky above mortals' heads. But how can one make sense of this strange familiarity? Heidegger replies that the sky is "everything that shimmers and blooms . . . everything that sounds and is fragrant, rises and comes—but also everything that goes and stumbles, moans and falls silent, pales and darkens. Into this, which is intimate to man but alien to the god, the unknown imparts itself, in order to remain guarded within it as the unknown."[3] As this description shows, skies are indeed the limitless, this unknown that guards itself always as the unknown and that helps mortals to measure themselves and everything else, including what needs no sight at all: sounds and scents.

Again, let's not worry too much about this limitlessness or unknown being some transcendental demarcation that allows mortals to go beyond (literally or metaphorically) the immensity of the skies. There is no indication here that contemplating the skies gets us closer to God or to any kind of divine or other realm. The measuring activities provided by what is limitless (i.e., the skies) is necessarily channeled through language and above all, but not exclusively, as we have seen, through the visible. The visible means here, as Heidegger tells us, "the sight and appearance of something,"[4] thus reductively confining this language back again to the work of retinas and their prosthetics. In this way, the skies, that is, this limitless, is mainly channeled through the sight and appearance of things, that is, anything from earths that surges in its self-seclusion and yet visibly exposes itself to light as something to be measured—as language. Again, there is no mysticism here. There is only a concrete reality. The skies allow us, because of their limitlessness, to measure everything that arises from self-secluding earths and appears above all—again, not exclusively—in my sight of vision.

The skies are not therefore some ether, heaven, or hell, but what precisely gives mortals the possibility of measuring everything. Heidegger writes: "The radiance of [the sky's] height is itself the darkness of its all-sheltering breadth. The blue of the sky's lovely blueness is the color of depth. The radiance of the sky is the dawn and dusk of the twilight, which shelters everything that can be proclaimed. This sky is the measure."[5] Note here how height and breadth, dawn and dusk, shelter each other in order to keep the skies always limitless, immeasurable, unquantifiable, unknown. Nothing constrains the skies, not even the darkness brought on by night on the horizon or deep space above. With such a lack of clearly defined boundaries, the skies are therefore the measure not in the sense of being a tool allowing mortals to ascertain the size, amount, or degree of things but in the sense of the measure of all measures: the limitlessness against which all limits are measured. If this were not the case, mortals would not rise up against the skies, and they would not look up into the skies hoping or planning for this or that. The skies are indeed the measure.

As the measure, as that which cannot be represented because it is not an object as such, the skies therefore stand for mortals' destinal trajectory. This does not mean that the skies stand for some kind of fate, fortune, providence, predestination, karma, or destiny. A destinal trajectory should simply be understood as the visible move of earthsbound mortals. In the process of measuring (and measuring themselves) in and against what is limitless, mortals direct themselves; they forge their trajectory. This directing is not a secret or independent movement. It simply follows and proceeds from the earths' self-secluding surge. Mortals would not have the lives they have if they did not measure themselves up, in, and against what is limitless and in doing so create their own destinal trajectories as visible expressions of earths' surges. For example, curators' work (cf. "Earths") most acutely marks this destinal trajectory. An exhibition, for instance, is always a visible expression of a set of destinal trajectories, surges of self-secluding earths—including artworks, curators, artists, museums, or income, for example—in and against the skies. This is what happens when earths visibly turn into skies or mark a destinal trajectory—a measuring surge into and against immeasurable skies.

But how can one illustrate this more concretely? What visible work can be put forward to show this destinal trajectory that rises up from self-seclusion into and against the skies? And in what concerns us here more specifically, what curatorial event can expose these skies as this limitless measure that gives mortals their destinal trajectory in the surge with earths? The example that follows is once again after Lorca as far away from Heidegger as is conceivable (so much so that Heidegger himself would most likely not approve). But the idea is simply, once again (cf. "Introduction"), of evading the atmosphere of Heidegger's work, thus giving skies not so much a more concrete reality but at least an off-key resonance that helps relate the curatorial with this measure of all measures. The skies as this measure and as mortals' destinal trajectory come across most clearly in Honoré de Balzac's novel *The Wild Ass's Skin*, and more specifically in that well-known description of the antique shop that resembles so much, for its exuberance, contemporary curatorial endeavors.

The scene in the shop takes places at the start of the novel, when the antihero, Raphaël de Valentin, determined to commit suicide at nightfall, enters an antique shop to relieve his last hours on earth. One of the crucial aspects of this last-minute visit to a shop is the fact that it occurs after places like the Louvre, Notre Dame, and the Ponts des Arts fail to entice him: "These monuments appeared to be taking on a dreary look as they reflected the grey tints of the sky, whose rare gleams of sunlight imparted a menacing air to Paris. . . . Thus nature itself was conspiring to plunge the dying man into a painful kind of ecstasy."[6] Raphaël thus rejects museums and architecture as a way of alleviating his suicidal tendencies. He aims instead toward "an old curiosity shop with the intention of finding something to occupy his senses, or else to pass the time before nightfall."[7] Balzac describes the shop with the following vocabulary: "It contained the debris of a score of civilization,"[8] "a chaotic medley of human and divine works,"[9] "a sort of philosophical midden in which nothing was lacking,"[10] "an ocean of furnishings, inventions, fashions, works of art and relics,"[11] "a vast palette on to which the innumerable accidents of human life had been thrown in a disdainful profusion,"[12] "a vast museum of human folly,"[13] "the immensity of space and time,"[14] "the whole of known creation."[15]

Raphaël's visit to this extraordinary shop has been analyzed in a number of ways: the shop exposes how the industrial revolution has brought an overabundance of useless objects, how works of art have become mere objects of consumption, and how wholesale inclusiveness has become more important than aesthetic discernment. The shop has also been analyzed through the shopkeeper's moral speech: instead of seeking power *(pouvoir)* or drive *(vouloir)*, the hero should seek knowledge *(savoir)* so as to usher in a peaceful contemplative life. Inevitably, the hero chooses power and drive when he acquires an ancient totem, this ass's skin, which magically shrinks every time its owner expresses a wish. The ass's skin gives him power and drive to continue until there is no more skin left—that is, until its owner dies. Balzac's morality is here all laid out: live not as if you held a shrinking ass's skin, but by seeking knowledge. In doing so, you will secure for yourself a long and prosperous life. I would like to suggest a slightly different reading of this shop visit.

Well before the fatal encounter with the shrinking piece of ass's skin, Raphaël encounters all of known creation in the shop. The crucial passage reads:

> For him, this ocean of furnishings, inventions, fashions, works of art and relics made up an endless poem. Forms, colors, concepts of thought came to life again; but nothing complete presented itself to his mind. The poet in him had to finish these sketches by the great

> painter who had composed the vast palette onto which the innumerable accidents of human life had been thrown in such disdainful profusion.[16]

Is this not a revealing account of the measure that the skies stand for? First, nothing is complete; all still needs to be measured. Sketches and poems, for example, still need to be completed. Then this ocean of furnishings is made up of innumerable accidents. These accidents expose the surge of earths against skies, this intimacy/enmity that mortals throw together as if on a vast palette of colors and shapes. Finally, Raphaël himself is required to continue the task of shedding more light onto what is already lit up, yet still needs to be given more light. Nothing can stop Raphaël from providing more light to what magnanimously arises from earths and already bathes in light. The limitless here always calls for yet more measuring.

But this is not mere spectacle. Raphaël's entire existence is engaged in this measuring without final measure. As he continues his tour of the shop, Raphaël's destinal trajectory takes a turn that highlights the way mortals measure themselves up in and against what is limitless: the skies. Balzac writes: "Pursued by the strangest of forms, by fabulous creations poised on the confines between life and death, he walked along as in the enchantment of a dream. Indeed, in some doubt as to his own existence, he felt himself at one with these curious objects: neither altogether living nor altogether dead."[17] The measuring here is clearly not some theatrical show but rather the delirious walk of existence: objects and mortals surging as and with the darkest confines of the earths in and against the skies—that is, whatever allows itself to be scrutinized in and by light. In this intimate yet conflicted encounter, the skies never leave these objects and mortals in full light. Their works are always in half-light, always in want of (more) light. Raphaël and these works are thus in unison and disunion in their surge into and against the skies, these skies that never establish or distinguish anything properly, not even the difference between life and death. As the measure of all things, the skies are indeed mortals' destinal trajectories, these trajectories that always extend themselves between the radiance of the skies' heights and the darkness of its sheltering breadths, revealing the strife for what it is: strife. The skies are indeed the limits, and yet there is no limit at all.

# Objects

**The belief that art has prophetic power is long-standing. • Kandinsky. • Artists are prophets. • There is no counterproposal, only a shift of perception. • The definition of prophecy is that prophetic knowledge equals natural knowledge. • Nature is understood here simply as what is free of cause. • Art is therefore as prophetic as nature. • Artists thus do not point to an elsewhere; they only show the event of matter. • Their work exposes strife overreaching itself as strife. • Weiner turns earths into skies. • There is a curatorial potential in nonprophetic approaches to art.**

One of the many events of matter rising up from earths into and against the skies is art. The belief that this event called *art* has prophetic power is long-standing. This belief is not exclusive to religious or spiritual art. Art is the medium par excellence capable of pointing to a truth or an elsewhere that no other medium can pull off. It opens up new vistas, illuminates life in unexpected ways, shines light on contemporary problems, elucidates current emotions, and gives us a glimpse of how the world truly is or should be. Likewise, art exhibitions attract hordes of people in the belief that they will be given an emotional, sensory, conceptual, participatory, or performative vision or experience (totalizing or partial) of how the world (or a portion of it) appears now or in the future. Utopian or dystopian, idealistic or apocalyptic, messianic or eschatological visions abound even if—and especially when—they hide under socially alert, politically correct, and/or moralistic stances that only aim to denounce the ills and wrongs of the world. From the moment art is exhibited in a gallery, museum, or in any adjacent contexts, it flirts with metaphysical connotations with prophetic aspirations.

One of the many culprits of this seldom recognized secret belief ("art is prophetic") is Wassily Kandinsky. In *On the Spiritual in Art*, Kandinsky famously compares the spiritual life of humanity to a future-oriented triangle:

> A large acute triangle divided into unequal segments, the narrowest one pointing upwards, is a schematically correct representation of spiritual life. . . . The entire triangle moves slowly, almost invisible, forward and upward and where the apex was "today," the second segment is going to be "tomorrow," that is to say, that which today can be understood only by the apex, and which to the rest of the triangle seems an incomprehensible gibberish, tomorrow forms the true and sensitive life of the second segment.[1]

On this changing upward and future-pointing triangle, the artist has a mission: lead the rest of humanity to the upper echelons of the triangle. During decadent periods, humanity sinks to the bottom because it ignores artistic endeavors. During enlightened periods, humanity rises up to the apex, listening to artists, these seers getting us all close to an all-time pinnacle of emotional, spiritual, political, sociocultural, moral, and/or material perfection. Not unlike a star bauble at the top of a Christmas tree, Kandinsky places Beethoven at the apex of his triangle as the ultimate example of prophetic vision in art.

Artists are therefore prophets. As Kandinsky says:

> [An artist] sees and points the way. Sometimes he would prefer to lay aside his power, as it is a heavy cross to bear; but he cannot do so. Though scorned and hated, he never lets go but drags the cartload of protesting humanity after him, ever forcing it forward and upward, over all obstacles in his way. . . . Each one of these artists, who can see beyond the limits of his present stage, in this segment of spiritual evolution is a prophet to those surrounding him and helps to move forward the ever-obstinate cartload of humanity.[2]

Alone, valiant, brave, and visionary, artists are prophets dragging the cartload of humanity toward the upper echelons of the triangle. This often secret aspiration never seems to give up, even today, when artists are supposedly more in tune with the harsh realities of a world facing its own annihilation. Which artist, however materialist and obstinately pragmatic, however socially and politically engaged, has not indeed dreamed of fulfilling, however modestly, Kandinsky's role? If they are honest with themselves, few would probably admit otherwise. The metaphysical dimension of art demands it and this, whatever the medium. In the art world, prophecies are thus stealthy, timidly, or brazenly de rigueur.

Yet as we all know, art objects are neither transcendental nor visionary, neither prescient nor predictive, properly speaking. There is no future-pointing triangle, and nothing can really conjure up superior strata of human evolution. Artists are neither seers nor prophets, and no cartload of protesting humanity is following them. This simple reminder does not reduce everything to some pragmatic "get real," as if the only thing that counts is the brute reality of everyday life. And saying this does not reduce the future to the cold predictions of accountants and business calculations. The aim behind this simple rejection of the commonplace perception of artists as prophets and their objects as prophecies is not to point in another equally false direction but to shift perspective, to alter the perception of the stuff that artists and curators exhibit: objects. The argument here is that art objects are not prophetic but are, most simply, objects that participate in the surge of earths into and against skies. Art objects do not point to an elsewhere; they do not aspire for an apex of human existence, or for a true revelation here and now. They simply point back to strife: earths/skies. What does this mean, and how can we make sense of it?

To answer this question, it is necessary to forget all of these unfaltering modernist delusions à la Kandinsky and start again with a reimagined definition of prophecy. Unsurprisingly, it is the least inclined to prophecies who provides us with a reinvigorating new definition of this term: Benedict de Spinoza. He writes in *Theological-Political Treatise*: "Prophecy or revelation is certain knowledge about something revealed to men by God."[3] This definition clearly posits that a prophecy is both a type of knowledge and that it is given—to use Spinoza's vocabulary for a moment—by God. However, Spinoza also points out, in a move that unsurprisingly reflects his consistent use of vocabulary, that his definition of prophecy could also mean "*natural* knowledge"—that is, knowledge detached from any kind of belief, superstition, or spirituality. As he says, "From this definition . . . it follows that the word 'prophecy' could be applied to natural knowledge."[4] Contrary to what one might expect, prophetic knowledge does not exclude natural knowledge; one and the other are not mutually exclusive. But how is one to understand this leap between knowledge given by God and natural knowledge? How can Spinoza assume such a similarity? As I will try to show, these questions point right at the heart of what we mean by this event of matter called the art object.

The only way to understand Spinoza's strange equation is to return to his well-known idea that God equals Nature. He writes: "The universal laws of nature, according to which all things happen and are determined, are nothing other than the eternal decrees of God. . . . Whether we say that all things happen according to the laws of nature or are ordained by the edict and direction of God, we are saying the same thing."[5] The equation God equals Nature, which he famously writes down as "*Deus sive Natura*—God or Nature," clearly and necessarily implies that when it comes to prophecies, there can therefore be no difference between what God sends down as prophetic knowledge and what is produced as natural knowledge. The equivalence is here not surprising, because it levels the knowledge of God with the knowledge of Nature, but also because it is above all radical. The two types of knowledge are the same; the leveling is unquestionable.

How can this make any sense in our archsecular world, proudly cleansed of all obsolete conceptions of (and approaches to) God and superciliously purified of all archaic notions of Nature? In order for this equation to make any sense today, it is necessary to recall the fact that when it comes to Nature, Spinoza is not talking about the natural world—that is, the phenomena of the physical world, including plants and animals as opposed to humans or human creations. For Spinoza, Nature is, as he famously says, *natura naturans*, that is, an immanent self-causing activity that knows no external power responsible for or in charge of it.[6] As he says, "By *Natura naturans* we must understand that which is in itself and is conceived through itself; that is, the attributes of substance that express eternal and infinite essence, or . . . God, insofar as he is considered a free cause."[7] In this way, all that takes place in the universe is Nature—not in a romantic or bucolic sense but as what is free of external cause, that is, as what proceeds from no external power whatsoever, bar itself.[8] Nature (understood as *natura naturans*) is therefore what knows no cause other than itself.

If we return to the vocabulary used throughout this book, this means that all that takes place as dark/matter; all that takes place as mattering events, such as earths and skies (cf. "Matter" and "Strife"); everything that surges in its self-seclusion into and against the skies, including mortals and gods and their art objects are therefore Nature in a Spinozian sense: free of external cause, proceeding from no external power whatsoever except itself. As we have seen, matter is an edge or indefinite horizon that knows no outside edge, no beyond the horizon. As edge, it expresses and reexpresses itself without anyone listening in, butting in, absorbing or absolving the dynamism of what is (re)expressed. In other words, matter sunders; as it sunders, the event unfolds without reason or why. This unfolding knows no originary or final fold. The event of matter depends, lacks, needs, and gives nothing. It simply is, without reason and for no one. So whether we call it Nature or the event of matter, the fact is the same: it is that which gives no ground for any external power.

In this way, we can only agree with Spinoza that there can be no prophecies tapping into some other world (parallel, future, or otherworldly). Prophetic knowledge is natural knowledge, and vice versa. Works of art—those sensory objects of reason and emotion—can therefore be understood both as prophetic and natural knowledge, with the two strictly indistinguishable. Part of the reason this is the case is that there can be no external position to Nature to use Spinoza's vocabulary or the event of matter to use ours. Prophecies or art objects cannot attune themselves to an elsewhere because there is no platform, window, or portal for getting out of Nature or the event of matter. This does not exclude the fact that *art*, like the name *God*, is still—to the great joy of Kandinsky and all his secret followers—a metaphysical term that points to an elsewhere (cf. "God"). But this pointing can open no vista properly speaking because no one and no object can surpass the happenstance of its taking place. Art is the name of a relation in which what is related does not exist. Inversely, no God can be seen to speak to prophets or artists because prophets and artists are Nature or the event of matter. Quod erat demonstrandum.

This leads us to conclude that artists, like prophets, can only show us the event of matter that they themselves are, that they manipulate or coerce into this or that art object. Or, to use our vocabulary here, artists can only expose the work of strife (cf. "Strife"). Art objects indeed express or reexpress the surge of earths, reflecting and refracting the light of skies about or through them: strife. This is their only function—a function that lacks any kind of transcendental or metaphysical potential, promise, or power. Art objects are just strife; they are what turn earths into and against skies. Their endless production maintains the strife as strife even if art history tells us that everything is engaged in a forward movement, evolution, or progress—(often dangerous) imaginary narratives based on hypothetical delineations of strife, biased surges of earths, prejudiced reflections of light in fanciful skies. Emptied of all these fables, art objects are just strife overreaching themselves as strife, and this whatever their symbolic, sociocultural, political, or financial value. The yardstick of prophetic power and all of its accompanying fables dissolve here to finally expose the only thing truly at stake: the enmity/intimacy of the event of matter leveling mortals and gods through work.

One way to simply think of these surges of self-secluding earths and measures by immeasurable skies that offer no prophetic power except the overreaching of strife by itself is to recall a famous conceptual art object. Lawrence Weiner's statement 462, *Many Colored Objects Placed Side by Side to Form a Row of Many Colored Objects*, was first exhibited in New York in 1979 as part of a one-man show at the Leo Castelli Gallery. It was then shown in a group exhibition at the Art Institute of Chicago, and it was later selected for inclusion in Documenta VII (1982) on the pediment of the Fridricianum. This work has been analyzed as an attempt to eliminate all references to authorial subjectivity (traces of the artist's hand, his skill, or his taste have all disappeared), a critique of mass consumerism (conjuring canned goods on supermarket shelves), a comment on museum visitors (standing side by side viewing art), and of course as a comment on exhibitionary and museological practices (paintings or sculptures lining up the walls of museums and galleries).[9] Whatever the perspective—Weiner's words are sufficiently indeterminate to be applicable to any series—the work clearly gives up on any prophetic ambition. It is a statement of fact; it announces what turns earths into skies: worded surges of self-seclusions into and against the limitless azure of interpretation.[10] Going back to Spinoza's vocabulary, Nature finds itself there without visions or revelations.

No curatorial event that attempts to estrange itself from artistic prophetic aspirations and their many accompanying fables can afford to either forget Weiner's word-objects or the work of strife as exposed here through a partial reading of Spinoza on prophecy. Reflecting on Weiner's row and on the equivalence of God, Nature and its knowledge(s) should always be the first step. Once free from the blinding sparkles of prophetic aspirations, art objects simply become reexpressions of Nature or the event of matter—that is, strife. If taken as such, these can only foster a type of exhibition or project that is no longer hierarchical (between the seer and the cartload of humanity) or ideological (pointing the way on the basis of fables misread) because the endeavor (strife overreaching itself as strife) simply renders these meaningless. Weiner's row, like any other art object, simply melts into Nature or the mattering event of strife. Of course, there will always be curators who choose to promote their friends because they supposedly have prophetic power or they simply fit imaginary art historical fables. But this does not necessarily need to be the case for all curators. Some might want to choose a road less traveled, where the objects of their exhibitions or projects embody the surge of earths into and against the luminous skies—this surge that brings together all mortals, these gods who paradoxically are no longer visionaries, prophets, or demiurges.

Inevitably, the last questions in this context are these: if they are not visionary, what does a row of nonprophetic objects express? And if they are no longer seers, what then are artists? The answers are straightforward. First, art objects are simply forms of natural knowledge (in Spinoza's sense). This natural knowledge has nothing to do with natural history or naturalism. It is the expression of an awareness of what is self-caused: objects laying bare the strife, exposing the surge into and against the skies, at one with Nature. Second, artists are therefore, more modestly, naturalists (or physicists; cf. "Dignifying"). Again, this does not mean they are experts or students of natural history or adepts of naturism or naturalism. To be an artist-naturalist or a curator-naturalist is to take part in the surge of earths into and against the skies—that is, to partake in the work of Nature. This humbling work affords no supernatural posturing, only the realization that the objects created are simply reexpressions of the mattering event of strife.

# Angels

**In the story of Abraham, Isaac, and the Angel, Abraham turns to the Angel and exclaims, "Here I am." • A new ethics is put forward, one that isn't a general answerability to society or faith in God. • It is an ethics based on recognizing placeholders for the future (Isaac). • However, two people are missing in this story: Sarah and Eliezer. • The need for their presence shows the impossibility of excluding ethics as generality. • Ethics is answerability to both the other (Isaac) and to society (Sarah and Eliezer). • Isaac and the Angel reveal themselves to be both mortals and gods. • This recognition leads curators to an ethics without God.**

One of the most intense, bloodcurdling, and frankly insane scenes in the Old Testament is the last-minute abrogation of Isaac's sacrifice (Genesis 22:1–11, Isaiah 6:8). Michelangelo Merisi da Caravaggio depicts this scene in a famous painting given to Cardinal Maffeo Barberini, the future Pope Urban VIII, in 1603.[1] The artist thrusts the action to the front of the picture, forcing the viewer to take in all the gruesome details: on the left the Angel, in the middle Abraham, to the right Isaac, and in the distance Abraham's wife and servant. The Angel is preventing the murder. His right hand stops the sacrifice, and his left hand points, as we will see, either to the substitute victim (the ram behind Isaac) or toward the distant scene in the background—one of Caravaggio's rare landscapes, perhaps the Alban hills in Rome. Abraham's startled face is turned toward the Angel, but his hands are still holding his only son, pressing a sharp knife against his skin. Isaac's frightened face stares at the viewer in a plea to make us stop this nonsensical murder. Caravaggio's chiaroscuro directs the viewer to scan the scene from left to right: from the Angel's face and outstretched arms to the startled face of Abraham, then, down his own arms, to the terrified face of Isaac, the docile ram, and finally the blurry scene in the distant background.

Caravaggio combines horror, violence, and irrationality with cold sensuality and pastoral beauty.

Emmanuel Levinas analyzes this last-minute thwarting of Abraham's murderous gesture in a blistering critique of Søren Kierkegaard's famous book[2] on the topic. His argument is that there is something missing in Kierkegaard's well-known interpretation of the story: the moment when Abraham decides not to kill his son, which is precisely the moment depicted by Caravaggio. This decision is not, for Levinas, the starting point of faith, as in Kierkegaard, but the moment when a new type of ethics emerges. This new type of ethics is the one that is solely concerned with the other, and here specifically with Isaac. This concern comes across in Abraham turning his head toward the Angel and saying, "Here I am." This response is the pivotal moment when Abraham finally chooses to abandon his unspoken one-to-one relationship with God—that is, his hereto unbreakable faith—and finally speaks, thus returning him to both language and life. In other words, with "Here I am," Abraham is no longer blinded by his absolute faith; he returns to the living. With this crucial turning toward the Angel and thereby his son, Abraham suddenly notices that he is no longer alone with God, that faith is not enough to be ethical.

However, responding to the Angel and recognizing the alterity of Isaac under his knife does not mean, for Levinas, returning to ethics understood as generality. The difference is crucial. For Levinas, the ethical means the general, what is negotiated, debated, and turned into rules, codes, precepts, laws (cf. "Introduction" and "Ghosts"). In this sense, the ethical is the spoken (cf. "Images"): the necessity of accounting for one's words and actions in front of others, of justifying and owning up to them. It demands a general answerability to society overall. The ethical as the general, as what is spoken, thereby elevates speech, negotiation, economy, and society above the one-to-one relationship same/other, or, in this case, Abraham/Isaac. Rules, codes, precepts, and laws trump one-to-one ethical relations. However, when Abraham turns to the Angel and says, "Here I am," he is not, according to Levinas, falling back to ethics as generality. He is not yet in an economic dialogue with others in general; he simply acknowledges that there is a responsibility that is higher than both faith and ethics as generality. As Levinas says, "Abraham's ear for hearing the voice that brought him back to the ethical order was the highest moment in this drama. . . . It is there, in the ethical, that there is an appeal to the uniqueness of the subject and sense is given to life in defiance of death."[3]

With this turning toward the angel, with this "Here I am," Abraham therefore enters a different type of ethics, one in which the relation to others is more important than both the relationship with God (and therefore contrary to Kierkegaard) and with society's rules, codes, precepts, and laws (and therefore contrary to Kant). In this way, regardless of what both reason (ethics as generality) and God (ethics as faith) tell us, we must first and foremost respond to the other person: "Here I am." The Angel's hand does not therefore simply interrupt the murder; it also and above all awakens Abraham to the importance of his relation to the other, which is nothing other than a questioning of his self as an ethical subject. Abraham's "Here I am" not only disrupts his one-to-one relationship with God but also literally puts his subjectivity in question: who is this "I" that says "Here I am" to the Angel? How does such positing affect the other? As Levinas concludes, "This putting in question signifies the responsibility of the I for the Other. Subjectivity *is* in that responsibility and only irreducible subjectivity can assume a responsibility. That is what constitutes the ethical."[4] In this reversal, nothing, not even religion or moral philosophy, can thereby surpass the ethical understood as absolute responsibility toward the other.

But who is this other? How is one to understand Isaac as the other? As is well known, Levinas provocatively and deliberately confuses the other with a small "o" *(l'autre)* and the Other with a capital letter *(Autrui)*. This signals that Isaac is both the other of exchange, this alter ego who exists in the realm of language as economy and who pleads to stop the sacrifice (by saying, for example, "Why are you sacrificing me?") and the wholly Other who shatters generality or language as economy and puts an end to the reduction of the other to the same. How is one to understand this wholly Other? Outside of all religiosity, the only way to make sense of It is by seeing Isaac as the Future, as the one who, by living longer than his father, shatters Abraham's singular subjectivity by pointing to a beyond his own being.[5] By the simple fact of being born and living, Isaac extends Abraham beyond death. Over and beyond a plea to stop the sacrifice, Isaac's traumatized and terrified face therefore shows the Future as what Abraham cannot anticipate: a future without him. In this way, with "Here I am," Abraham responds to the Future—literally, to the possibility of a life lived beyond his death embodied in his own flesh and bones, his progeny, Isaac (cf. "Fraternizing" and "Conclusion").

Hence Caravaggio's subtle painting artfully showing where the future lies: with Isaac. The Angel mostly points to Isaac—that is, to Abraham's Future, to what extends beyond his own subjectivity—and thereby establishes an ethics beyond faith and generality. The crucial thing in both Levinas's interpretation of this biblical scene and Caravaggio's painting is precisely the fact that the Future does not lie ahead or in front of Abraham but behind him, with his victimized son whom he no longer sees because his head is turned toward the Angel. Abraham's turning away from Isaac is what is at stake here. As is well known,[6] in Hebrew, the future is not ahead of us and the past is not behind us. With words such as *qadam* and *akhor*, the future is necessarily behind us and the past is in front of us where we can scrutinize and analyze it. By pointing behind Abraham, toward Isaac, the Angel therefore directs him to ethics understood—in this Levinasean sense—as engagement with the Future, the wholly Other, the face of the other. It is in this turning, in this recognition that the Future lies behind him in the Other (that is, in Isaac) that the ethical begins.

There is, however, one thing missing in this, and Caravaggio's painting subtly points to it. The index of the Angel points in fact in a vague direction: not only toward Isaac but also toward the ram, which, as is well known, is included as a sacrificial substitute for Isaac, and toward the blurry background scene where one can distinguish in chiaroscuro two dark silhouettes standing next to a house in sunlight. Who are they? In his own reading of this scene, Derrida is quick to point out the absence of women in this bloodthirsty biblical narrative. For him, the fact that Abraham says nothing of his planned sacrifice to either his wife, Sarah, or his servant, Eliezer, shows a crucial rejection that alters Kierkegaard's and Levinas's reading of it. As he writes: "Abraham does not speak of what God has ordered him alone to do, he does not speak of it to Sarah, or to Eliezer, or to Isaac. He must keep the secret (that is his duty)."[7] Later he asks: "Would the logic of sacrificial responsibility within the implacable universality of law, of its law, be altered, inflected, attenuated, or displaced, if a woman were to intervene in some consequential manner? . . . In the case of the tragic hero or the tragic sacrifice, woman is present, her place is central, just as she is present in other tragic works referred to by Kierkegaard."[8]

What Derrida's own reading of the biblical narrative shows, and what Sarah and Eliezer's shadowy presence in Caravaggio's painting illustrates, is basically a return to the ethical as generality—that is, as rules, codes, precepts, and laws, and therefore speech and dialogue within Abraham's community. The vague pointing of the Angel's left-hand index finger in the painting shows the impossibility of deciding between responsibility for the Other, for the Future as Levinas understands these terms and responsibility as generality. As Derrida writes: "Such is the *aporia* of responsibility: one always risks not managing to accede to the concept of responsibility in the process of forming it. For responsibility . . . demands, on the one hand, an accounting, a general answering-for-oneself with respect to the general and before the generality, hence, the idea of substitution, and, on the other hand, uniqueness, absolute singularity, hence non-substitution, non-repetition, silence, and secrecy."[9] This, contrary to what many critics of Derrida say, doesn't leave us in some kind of undecidable hell: should I obey the ethics of generality or the ethics of responsibility to the other, the Future? Should I obey norms and codes or the promise embodied in my son, Isaac? Should I return home and speak to Sarah and Eliezer, or should I simply pay attention to Isaac, who alone binds me to the wholly Other?

Neither Caravaggio's Angel's undecided index finger nor Derrida's reading of this gruesome biblical scene leaves us stranded because an aporia is always a *poros*. The *poros* to the story of Abraham and Isaac is really a twofold task: that of taking responsibility for the other (that is, for the future progeny who disrupts my subjectivity and destabilizes all totalities) and for the spoken, the necessity of accounting for one's words and actions in front of others and society. Abraham cannot get away with murder. His irresponsibility (his secret faith) becomes a responsibility ("Here I am"), and such responsibility (toward Isaac) becomes in turn a general responsibility (toward Sarah and Eliezer or society). This is not a progression but a necessary double game: what ties us and makes us answerable to one another as Futures and as society. The violence and strong-willed singularity of Abraham's subjectivity is shattered with Isaac and returned to humanity with Sarah and Eliezer. God in all this not only remains below ethics but also no longer has a role to play. No (Kierkegaardian) faith can either substitute responsibility toward others/Other or toward speech, the ethical concept, the general.

The crucial player in this spine-chilling biblical story is neither Abraham nor Isaac, neither God nor Sarah and Eliezer. It is of course the Angel. The Angel is God's messenger, but not in the sense of a spiritual being acting as an attendant or agent of God. With barely visible wings, Caravaggio's Angel is locked in a face-to-face struggle with Abraham. Unlike other painterly descriptions of this story that always place the winged Angel flying down from the skies,[10] this Angel is an equal, a peer: Abraham's alter ego. He is situated at the same level as him. He intervenes, speaks, and expects a response from Abraham. As such, unlike God, he is engaged in the economy of language; he is like any other mortal having to use language to stop the sacrifice. Yet at the same time he is sent by God. His message comes from what could be understood as the wholly Other or the Future. So is the Angel divine or human? The a-poretic nature of the Angel is crucial. He is, like the other protagonists, both human and divine; he is at once a mere mortal and the placeholder of a Future unimaginable (cf. "Introduction," "Mortals," and "Gods"). As such, and this is really the moral of the story, mortals are effectively gods to each other, and they alone can save each other from death. Caravaggio's painting exposes this exchange at the limits between mortals who also happen to be gods, an exchange crucially without God in sight.

How is this evident? Again, Caravaggio shows the way. Art historians have confirmed that the model who posed for Isaac was Cecco Boneri, who also appeared in other paintings by Caravaggio. Recent X-ray analyses also showed that Caravaggio used Cecco Boneri for the Angel, and later modified the profile and the hair to hide the uncanny resemblance. Could this be mere coincidence? How could Caravaggio assume that the face of Isaac could also be that of the Angel? This question will probably never be answered. What matters here is this: if God plays no role in human ethics, and if everything revolves around mortals who are also gods, then should not we pay more attention to these Angels and Isaacs, the faces of others in our lives, these placeholders of a Future unimaginable? In other words, should not we pay more attention to these Sarahs and Eliezers in our lives? Or again, more prosaically, should not we respond "Here I am" every time we sense that an ethical finger is pointing to a frightened child, ram, or silent witnesses? Ethics starts there, in this "Here I am," in this primordial use of language that uniquely responds to this Future beyond death, to these gods who also happen to be mortals and speak of generality. Ethics starts with this most intuitive of acknowledgments (cf. "Intuiting").

Caravaggio's exchange between mortals who also happen to be gods—that is, between men and women who are able to interrupt murder by referencing both generality and what escapes generality—indeed confirms the framework of the ethics of this book as established in the Introduction. The exchange between Abraham and the Angel as well as the renewed relationship between Abraham and his family operate precisely as a midwifery (cf. "Midwifing") inasmuch as it emphasizes not only the rationality of the economy between mortals ("Here I am" expects a reply) but also the birth of "more"—that is, the possibility of what escapes rationality ("Here I am" Angel, Isaac). This midwifery, one that can never be learned or imposed, one that suffers no dictatorial absolute value, thus works ethical dilemmas by balancing both the economies of life (Abraham's future life in society) and what can no longer be called "life" (Abraham's unhoped-for Future embodied in his son). Free of good intentions and good consciences, and free of any standards of right and wrong, ethics is here given over to the Future. It is given back to these mortals who also happen to be gods, who alone are able to open up the immemorial or the unhoped for, and this without a paradise to be gained after a lifetime achieving good deeds (cf. "Conclusion").

All this seems far away from the curatorial. But it really is not. Because it always engages more than one, the curatorial necessarily adheres, sometimes unconsciously, to this midwifery that emphasizes not only the rationality of mortals' economy but also the birth of "more," the possibility of what escapes rationality and economy. This "more" can, of course, be another set of economies to be traded and/or shared (views, likes, etc.), but it can also be what necessarily evades all forms of economies, what can never be guessed in the face of the other, in the emblematic unknown that is, for example, viewers or subscribers. In this way, whether in the old gallery setting or online, curators always give birth to "more" that is to both economy and what escapes all forms of returns. As such, they always address themselves to other Isaacs and other Angels, placeholders of a Future never future enough. They open up the unexpected amid the harshest of autistic economies whereby everything, of course, has a price tag and incurs a return.

This cannot be said of everything new and tradeable because only what leads viewers or participants to think more than they can (and this even if it is a selfie) has the ability to point to a Future beyond economy and death (cf. "Contents"). Isaacs and Angels need to be provoked not with the same but with what defies expectations, what can never be commodified as the unexpected. As we have seen, the midwifing actions of curators can never be channeled into prescribed avenues to yet again "épater les bourgeois," as the saying goes. As we will see (cf. "Midwifing"), this unique act is one that necessarily takes place as if lives are at stake, in situations whereby nothing is expected to return as safe and sound, profitable and self-serving. Recognizing that there are Isaacs and Angels, and recognizing that the curatorial can raise itself above the fray of practices by engaging others to think more than they can, can only allow curators to better work the moral and ethical predicaments they face every day.

# Words

**What does it mean for a curator to be just? • First, curators are utterers and addressees. • Amid their utterances, some are unrecorded, especially the obligation "be just." • This obligation takes place before will and power. • Is only discernible after the event. • Is always anonymous. • Is always left in midair. • Overall, obligations happen without "why." • They happen without guarantee of justice. • They happen by fits and starts. • Only mortals who know each other as gods can realize this passing of justice.**

In order to counteract the greatest of all platitudes in curating, namely that curators should always put artists first, Peter Eleey suggests that curators should be more irresponsible. As he says, "We should feel emboldened to act as badly as we can justify, and grateful if we can find people who still care enough about what we do, to complain."[1] With this suggestion, Eleey highlights a crucial ethical issue: How do curators retain their freedom and yet remain just? By calling to irresponsibility, Eleey basically wants to give himself and fellow curators as much freedom as possible and yet expect this freedom to be curbed in case it becomes excessive. But how does Eleey or any other curator navigate the right and wrong of curatorial situations in a just way? This question does not refer to either religious commandments (prescriptions helping you to lead a just life, for example; cf. "Angels") or atheist regulative principles, codes, and customs (Kant's universal maxims or curators' codes of ethics, for example; cf. "Ghosts"), but rather to a question of justice: what does it mean for a curator to be just?

In order to address this question, allow me to start from a simple premise. If, as we have seen, an exhibition, like that of the antique shop in Balzac's novel (cf. "Skies"), is a measure against what is immeasurable, then it is most simply an utterance.[2] An exhibition indeed utters a measure of earths' surge into and against the skies (cf. "Skies"); that is, it puts forward a measure of what surges from darkness into and against lightness immeasurable. The curator in turn is therefore an utterer, someone who says something, who relays a measurement of a particular surge. Let's take a well-known example from the history of curating: in 1969, Harald Szeemann uttered a measurement of the late 1960s conceptual art scene with his famous exhibition, Live in Your Head: When Attitudes Become Form (Works–Concepts–Processes–Situations–Information).[3] The exhibition has a message. It constitutes a measurement of a specific surge, thus making Szeemann an utterer: he uttered a turning point in art history that brought to light (or preeminence) works by sixty-seven men and just three women: Hanne Darboven, Eva Hesse, and Jo Ann Kaplan. For good or bad, this was the measure he took. The premise is therefore pretty straightforward: exhibitions are utterances and curators are utterers, both of which are visible expressions of earths' surge into and against immeasurable skies.

Now, as an utterer, a curator is also, and inevitably, an addressee, someone who is spoken to. As Jean-François Lyotard says in his book *Just Gaming*, a book that will pretty much structure how we address this topic of justice, "An utterer is always someone who is first of all an addressee, and I would even say one destined."[4] Indeed, a curator first needs to have been addressed before being able to become an utterer, a curator with something to say. This is pretty basic. After graduation, for example, curators always arrive in the middle of conversations about art, history, theory, culture, politics, and so on. They enter their chosen language (art activism, for example) always halfway in its articulation, development, or progress. Whether they curate stuff online, in picket lines, or in pristine galleries, curators always take up conversations heard or discussed elsewhere, adding their voices (if they have anything to say), making the conversations their own (if they have ambitions of authorship), and then presenting, sharing, and/or selling it (well or badly) to viewers, spectators, surfers, onlookers, or participants. As such, they are both addressees and utterers.

In what concerns us here, namely this question of justice, the crucial thing about this game of addressee/utterer is that the information communicated is not always what is on display on a screen or in a gallery. What you see is not always what you are told. A curator also passes on other kinds of utterances that are not visible, that do not automatically participate in the economy of what is presented, displayed, and seen. But what is being uttered yet remains invisible? The most common of these hidden utterances are obligations, and most specifically the words "be just," as in, for example, "Be just when judging this exhibition." In other words, and in what concerns us here, amid all their exhibitions or expositions, curators also utter things that are not always part of the show and that include above all this issue of justice, which is also, of course, the issue of injustice: "Do not be unjust in your judgment."

It would be wrong to imagine that these kinds of unheard ethical utterances ("be just," for example) are unique to exhibitions or curators. The obligation "be just" is in fact already secretly contained in most forms of speech. In other words, there is a covert obligation every time there is an utterance, every time something is said. When I say, "Listen to me," for example, I am also saying, "Be just in your response." Again, as Lyotard remarks, "This is the question of obligation in the sense that there is a kind of imperative in which, as soon as I have been spoken to as well as spoken of (in the sense that I have a name, etc.) I have to speak."[5] All utterances therefore come with obligations attached to them: the obligation to respond, repeat, relay, and gossip about. There would be no conversation about art, history, culture, or politics in the art world, on social media, or elsewhere without this hidden obligation. Furthermore, there would be no curating without obligations to view, react, respond, or retell. Even boredom is a response—not only to the contents of an exhibition but also to its hidden obligation: "be just," for example.

The curious thing about this obligation that always seems to appear every time one has been spoken to is that it literally comes prior to any will power. Curators always think they know best; they always tell artists what to do; their egos, as is well known, usually get the better of them. Yet notwithstanding their egos, they still obey an obligation that comes from before they put themselves forward as utterers with a will to curate. Lyotard explains this odd premise: "The will is never free, and freedom never comes first. . . . [The] will can be exercised only against the backdrop of an obligation that comes first and is much older, much more archaic, and it is not subject to legislations; it has not been the object of a decree."[6] This does not mean that curators do not have will power, autonomy, or freedom. This simply means that prior to any of that, there must be an obligation. Without this preliminary condition, there would be no will, power, autonomy, or freedom. This obligation (in our case, "be just") is indeed archaic, knows no legislation, evades jurisprudence, and escapes all laws because it simply comes before any attempt to participate in this game of addressee/utterer. It is the condition for speech itself, including the speech of exhibitions and curatorial projects.

Another important thing about this obligation is that it can only be understood after the event. A curator, for example, realizes that he or she has stealthily uttered the obligation "be just" only after the show opens the doors to the public or the images have been posted online. Similarly, viewers can only understand that they have been obligated to respond after being addressed, after the show or exposition is starting to make sense. Lyotard says this in the simplest of terms: "It is clear that it is not a question of first understanding, no! First, one acts from the obligation that comes from the simple fact that one has being spoken to . . . and then, and only then, can one try to understand what has been received. In other words, the obligation operator comes first and then one sees what one is obligated to."[7] There is no hierarchy here. The obligation is not superior; it simply comes first, before understanding, even before obedience or rebellion. So if I ask myself, "What on earth is this exhibition about?," I am already obeying a hidden obligation from the curator to raise this very question and respond. The obligation "be just" is in this way received before the exhibition or exposition is even viewed.

Finally, another curious aspect of this obligation that seems to appear every time a curator utters an argument in the form of an exhibition is that it is, as Lyotard says, anonymous. He asks pointedly, with reference to the oldest of all obligations, namely biblical commands, "Why do we find it natural—and we always seem to find it natural—that the first narratives, that the oldest narratives we know, are anonymous? It is not by chance, it is because the pole of the author is not the most important one, something we find almost unthinkable today."[8] Obligations—"be just," for example—must therefore avoid the author function in order to work. This does not divorce the obligation from the utterer. This simply emphasizes the fact that although obligations are to some degree authorial, they are always expressed anonymously. The anonymity of the obligation that comes every time I am spoken to or every time a curator opens the doors to an exhibition is crucial. It shows that over and beyond what is exhibited, anonymous obligations are also part of the show, invisibly enjoining addressees or viewers to respond.

The questions that inevitably will be on everyone's mind are these: why on earths and under the skies are these obligations kept? Why are they heeded and not simply analyzed alongside other comments about exhibitions? Because their force of generality prevents it. If obligations are commented on and analyzed, they lose their power and purpose. As Lyotard says: "It is proper to obligations to be left hanging in midair, if I may put it thus. Any discourse meant to account for obligations, transforms them into conclusions of reasonings, into propositions derived from other propositions. . . . The proper of the prescriptive is that it anticipates or at least precedes its own image."[9] In order to retain their power and purpose, obligations must not therefore be commented on or analyzed. If by chance a curator comments on or analyzes the obligation that structure a curatorial statement, he or she then ceases to prescribe and curtails the response. Everything on display becomes then already conclusive discourses, closed statements of facts without obligation. In this way, obligations are necessarily, as Lyotard says, always left hanging in midair; otherwise they would not be kept.

Without commenting on or analyzing them, curators thus utter obligations ("be just") without really knowing why. With every show, they say anonymously "be just" without at any moment asking the question, "Why am I asking viewers to be just?" or "Why should viewers be just?" We reach here the heart of the question of justice. As Lyotard says: "We do not know what it is to be just. That is, we have to be 'just.' It is not 'Abide by this'; it is not 'Love one another,' etc. All of that is child's play. 'Be just'; case by case, every time it will be necessary to decide to commit oneself, to judge, and then to meditate if that was just."[10] The question "why?" is therefore also absent in the obligation that enjoins us to respond, in the curator's injunction that a response is requested. In this way, the request to "be just" always happens without "why." It is only, as we have seen, afterward, after the judgment, that understanding and reasoning take place, that the obligation has the potential of being commented on, analyzed, and/or dissected.

But even if the obligation is always uttered without reason, this does not necessarily mean that, if heeded, it will automatically lead to justice. The obligation "be just," for example, can generate injustice. As Lyotard says, "Obligations are not always to be taken literally, and they may result in the most extreme injustice. They must be taken as much as traps as obligatory obligations."[11] Why is this the case? The problem with obligations that come with speech or exhibitions is that they can never be tested in advance of their taking place, before they reach their targeted audience. Again, as Lyotard says, "There is no test for the just whereas there is for the true. . . . It is proper to prescriptions not to make commensurate their discourse with a reality, since the 'reality' they speak of is still to be."[12] So obligations not only fall on us without why but they also happen without the possibility of being tested in advance. A statement of fact or a reasoning can be tested as true or not. Obligations such as "be just" evade this, and that is their danger. However much I enjoin my exhibitions with hidden calls to "be just," there is indeed no guarantee that I will not incur the most horrendous of injustice. No reality can vouchsafe the obligation that enjoins a speech or exhibition.

Does this thus mean that unlike other utterances (statements, comments, discourses, or descriptions, for example), obligations open onto a future that cannot be anticipated? Lyotard intimates this in the sentence just quoted when he says: "The 'reality' [obligations] speak of is still to be." Obligations indeed open onto a future of justice or injustice always unknown. The reason for this leap into the unknown is simply that, looking back, they actually come as if from nowhere; they are indeed, as we have seen, anonymous. As Lyotard says: "What is being called the transcendence of the prescriptive is simply the fact that the position of the sender as authority that obligates is left vacant. That is, the prescriptive utterance comes from nothing: its pragmatic virtue of obligation results from neither its content nor its utterer."[13] Anonymous, that is, without a properly identified origin, and futural, that is, always directed toward what is "still to be," obligations are without arche or telos. In other words, they go from anonymity to the uncharted, from a prelinguistic darkness to the immensity of the skies—a curious state that will infuriate all those who long for clear, safe, and repeatable methods of justice.

Without origin or destination, the obligation ("be just") thus moves from artists to curators, from curators to viewers, and between viewers. The obligation takes place with only one task: that of passing on the obligation without questioning its origin and without a specific aim in sight. We do not comment or analyze obligations; we simply pass them on, not knowing where they come from or lead to, not knowing whether they are right or wrong. This does not turn the hidden play of justice into the governing mechanism structuring all utterances, all expositions, and therefore all world events. This simply highlights that justice passes. It passes not as if a judgment, but always awkwardly, as Lyotard clearly concludes, "by fits and starts."[14] To pass by fits and starts is not very satisfactory, but it is crucial because it highlights, going back to our vocabulary, the way the earths surge into and against the skies. In that surge, justice passes; it proceeds between utterer and addressee, pushing the surge further and further into immeasurable skies. As such, the obligation "be just" can never be turned into the judiciary. An obligation is the antithesis of orders, edicts, and decrees proclaimed by judges, magistrates, lawmakers, or lawyers. It is the lubricant of earths self-secluding themselves into and against the skies.

Amid all the curatorial work (raising funds; choosing artists, artworks, images, sounds, scents, or foods; working with locations or modes of display; articulating an argument or not; advertising the project; welcoming visitors; viewing and reviewing; and closing, storing, and forgetting), the obligation "be just" then simply proceeds. It does not proceed sporadically or randomly; it simply passes in the intangible space between addressor and addressee, between the moment it has been addressed and the moment it is heeded or not. Because it has no origin or destination, because it is always anonymous and futural, the obligation "be just" indeed proceeds without ever being experienced as present, without establishing itself as presence—that is, in a supreme irony, as morally or ethically acceptable. Because it is at heart an exteriority that always excludes itself, an obligation therefore evades all ontological and moral axes. This is the extraordinary aspect of the obligation "be just": it is never "there," it is never identifiable as wrong or correct, and yet we pass it on at every stage of our communications, at every stage of any curatorial work—and this even if we have nothing specific to say, show, or argue.

Ultimately, and this is what all the arguments above lead to, only mortals who know each other as gods (cf. "Mortals" and "Gods") are able to pass on this obligation in full awareness. Realizing its anonymity and its unfathomable destinal trajectory requires not self-contained mortals embattled with alienating commandments, codes, and principles, but rather mortals who are able to midwife (cf. "Midwifing") or pass intuitively (cf. "Intuiting"), by fits and starts, this game of hidden justice. In other words, only mortals who are also gods can accommodate what has no origin and no destination, what simply happens without "why" and yet must be passed on. This does not free us of duties, responsibilities, or principles (cf. "Ghosts"), and this does not exempt us from justice as the institution adjudicating rights and wrongs. It does, however, allow us to glimpse the possibility of acting without necessarily putting forward an upstanding or moral posturing (or taking credit for it). By fits and starts, we consciously oblige each other, here, now, and every day, not imperiously, not commandingly, but as a midwife opening up, slowly or at great speed, the immemorial or the unhoped for. Recognizing this reveals us as the gods that we are because in the end, we are all the passers of justice.

As such, even the most unprincipled curator can "be just" because it is not a question of morality or ethics but of justice—a justice that takes place as curatorial statements and discourses are proffered. To be unprincipled is to avoid moral contents, the diktats of reasonable behavior, the stifling orders of moralizing codes and doctrines. To "be just," in the way Lyotard helps us to articulate, is to recognize instead that justice occurs from the moment communication takes place (from the moment a curatorial statement is put forward, for example) not as a ruling, decree, or sentence, but as what transits from darkness into light, from anonymity into futurity, a transiting or passing that no reductive interpretation of humankind (being, subject, citizen, identity, for example) can truly perceive or appreciate. However, once this anonymous and blind transiting is recognized, curators, and Peter Eleey in particular, can then be gods—that is, passers of justice—because with such recognition, they align themselves in fits and starts with the surge of self-secluding earths. The obligation "be just" will intuitively pass through them to artists, viewers, and all other mortals, and this without raising too many objections or complaints precisely because anyone attuned to the fourfold will recognize that justice is indeed passing in the surge of earths into and against the skies.

# Ghosts

**Can we evade moral principles inherited in a community? • Example: "to serve the public good." • This is at once majestic and cloaked in ridicule. • But what does it mean? • Before meaning anything, it enjoins respect. • This respect binds mortals to the principle, even if this principle ends up being false or evil. • It is thus always a subjective commitment. • It is also a matter of sovereignty. • It reins in freedom. • This is what haunts us: subjective principles as ghosts making demands and yet withdrawing. • Mortals/gods are therefore in a double bind: "be just" and obey principles.**

Can we simply "be just"? Can we really hand over the issue of justice to gods, even if these are mere mortals? Is it at all reasonable to sidestep the dictates of what is right and wrong, what seems like a good moral principle or what appears like an ethical code, principle, or maxim? Even if gods are permitted to play their part in this game of fits and starts that aims at "being just," is there not always some moral code, principle, or maxim also hovering somewhere on the horizon and imposing its ubiquitous law? These questions are not intended to contradict what has just been written about the words "be just" (cf. "Words") but to see that it is not just a matter of allowing mortals/gods to be passers of justice without asking why. It is also a matter of negotiating what is inherited in a community, what imposes itself like a certainty to this community (equality or freedom, for example), and what directs this same community ahead of itself, even if this "ahead" is uncertainty itself. So the issue now is to see how this negotiation takes place, how codes, principles, and maxims impose themselves as worthy economic deals, how they lead mortals/gods into the future, even if they themselves play, at the same time, in fits and starts, at "being just."

One way of doing this is to look at a seemingly solid ethical principle that contemporary curators follow. I use the term *principle* not in the sense of a fundamental truth that serves as the foundation for a system of belief or behavior but in the sense of a pervasive proposition or suggestion that more often than not remains unchallenged. I would like to focus more precisely on a principle that often appears in codes of ethics for curators. Here is one version of this principle: "Curatorial work is guided by the following value: To *serve the public good* by contributing to and promoting learning, inquiry, and dialogue, and by making the depth and breadth of human knowledge available to the public."[1] As this shows, the principle in question here is the public good. All self-respecting curators should abide by this fundamental principle. Their work has to benefit not one or two people in particular but the public in general. But what does this principle, hovering as it does on the horizon of all curators' work ethos, actually mean?

First of all, there is no doubt that although this expression is inscribed in this recently formulated code of ethics, the words "public good" have come to acquire a certain ambivalence whereby one is not too sure whether one should take them seriously or not. "To serve the public good" sounds as if curators need to abide unreservedly to some general truth, the formidable majesty of a principle surpassing all other principles. Yet at the same time this expression has also come to be cloaked in a degree of ridicule whereby one is no longer sure what it means, as if heralding from a forgotten past unrelated to the concerns of today's multifariously wired communities. The result is that either we follow this principle in protracted seriousness, or we smile at it, mocking it for its old-fashioned overtones. In either case, the expression stands for a principle that seems inaccessible ("am I ever serving the public good?"), impossible to execute ("am I really only serving my self-interests?"), and effectively unknowable ("do I really know what the expression means?"). Majestic or ridiculed, the "public good" nonetheless remains in our vocabulary as a powerful and inescapable term. No curator would want to be seen as serving the privileged or the excluded, even if, as we all know, they often do.

So the question remains: what does this principle mean? What gives it power? Why do curators follow it without ever questioning it? In order to address these issues, I will read a few short passages from a book that Jean-Luc Nancy dedicated to Immanuel Kant's categorical imperative.[2] The intention here is not to equate a curatorial principle put forward by a committee of curators with Kant's categorical imperative. As is well known, Kant's imperative stands (or is an attempt to stand) for the ultimate condition of possibility of morality, a kind of supreme rational maxim that remains absolutely constant notwithstanding circumstances or experiences. As such, Kant's imperative suppresses freedom of choice and prevents deliberation. It is the harshest of all economic deals: one that cannot be altered or revoked. Nothing of the sort is obviously at stake in this principle of "public good" put forward by museum curators. Yet there is no doubt that although not formulated as a categorical imperative, the idea of serving the "public good" reverberates with the same connotations as Kant's universal maxim. The question will be therefore not to compare the two but to analyze the "public good" on its own while keeping in mind, in the background so to speak, Kant's ultimate maxim.

The first thing that must be highlighted when it comes to these codes of ethics is that they must be respected. Moral principles such as "serve the public good" enjoin respect; otherwise there would be no point in putting them forward. This respect, as Nancy says, "forms the very relation to the law. . . . Without this relation, we could speak neither of 'good' nor of 'evil.'"[3] In other words, notwithstanding the meaning of the expression "public good," respect comes first. The reason respect comes first is because contrary to its object (i.e., the actual meaning of "public good"), respect remains constant. I can, for example, lose respect for the law. I can find that the law does not affect or oblige me. I can go as far as thinking that I prefer to be bound by other laws. However I go about it, I still have respect binding me in one way or another. This is what remains constant even if the law changes, or is ignored or replaced. Respect therefore not only comes first; it is what inaugurates codes, principles, and maxims; it is what gives them power. The position of the principle "public good" at the top of the code of ethics for curators testifies to the importance of this respect: it is what founds the other principles in the remainder of the code.

So it does not really matter what the "public good" means, as long as there is respect. This respect forms the code and inaugurates the "good," even if this "good" is not simply undefined or changing but, however paradoxical this is, evil itself. To take a well-known example, Adolf Ziegler's Degenerate Art Exhibition of 1937, which presented 650 works of art confiscated from German museums as a counterpoint to the concurrent Great German Art Exhibition, was curated in some twisted ideological strategy "for the public good." It declared a "merciless war" on works of art that insulted "the good" of the German people. One million people attended the exhibition in its first six weeks. The respect of the principle is therefore clearly what enjoins authority, not the principle itself. As Nancy says, "[Respect] is the law of the law, prior to any legislation and more archaic than any legislative subject. It is paradoxically, the law of what has no law."[4] Curators are therefore principled not because of a beautiful and universal maxim or law but because of the injunction that comes with the principle they abide to: respect. This is not because such an injunction has the power to command but because it is precisely incommensurable with any power of constraint or propensity. As Nancy says, it itself obeys no law.

The curious thing about this primordial respect that gives force to a vague, questionable, and changeable principle is the fact that it remains entirely and exclusively tied to the subject who abides by it. Respect matters even if it is not accepted by all, even if the meaning of "good" is unacceptable to many or has become lost, obsolete, or irrelevant. The reason it matters in this way is because it enjoins singular and subjective wills over and beyond any supposedly national, international, or universal will. Respect is a question of subjective commitment and not of collective will. It starts from the subject who alone decides, for example, to respect the principle of "serving the public good." As Nancy says, respect "doesn't prescribe submission to the universal but prescribes that *I* make universal law."[5] In other words, I alone render universal the principle that I follow; I alone enjoin the "public good" by respecting it, even if no one else follows it or if history proves it to be utterly pointless. The singular and subjective commitment to respect is what gives the principle its force of generality, its supposed universality.

This means that the respect called upon by the ethical principle "serve the public good" is really a matter of sovereignty and not of a universally accepted good as such. Through me—that is, through the subjective—I impose the "public good." Discussing the much wider remit of the "sovereign good," Nancy writes: "The Sovereign Good, needs to be understood less in terms of the good than in terms of sovereignty; that is, according to a difference that is incommensurable with anything that could be or make 'good.' The Sovereign Good not only reduces to nothing goods in general, it also consists in nothing other than this reduction to nothing."[6] So when museum directors ask their curators to "serve the public good," they ask nothing other than to impose the sovereignty of respect over and above the principle itself. In this way, the only thing that matters is the sovereignty of the imposition coming not from on high (the aforementioned museum directors) but from each subjective obedience to the injunction of respect. "I serve the public good" really means "I privately serve to universalize the sovereignty of respect."

But surely there is such a thing as the "public good," and the aim of this curatorial principle is to counteract, if not "evil" in general, then at least an "evil public" that only seeks its own self-interest. In other words, the good must be included in codes of ethics because there is such a thing as evil. The contrast is here not so much between two opposites (good/evil) but between what knows no restraints (freedom) and what is reined in by the sovereignty of respect. Nancy, again, is very clear on this:

> We need to distinguish recognized evil, localized by a law that takes it into account as a fact, and the evil disposition implicated in law. . . . If evil were a law of nature (we tend to view it this way when we confuse the ferocity of an animal or the devastating force of a volcano with the cruelty of humanity); the prescription of the good would be absurd, and futile . . . [because] evil is incomprehensible. But this is why evil, as an incomprehensible possibility, is evil, which is to say, free. If it were not free, it would not be evil.[7]

The correlation evil/freedom is thus necessarily implied in the principle as what needs to be reined in by the sovereignty of respect. The "public good" in curatorial codes of ethics implies a "bad public," not in the sense of an inherent wickedness in people but in the sense of a free public. So curators who claim that they are laboring for the "public good" are really only working as a way of counteracting the possible excesses of freedom: excesses that can easily and quickly become incomprehensible—an "evil public," for example.

Although curators only serve the sovereignty of respect—a sovereignty that only posits itself as the guardian of the limits of freedom—"the good" in "public good" thus becomes not so much a vague and changeable principle but above all something unreachable, an extremity that effectively knows no measure. "The good" indeed points to something that, as Nancy says, is "the immeasurable extremity of an elevation . . . the highest, supreme, or sovereign good, which, in fact, is no longer measured in terms of 'height' of any sort."[8] So on the one hand there is respect curbing dangerous freedom, and on the other there is a "good" as an extremity that can never be measured. In a way, no one, not even curators and their public, can measure this extremity; "the good" always evaporates higher up in the skies every time an attempt is made to make sense of it. The crucial thing here is the fact that this extremity must be understood not as a metaphysical ideal (a supreme or divine good, for example) but as what defies reason: an intelligible extremity paradoxically defying all measurable extremities. In other words, "the good" makes sense, and yet we do not know what it means.

This is precisely what haunts us. "The good," as this extremity that defies reason, is in fact a ghost that makes a demand of us and yet withdraws or disappears as soon as an attempt is made to gauge or measure it. As a hovering ghost that defies reason, this "good" haunts our lives, and here specifically the lives of curators, who only obey the sovereignty of respect. However much they try to obey the principle of the "public good," they can never quite domesticate the ghost that structures it: "the good." It slips in and out of view, in and out of reason without a moment's notice. In this way, "the good" in our principle can never be rendered familiar or natural. It is something domestic that paradoxically can never be domesticated. It haunts the corridors of museums and galleries and yet can never be seen or felt. As a ghost, "the good" thus never allows us to settle comfortably, and this is why it can so easily become evil—that is, (often retrospectively) unreasonable or illogical, serving, for example, the ideology of the Nazis. As long as we obey the sovereignty of respect embedded in the principle of the "public good," we run the risk of letting the ghost known as "good" become "evil."

I asked at the start: Can we really live without moral codes, principles, and maxims? Can we simply rely on a justice that occurs in fits and starts and that only mortals who realize their godliness are able to embody? The answer is no. We also need codes, principles, and maxims. Unfortunately, however, these do not necessarily exist, properly speaking. The one principle we identified in curating (the "public good") can only haunt us like a ghost, never quite present but never quite absent. This does not mean that we are stuck with ghostly codes, principles, and maxims that challenge reason. Not unlike when Caravaggio's

Angel points in an undecided manner to either Isaac or to Sarah and Eliezer—that is, to either ethics as responsibility toward the other or ethics as generality (cf. "Angels")—our relationship to "the good" is another double bind that ties us and makes us answerable to one another. We cannot live without ghosts (otherwise absolute freedom runs the risk of becoming evil), yet we must get rid of ghosts (otherwise they themselves run the risk of becoming evil). The double bind leaves us stranded with ghosts that effectively can never be accounted for. So what are curators to do with these extremities that haunt them, with these ghosts that run the risk of becoming the opposite of what they supposedly stand for?

The problem with a ghost is that it always requires a certain degree of midwifery or intuition (cf. "Midwifing" and "Intuiting") in order not only to be accepted as such but also to be made sense of. If ghosts ride at the cusp of reason, if they defy all forms of measurement, then reason alone is ineffective. Contrary to Kant, a principle cannot be entirely rationalized. A principle like the "public good" necessarily calls not only for a subjective sovereignty of respect but also for a midwifery or intuitive approach that keeps the ghost ghosting so as to retain the meaning of the word "good" from straying too far away from its intended sense, that is, from its intelligible extremity. Obviously, like for reason, midwifery or intuition cannot guarantee that the principle will not (eventually) become "evil," but it at least can help in saving us from respect as sovereignty for sovereignty's sake, and it can assist us in staying away from dangerously shifting forms of universal and rational "good." If this is the case, then only mortals who happen to be gods—that is, only mortals who are able to intuit or midwife that the "good" is not (yet) "evil"—can save us from the worst violence: the violence of senseless respect. In other words, only a mortals/gods approach to these unsettling and undomesticated ghosts can attenuate the possible dangers that the "good" shifts extremities and becomes "bad." If this is indeed the case, then mortals/gods can rest assured that the "public good" of curators will no longer raise a few smiles.

# Images

**Ethics is mostly dialogical. • This includes curatorial ethics. • How does the visual convey an ethics? • Tenier's curated collection is discussed. • A first arbitrary reading reinforces dialogical ethics and excludes the visual. • Can there be another reading? • Inspired by Paul Claudel's juxtaposition of maple and pine, Lyotard puts forward a sylvan, plastic, and libidinal obligation. • Feelings obligate us. • The "it happens" constitutes another nonmarked, nondialogical obligation. • Visual ethics is thus a driftwork. • Or it is an *ars vitae*, which curating cannot afford to ignore.**

How does the visual transmit an ethical message? More precisely, how does a painting or image convey an ethical message without recourse to words, texts, discourses, or narratives? Anyone who has reflected on ethical issues usually turns to a dialogical understanding of ethics. Ethics mostly takes place orally and aurally, not visually. It is an impassioned play of voicing and hearing in which the visual plays a small role, or no role at all. The reason for this rejection of the visual is because the voice and the ear basically better de-essentialize the monadic subject, thus emphasizing the importance of dialogical intersubjectivity over any other form of communication or exchange. With voice and ear, an ethical obligation becomes immediate, prior to any intellection, residing, for example, in the spontaneous "welcoming of the stranger," this prereflexive and prejudgmental verbalization addressed to the other.[1] Ethics indeed starts with and plays itself out through voice and ear, listening and voicing. For all intents and purposes, ethics is therefore in most cases dialogical ethics.

In a previous chapter (cf. "Words"), I emphasized, following Jean-François Lyotard, that every time there is an utterance, there is an obligation. More specifically, I emphasized the fact that as soon as I have been spoken to, I have to speak. This emphasis on utterances and speech clearly pitches ethics within this remit of voices and ears, of dialogical attentiveness and responsiveness. There would be no conversation about art, history, culture, politics, and so on without this secret obligation, this unheard imperative that founds social dialogue and—hypothetically—a just society. In what concerns us here, curating participates in this dialogical perception of ethics in the way it presents exhibitions as utterances to which viewers must respond. A good curator listens to the zeitgeist of the times, voices particular statements, and expects viewers to hear (or not) the well-founded nature of his or her statements. In this way, curating participates in this oral, aural, and therefore discursive dialogical exchange in which ethical obligations play their part.

So is it possible for works of art, paintings, sculptures, or simply images to convey an ethical message without accompanying dialogical discourses? An immediate response would be that art or any visual expression is basically language, and as such, it participates in this dialogical exchange. To determine whether it can convey an ethical message without accompanying dialogical intersubjective listening and voicing is thus self-defeating and ultimately meaningless. The visual is the textual, and vice versa. In other words, the visual is entirely dialogical. There is no need to ponder the question further. Yet is this really the case? Without falling for the hackneyed view (common among artists) that art or the visual is prediscursive and therefore untranslatable into words, texts, and discourses, the question still beckons: How does the visual convey an ethical message in its own language (i.e., within its own communicability), and how does it differ from dialogical exchanges of voice and ear? In order to address this thorny question, I would like to focus on just one curatorial painting and to perform a reading of it with the help of a specific passage taken from another book by Lyotard, this time *Discourse, Figure*.

The painting is *The Art Collection of Archduke Leopold Wilhelm in Brussels* (c. 1651) by David Teniers the Younger. It is an oil on canvas currently in the Kunsthistorisches Museum, in Vienna.[2] The canvas depicts a selection of paintings belonging to Archduke Leopold Wilhelm. At the time, the archduke was governor of the Low Countries (1647–56). In 1649, he appointed the son of Antwerp painter David Teniers the Elder as court painter and curator of his personal collection. In this capacity, Teniers was charged with acquiring works of art, cataloging them,[3] and painting a number of grand views of the acquired works, one of which is this painting of 1651. The harmonious, symmetrical, linear, and precisely curated wall hanging in the background shows a selection of the archduke's private collection, partially acquired in England from the collection of the duke of Hamilton (executed in 1649 after the royalist defeat in the English civil war). It includes paintings by Holbein, Bruegel the Elder, Van Eyck, Raphael, Giorgione, and Veronese, as well as a number of works by Titian. In addition to the carefully curated background, the painting also depicts Archduke Leopold Wilhelm himself, dressed in the fashion of Spanish royalty, standing with Teniers, who is pointing at a number of paintings purposefully displayed on the floor for his attention.

In this painting, I would like to focus on this careful layout of paintings that Teniers presents to the archduke. It consists of the following paintings: Catena, *Portrait of a Man with a Book* (c. 1520), Titian, *Violante* (c. 1515), Carracci, *Pietà with Two Angels* (c. 1603), Titian, *The Bravo* (c. 1517), Raphael, *St. Margaret and the Serpent* (c. 1518), and Veronese, *Esther before Ahasuerus* (c. 1575).[4] If one were to use conventional art historical methodologies, then one could easily interpret this arrangement of paintings by saying that it puts forward an ethics; it shows the ethical choice that Teniers presents to the archduke. It hypothetically asks, for example: "With this new collection of works, what kind of ethics are you going for?" The choices are all laid out: a learned approach to ethics (Catena, *Portrait of a Man with a Book*), an ethics of love (Titian, *Violante*), religiosity and devotion (Carracci, *Pietà with Two Angels*), manliness, dignity, and honor (Titian, *The Bravo*), faith, grace, and strength (Raphael, *St. Margaret and the Serpent*), or forgiveness and tolerance (Veronese, *Esther before Ahasuerus*). Which will it be? If one only casually glances at the painting, then the fact that the archduke points his walking stick at Catena's *Portrait of a Man with a Book* seem to provide the answer: he is a learned man, so he chooses an ethics based on reason. However, if one pays a more formalist attention to this painting, one then notices that Archduke Leopold Wilhelm points his stick in the same direction as King Ahasuerus's own stick in Veronese's painting. The fact that it forms the backdrop of Teniers's display clearly indicates therefore that the choice rests on both reason (Catena) and forgiveness and tolerance (Veronese).

However, this interpretation is effectively arbitrary, the simple process of putting forward a formalistic and therefore highly subjective reading of this unusual display of works of art for the attention of the archduke. It is only a hypothesis. It is more likely that the archduke chose Catena's *Portrait of a Man with a Book* because he just needed to fill an empty wall in his study, and this painting fit the bill. It is also likely that there could be another explanation for the display. In any case, the arbitrariness of this or any other art historical narrative to interpret Teniers's selection of paintings only shows painting's dependence on discursivity when it comes to ethics. The visual is effectively excluded in the task of conveying an ethical message. My interpretation translates the paintings into a discourse that is effectively utterly unnecessary, a gratuitousness that will no doubt obligate future art historians to contradict or correct my readings of Teniers's famous painting.

But such arbitrariness also returns us to our main question: could there be an ethics that solely rests on the visual (i.e., here, from and between paintings), and if yes, then how can it be made sense of? In order to address this question more accurately, I feel it is necessary to refer to Lyotard's own unique way of pitching the issue. In his own attempt at reading the visual as such and how it conveys an ethics, he begins by referencing Paul Claudel's book *Poetic Art*, in which the poet attempts to pitch against one another two logics: that of discourse and that of the sensory. The former incurs an obligation through a linking of phrases in dispute (cf. "Words"). The latter incurs a strange obligation that curiously evades discourse. Lyotard focuses on the latter with this sentence in Claudel's book:

> A long time ago, in Japan, while going up from Nikko to Chuzenji, I saw, juxtaposed by my line of vision, although at great distance from each other, the green of a maple filling the separating space, in order to answer the appeal of a pine, asking for agreement.[5]

Lyotard explains:

> Claudel does not say juxtaposition of pine and maple, but juxtaposition by the line of vision. The two trees stand "at a great distance from each other," yet the stem of the gaze skewers and sticks them together on an unspecified background on any canvas. Very well, but this flattening makes the "picture," not a page covered in writing, which

> is a kind of table. One does not read or understand a picture. Sitting at the table one identifies and recognizes linguistic units; standing in representation, one seeks out plastic events. Libidinal events.[6]

The pitch is given: the aim is to move away from desk and books and immerse oneself into a sylvan, plastic, and overall libidinal event—the three crucially confused by the eye so as not to demarcate a false nature/culture division.

The question, then, is how does this sylvan, plastic, and overall libidinal event oblige without discourse? How does it convey not only this agreement of pine and maple leaf, this harmony of silhouette, tone, value, and position, but also, as Lyotard says, quoting Claudel, this "knowledge of each other, [this] obligation between them"?[7] Lyotard responds by first suggesting silence. As he says: "What cannot be tamed is art as silence. The position of art is a refutation of the position of discourse. . . . Art stands in alterity as plasticity and desire, a curved expanse against invariability and reason, diacritical space."[8] If there is no discourse, then silence must be what conveys an obligation. But Lyotard is quick to dismiss this approach: "The silence of the beautiful, of perception—a silence that precedes speech, an innermost silence—is impossible: there is simply no way to go to the other side of discourse."[9] So silence is just another phrase, a negative phrase intrinsic to discourse. The sylvan, plastic, and overall libidinal event cannot therefore oblige through silence.

Maybe this libidinal event can oblige through what we call a feeling. But this feeling is not an emotional state or an irrational belief. This feeling is the one that summons language, that calls for a linkage of phrases. It is a feeling that signals that something must be said, just when one cannot yet find words. This feeling is also the one experienced when one expects something but does not know what exactly. It is the feeling of an "it happens"—that is, the feeling of what cannot (yet) be phrased, the immediate incommunicability of something that ought to be communicated. The proof that this type of feeling is not yet dialogical discourse and yet obliges comes from the fact that it stands for an "it happens" and not for a "what is happening now." As Lyotard explains elsewhere, "It happens is not what happens, in the sense that *quod* is not *quid* (in the sense that the presentation is not the situation)."[10] The agreement or harmony of pine and leaf thus comes from a feeling, an "it happens" that provokes verbalization and exchange. The sylvan, plastic, and overall libidinal event happens, and this is what obliges before *quid*—that is, before discourse ends up taking over.

In this way, and to focus once again on Teniers's mini curated show, an image (or a painting) obliges another and obliges us because an image is effectively—to return to our vocabulary—an event of matter (cf. "Strife"). As an event, it is structured as an "it happens." This obligation (the obligation of the event) does not have the same structure as an obligation that takes place orally and aurally or through exhibited utterances. As we have seen (cf. "Words"), speech—and exhibition speech in particular—are phrases in dispute; they link "oughts" together. "You ought to" is a phrase whose occurrence is preserved by a rule of linkage. It is preserved because it is sheltered in conceptual content, in the recognizable mark that constitutes the utterance, even if no text has been printed. By contrast, an obligation arising in nature (as in Claudel) or in a display of works of art (as in Teniers) is an event, an "it happens" that is effectively not marked. It is not a deictic gesture with a conceptual content. It is an occurrence without content. That Veronese blue, for example, sits next to that Titian blue, obligating each other, and us, by a line of vision. Not unlike Claudel's maple leaf and pine, these events obligate us and each other by their very happenstance, their "it happens."

So an image can convey an ethics without recourse to words, texts, discourses, or narratives. The archduke and we, the viewers, are presented with a curated exhibition of works that offers, as we have seen, both an ethically charged message (albeit highly subjective) and a visual ethics by the sheer force of its event, by the simplest fact that "it happens." Lyotard says that when there is no discourse, when there is no utterance, "there is a 'there is' that is not originally a heard utterance, but the product of a driftwork that tears the element in two [discourse/sensory], leaving the flanks in the imbalance that the ethical life indeed speaks of, but that belongs to the seer and the visible, that is unheard speech."[11] In other words, when there is an "it happens," it does not take place as if out of nowhere but rather between the libidinal and the discursive. Always flanked by discourse, visual ethics effectively edges with speech, exploiting the driftwork, this wanton abandonment between discourse and the sensory. As a visual practice, curating, understood here simply as presentation of works, prior to any formulation or argumentation (and therefore prior to any press release, wall text, or catalog), can thus be an ethical driftwork ready to be caught by the heavy weight of speech and by intersubjective and dialogical work. No righteous, morally correct, or upright curator can ignore it. To do so is to give preeminence to discourse, to phrases in dispute, and no self-respecting curator would ever admit to that.

As a result, the overall libidinal ethics in question here, this ethics that lies in neither a dialogical intersubjective oral and aural exchange nor in codes, principles, precepts, or maxims, cannot proclaim or broadcast any new interpretation of "the good," not even understood as an extreme ghost that cannot be domesticated (cf. "Ghosts"). The circulation of wordless affects, these "it happens," is empty. The maple and the pine, a Veronese or Titian painting obligate themselves and others without asking why or for whom. The curious thing about this ethics is that no "good" or "evil" are promoted by the sensory. As such, it cannot be an ethics in the conventional sense of the term. It is, as Lyotard says, "an *ars vitae* . . . but then one in which we would be the artists and not the propagators, the adventurers and not the theoreticians, the hypothesizers and not the censors."[12] If this is the case, then mortals—that is, these gods—are the only ones who, again, can take up the task and proceed by fits and starts (cf. "Words"). Once more, we touch here on an ethics as midwifery (cf. "Midwifing"), an *ars vitae* that intuitively knows the dangers of discourse and can thus proceed by exploiting this driftwork, this wanton abandonment between discourse and the sensory, what is ruled by reason and what defies it altogether.

# Gnoses

**Can the curator's work be something more than just a confession? • A confession doesn't affirm sovereignty but objectification ("he" or "she"). • This objectification can be transformed into an "us." • This "us" fights "them" and all hegemonic reductions. • But something more is needed. • Mudimbe and the fight against "them" is discussed. • Confessions turn into gnoses. • Gnoses are the path toward an "us" open to invention. • It is the strongest tool against "them." • Curators have the potential of gnoseology.**

Claude Lévi-Strauss once asked: "As for the anthropologist, are their writing, anything else but confessions?"[1] Could one equally ask: "Is the work of curators nothing but confessions?" With this question, the issue is not about curating as anthropology or vice versa, but about the curatorial as a mode of confession. The act of confession is not here understood as a formal statement admitting guilt or sin, an acknowledgment that one has done something wrong or an intimate personal revelation. In the context of the curatorial, a confession is simply the deliberate act of admitting having put forward knowledge (about artifacts, artworks, artists, images, art movements, and financial, environmental, or sociopolitical and cultural concerns, among others), and in the same gesture of having also put forward a lack of knowledge (what has been omitted, ignored, evaded, etc.). Who has not, at least once, been both impressed by the knowledge put forward by an exhibition and at the same time frustrated by what has been omitted, ignored, or evaded? If the answer is yes, then curated exhibitions are indeed confessions of both knowledge and nonknowledge. Lévi-Strauss's question about anthropologists thus needs to be taken seriously. How are we to understand this confession that characterizes the work of curators, and how can it be transformed so that it is more than a confession, a gnosis for mortals, these gods? To address this issue, I will read a few short extracts by

Lévi-Strauss himself and by one of his most diligent readers, Congolese philosopher Valentin Y. Mudimbe.

Let me start from scratch: what is a confession? Paradoxically, a confession does not start with an "I." It starts with a "he" or a "she." If I write a confession, for example, I do not treat myself as a subject but as an object that needs to confess. Lévi-Strauss is remarkably clear on this. He starts by raising the crucial issue of how an "I" constitutes a subject through a series of questions: "To Montaigne's question 'what do I know?' . . . Descartes thought he could provide the reply with his 'I think, therefore I am.' To this Rousseau retorted with the query 'what am I?' which cannot be answered until another, more fundamental, question has been resolved: 'am I?'"[2] Let's leave the last segment of Lévi-Strauss's sentence ("am I?") aside for now. Up to this fundamental point, we have this: through Montaigne's and Rousseau's questions, Lévi-Strauss dismantles Descartes's delusion that one can treat oneself as a sovereign subject. Unable to truly think and speak as "I," one has therefore no choice but to take oneself as an object ("what am I?"). This first move leads one to treat oneself using the third person singular pronoun ("he" or "she"). As Lévi-Strauss concludes: "And the answer that personal experience has given is the 'he' concept that Rousseau discovered and which he proceeded at once to explore with consummate lucidity."[3] A confession is therefore not an exercise in the affirmation of a sovereignty but is above all an attempt to make sense of an "I" who can only be understood through the objectification of a "he" or "she."

At this stage, the questions are these: is it possible to transform this description of a "he" or a "she" into something a little less narcissistic or self-centered? Is it possible to confess so as to address a wider spectrum of experiences? In his reading of Rousseau's work, Lévi-Strauss suggests a second move to ensure that a confession becomes more than the assertion of an objectified "I." This second move consists in highlighting the importance of transforming one's objectified "self" into what he calls "the most humble of others": "Rousseau's thought . . . evolves from two principles: identification with another . . . and the rejection of identification with oneself, that is to say, the rejection of everything which might make the self seems 'worthy.' These two attitudes are complementary, the second actually being the springboard for the first: I am not 'me' but the weakest and humblest of 'others.' Herein lies the true originality of the *Confessions*."[4] The second move is clearly that of giving up on the rational mind who always insists on saying "I am" or "he or she is" to reach this most "humblest of others" that is neither subject nor object, neither worthy sovereign nor oppressed other, and who can only exclaim, as in the earlier quotation, "am I?" But what does this "humblest of others" who says "am I?" really lead to? Let's look at Lévi-Strauss's third step.

Lévi-Strauss believes that if anyone who confesses achieves such a humbleness, then he or she has the power to slowly turn from being narcissistic and self-centered to becoming the possibility of an "us" that can rally against all forms of hegemonic reductions. Lévi-Strauss details this third step again in Rousseau's work:

> Rousseau's revolution . . . lies in the repudiation of . . . an individual member of a culture with a figure or role which that culture seeks to impose upon him . . . the "I" and the "he," freed from the distinction that only philosophy has sought to encourage are once again united and merged. With their original unity thus restored at last, they can forge together the "us" against the them, that is, against society antagonistic and inimical to man.[5]

In other words, if one repudiates the perception of oneself imposed by culture, then one can unite "I" with "he or she" to form the most humble of self, strong enough to constitute an "us" ready to stand against any further reduction. The confessional move to an "us" thus takes place through the refusal of identifying with both a self-governing subject and an objectified "self," a refusal that ultimately leads (via the "humblest of others" awakening) to the forging of an "us" pitched against all reductionisms imposed by "them." Lévi-Strauss's third step transforms the confession into an agent of change able—finally—to rally others against all forms of conceptual imperialisms.

Lévi-Strauss's hegemonic "them" is a curious one because it refers to no community, collectivity, or controlling power as such. This "them" targets in fact any attempt, even a random one, at reducing mankind to a predetermined rational concept. The enemy is this easy reductionism that is antagonistic and inimical. Against this "them," the confession thus becomes not a personal revelation against an oppressor but the work of an "us," a work whereby no one ("I," "he," "she," or even the "humblest of other": "am I?") is engaged individually, but together. In other words, it is a type of confessional work whereby one no longer has any distinct notion of identity fighting against "them." Allergic to all forms of compulsory subjections and objections, the "us" that emerges in this new type of confession thus becomes an agent of societal transformation who can finally operate without fear of being appropriated, violated, reduced.

But are we still talking about a confession? If this confessional work is to bypass mastery and ignorance, if it is to become a true agent of transformation, then it needs to be something much more substantial and revolutionary. What could it be? There is one faithful reader of Rousseau and Lévi-Strauss who has a profound experience of this antagonistic and inimical societal reduction: Mudimbe. Inspired by the work of anthropologists and philosophers, historians and theologians, Mudimbe also writes in a confessional mode, but his writing is not, like for Rousseau, a personal statement about identity written in the hope of awakening the same in the reader. Mudimbe's confessional writing is more precisely a textual self-presentation that also moves from an "I"/"he" to a "humble other" and to an "us," but this time, the "us" in question is clearly pitched against the most violent of ontic hegemonies: the reductionism imposed by colonialism. Mudimbe is indeed the ultimate example of an agent of profound self and world transformation. He offers his readers not only a history but also the tools for transformation, and this against all odds. But how does he go about it if not through a confession? How does he transform a confession into an agency of transformation?

One of the most famous of Mudimbe's critiques is the one he directs against what he calls the Colonial Library. This Library is the perfect example of this hegemonic, antagonistic, and inimical reduction of the other by a "them." It stands, as he says, for "the scientific knowledge gathered by the colonial experience. A knowledge that objectifies Africans and provides an ordered caricature of African socio-cultural realities: primitive, unruly, superstitious, etc."[6] It is against this racist and violent Colonial Library that Mudimbe mounts his confessional investigation and transforms it into an agent for change. It is this textual self-presentation/investigation that becomes a gnosis, a type of undertaking that frees himself and his readers from the constraints of all forms of unwanted or unwarranted reductions. The word *gnosis* is a difficult one because it is always associated with either gnosticism or mysticism. Mudimbe uses it in neither sense. If one wants to move away from self-serving confessions, then one needs to hear Mudimbe's interpretation of this word carefully.

Mudimbe is an avid reader of ancient Greek texts. Having read Aristotle's *Posterior Analytic*,[7] he knows that gnosis embraces sense perception *(aesthesis)*, memory, experience, and scientific knowledge *(episteme)*. But he also knows that gnosis is related to *agnostos*, what is unknowable. The latter is important because it does not refer to what is unknown but to what is as yet unknowable. The difference is crucial. It allows one to leave knowledge open, to never be in a state of certainty, to never affirm a *doxa*, and thereby to evade all forms of reductionism. As he says, "Gnosis is different from *doxa* or opinion and cannot be confused with *episteme*, understood as both science and general intellectual configuration."[8] Gnosis is therefore a departure from what one supposedly is ("I am"/"he or she is"); it is a withdrawal from knowledge and nonknowledge ("am I?"), and it is a move toward what can never be anticipated ("us"). As such, it can never lead anyone to become an agnostic—that is, a person who believes that nothing is known or can be known (of God or anything else). A Mudimbean gnosis is an immanent form of transcendental insight; it is a knowledge that leads to an "us" unbound.

Hence the extraordinary transformative power of Mudimbe's reading of Rousseau and Lévi-Strauss. He offers us not an already well-trodden passage from one plane of subjectivation to another, from one oppressed culture to another; he offers us instead a breaking out of what we are, of what we believe we are. Mudimbe's gnosis is, not unlike Levinas's desire to escape the weight of Being, a "liberation"[9] from all that is inherited, all that constitutes already established knowledge and what is being overlooked, ignored, or disregarded. In this way, in lieu of a confession, we have a gnosis, an invitation to move out of any cumbersome libraries, not toward another form of subjectivity (which would then constitute yet another library) but toward an "us" as what cannot be anticipated, what needs to be invented—*agnostos*. This means that in order to pull away from the confessional mode, in order to give a chance to an "us," it is necessary to be suspicious of our own libraries, and in doing so, it is necessary not just to confess but to create gnoses, for which what comes together as "we" is never quite in full sight.

As such, a gnosis is effectively a question mark, an invitation to know more, to open ourselves up to what is as yet unknowable. As Mudimbe says, "What this gnosis attests to is thus, beyond its will for power and its conceptual apparatus, a dramatic but ordinary question about its own being: what is it and how can it remain a pertinent question mark?"[10] This invitation is the strongest, most powerful tool against self-centered confessions of victory/defeat and against all hegemonic reductions by a "them": it bypasses the will to power of the monadic subject ("I am"), it evades the comfortable certainty of all objectifications ("he," "she"), and it participates in this adventure that is an "us," constituted by humbling others ("am I?"), and this at the limit of knowledge. As such, Mudimbe's gnosis, this dramatic question mark always at risk, is what gives "us" the strength to evade all and any masteries of knowledge and the many stupidities that come with it.

As stated at the start, the curatorial knows many confessions. It is filled with admissions of mastery and ignorance. Curators know about artworks, artists, art movements, images, and sociopolitical, financial, cultural, and economic issues. Curators also know that they do not know, that after all, it is just a show, with all its failings and shortcomings. As such, the curatorial is filled with ambivalent confessions. Yet sometimes it is also filled with gnoses in a Mudimbean sense. The few curators who create gnoses have abandoned their "I am"; they don't pretend to be anything other than the "humblest of others," a humility that allows them to hear a transformative "us" open not to the "other" as an imaginary or projected entity (a public, an audience, a statistic, etc.) but to what can never be anticipated, what evades the hegemonies imposed by "them." Here is an example that constitutes a set of artistic-curatorial confessions turned into gnoses, whereby objectified "selves" (artists turned curatorial activists) are no longer in play and an "us" is clearly put in place as an agent of transformation.

I am thinking here of the artistic-curatorial venture called Flood that took place as part of Mary-Jane Jacob's site-specific multisite project for Sculpture Chicago, Culture in Action.[11] Flood was set in place by a group of twenty or so artists (originally set up by Richard House, Wendy Jacob, Laurie Paler, and John Ploof under the denomination Haha) who built and maintained a hydroponic garden in a storefront on the North Side of Chicago in the mid-1990s as a way of counteracting the disastrously lame politics against the AIDS crisis in the United States at the time. They grew vegetables (kale, collards, mustard greens,

Swiss chard) and therapeutic herbs for people with HIV/AIDS. For several years, Haha provided meals twice a week, educational activities, meeting spaces, public events, and information on alternative therapies, nutrition, and horticulture, as well as a place to garden. Such a project not only questions what artists-curators do (they do not always make or stage artworks) but also acknowledges that a project can do more than just create economic returns to be listed on CVs. It can be a gnosis in a Mudimbean sense, whereby the artists-curators' confessional "I" has been transformed into an "us" as an agent for change open to the unknown provoked by the AIDS crisis (the search for a cure, ways of addressing it, healing, compassion, love, etc.). In this way, Haha clearly bypasses the will to power of the monadic subject; it evades the comfortable certainty of objectification and participates in this adventure that is an "us" over and beyond the violence of President Ronald Reagan's "them."

It is this kind of artistic-curatorial work that characterizes mortals who also happen to be gods. This type of confession turned into gnosis—that is, this type of gnoseology—indeed turns earths into skies and acknowledges that we are all mortals—that is, gods. How? Simply because they focus on an "us" that is not already reduced by a "them" as this or that (gay, straight, artist, curator, person with AIDS, etc.). They focus on an "us" open to invention, open to a future beyond death (cf. "Introduction," "Angels," and "Conclusion") and this, even if there is no or little future ahead, as was then the case of those with AIDS. Mortals who also happen to be gods are indeed, following Mudimbe, the midwifing and intuitive players of *agnostos*—that is, what is as yet unknowable. Against the "them" that always tries to foreclose the future, these mortals/gods (here called Haha) let what is as yet unknowable play its part in the work of "us," extend a hand to the ill, helping them find healing solutions and addressing their plight. They leave knowledge open not in order to stay in a permanent state of uncertainty but in order to fight against all forms of *doxa*. The "us" of gnoses is perhaps the only aim for curators who finally want to leave hackneyed confessions aside and finally embody these godly selves for a world free of all forms of hegemonic reductionism.

# Contents

**There are different types of content curating. • The focus is always on content, but rarely on navigation. • Amid the process of navigation, hyperlinks are key. • Following Gruber/Lyotard, hyperlinks are hyphens. • Hyperlinks are signs with promises. • They are always in retreat from contents. • They stand in for the passage of time. • Witness the frenetic standstill of Web surfers. • Such surfing keeps ourselves in childhood. • It results in self-incurred tutelage and emancipation. • The blank is the beginning of the end for the frenetic standstill. • Curators must move from "what can I know?" to "who do I want to be?" • This is the only move out of childhood.**

Among the many different types of content curation, one can perhaps distinguish three kinds. The first is performed manually, usually by a paid employee, called a content curator, who sifts through megabytes of data, identifies relevant content, and shares it across the company or organization's Internet platforms for immediate or deferred public consumption. In this case, the content is specifically aggregated for a demographic that is as wide as possible, even if it is a specialized segment of the population. It is difficult to provide examples here because most companies with a functioning website, from Coca-Cola to the smallest local corner shop, curate contents for their customers, viewers, or readers. In all cases, most of these websites are designed with a curated section not only in order to bring in more customers, viewers, or readers but also, above all, in order to generate more profit, either by selling advertising space or user data and/or metadata.

The second kind of content curation is also performed manually by one or more (most often unpaid) individuals for their own enjoyment and that of their followers. The purpose of this aggregation of information (texts, images, videos, data, etc.) is to identify, select, edit, correct, compile, assemble, prepare for publication, and share content that reflects these individuals' own interests. Examples include the many users of social media platforms such as Instagram, Pinterest, or Tumblr. This type of content curation has no intended audience other than the curators themselves and their immediate social network. This lack of target in turn gets instrumentalized for valuable metadata by algorithmically driven advertising technologies. The curators in this case are monetized on the terms of the platform on which they have built their curated content. If they have a large enough following, the curators monetize their own aggregation as a branded identity.

The third type is algorithmically generated content. This can be understood on at least two levels. First, there are content curating companies specifically dedicated to sifting through petabytes of data to satisfy content curators themselves. These companies include Paper.li, Curata, Scoop.it, and ScribbleLive. Their aim is to ensure their paying content curators (with websites, blogs, social network pages, and e-newsletters) expand their networks by providing "interesting" contents to generate more sales, likes, or returns. These companies' sophisticated tools operate like social media assistants churning out millions of pages of the freshest, most original, and sifted-through content to be shared. Second, there is content curating software used by most large companies to attract consumers, convert products into sales, and/or expand and retain their audiences and followers. Such software, which can often be spotted under the rubric "Recommended for You," creates scalable, premium-content, interactive experiences as well as real-time audience engagement in order to optimize performance and drive better business results. As both of these methods of curation indicate, this type of algorithmically generated content no longer quite (as yet) counts as curation, properly speaking, because it more resembles automated marketing strategies than manual curatorial endeavors.[1]

The consequences of the first two types of manual content curating are many. First, content curators usually focus on their own taste or that of their targeted audience before putting forward an articulated argument about the chosen content. Most often the aim is user satisfaction before the communication of messages or arguments. Second, content curators edit out context in order for the content to fit the size of the screen and/or the needs of the users' immediate consumption. The aim is therefore Web page readability over the meaningfulness of what is treated as content. Third, content curators discard any type of content that does not photograph, visualize, or sound well. The aim is online digestibility over cultural weight or signification. Fourth, content curators participate in a general homogenization (social, cultural, political, etc.) of content that is then fragmented into demographically pre- or self-determined consumer or interest groups. The aim is the reinforcement of clichés, truisms, stock phrases, and hackneyed contents ruled by the ever-pervasive tagging process. In other words, confirmation of the same is the sole aim, and this even if (and especially when) difference is what is curated. Finally, but most importantly, content curators more or less reject any kind of responsibility. They usually use pseudonyms, or—especially in the first type—they remain nameless, invisible, and/or mute in order to embrace a warped utilitarianism: giving targeted users what they want. The aim here is overall shareable satisfaction over any responsible consideration.

In this bleak picture of the work of manual content curators, one thing, however, stands out. This thing is often forgotten in this newly defined profession. The focus is indeed always on the content curated and how it is presented visually on Web pages, and rarely on the process of navigation between content. Click, tap, hover: three common ways of moving from content source to content target and back. Click, tap, hover: three gestures that concern both online curators and the targeted audience. It is what unites them in the pervasive use of the Internet. Although individual and unique, these movements are paradoxically not done alone. They come with crawlers monitoring movement, gathering data and metadata about the surfers' personal moves. How is one to make sense of these movements in this vast ocean of contents? Content curators, not unlike their cousins, gallery or museum curators, want their targeted audiences to focus on what is presented to them, yet online, this focus would not exist without these nonlinear moves across potentially endless pages of contents. There is always talk of content but little of what allows this content to be seen, appreciated, tabulated, bookmarked, minimized, maximized, ordered, closed, or discarded. In a way, click, tap, and hover rule contents, curators, their work, and its reception. How is one to make sense of this?

In order to address this question, I will perform a type of reading that is usually unacceptable among philosophers: to read two authors on the edge of their discourse—that is, without actually addressing the content of their work. The aim is not to be disrespectful or unethical. Rather, the aim is to read their text not on the surface but as it comes into view or eclipses out of sight—basically, before content takes over. The two authors in question are Eberhard Gruber and Jean-François Lyotard. The content of their jointly written book can be summed up with this question: what unites and separate Judaism and Christianity? The edge of their essays and conversations is the hyphen in "Judeo-Christian" and its many derivations. The hyphen is basically a link between the two religions. In what concerns us here, I will read Gruber and Lyotard's study of the hyphen as a way of making sense of the hyperlink, these highlighted and underlined words, symbols, or images that allow curators and audiences to move from content to content, surfing their unique paths into or through homogenized hypertexted contents.[2] Treating the hyperlink as a hyphen allows for an understanding of what is so often forgotten when moving from page to page: the actual movement itself. So let's follow that small hand with a pointing index finger.

A hyperlink or a hyphen is basically a sign. As Eberhard Gruber says of the hyphen, "It is a *sign* with an affirmative, differential, interrogative, or metaphorical effect."[3] When thinking of the hyperlink as a hyphen, it is indeed, first of all, affirmative: it says, "That's where you need to click, tap, or hover in order to reach a new page—that is, what promises to be even more informative and desirable"—and this even if the positive aspect of this link is full of danger, as in the case of corrupted or hacked linked websites. It is also differential: it says, "Here is something else, something different from the present contents, something that has not yet been seen, read, watched, heard." It is also interrogative: it says, "What is it that you do not yet know? Could this be the answer?" The icon of the small hand invites the targeted audience to seek out more, leading the way to other content, another hypertext page. Finally, the hyperlink is metaphorical: the easiest way to understand this is with the use of the expression "here," as in click or tap "here." This "here" is a metaphor because it is representative or symbolic of what is not "here," namely another page or window. More could no doubt be said of this sign that opens up further contents. Overall, the issue here is simply that, like the hyphen, it marks a passage; it is a *poros* to the aporia that is content—what has already been seen, read, commented on, digested, and therefore already defunct.

A hyperlink is indeed a passage between two contents, but it is also much more than that. It has two further characteristics. First, it is a sign that withdraws itself. It not only signifies something (it is usually a word, image, or symbol) but also leads elsewhere, thus retreating from what it signifies in the first place. Again, as Gruber remarks about the hyphen: "It is a trait in retreat, in withdrawal of the thing, or more precisely of the things whose composition it underpins or supports."[4] This retreat or withdrawal not only renders the hyperlink somehow indifferent to either contents but also places itself *sous-rature*. However, it is not literally under erasure but rather under threat of erasure. It is both legible and necessary, yet not enough for the contents in which it is embedded. The hyperlink is in this way a typographical expression that marks an absence right at the heart of what appears to be full presence, contents on screen. As such, a hyperlink does not signify the passing of time but its passage. Being inscribed or embedded in hypertext, the hyperlink signals a "pass here toward an elsewhere." In this way, the hyperlink invites a temporal movement toward an unknown future, even if this future is easily predictable. There has perhaps never been a more visible sign of the passage of time as *sous-rature* in history.

Of course, if one says that a hyperlink marks the passage of time and that this passage necessarily points to an exit in the form of another content, one also automatically assumes that there can be a way back: the back button. The return arrow implies a certain reversibility of time; one can always go back to previously seen contents. Unfortunately, because the hyperlink is a sign amid signs, the return or back button only reinforces a false exteriority. Hypertext users in fact go nowhere in their endless clicking. Gruber talks of the duplicitous nature (*aufhebend*[5]) of the hyphen, the fact that it allows both passage and return, and that such duplicity gives an illusion of transport. Transposed onto hypertexts, Web users are simply duped into believing that they are going somewhere in their surfing. They are not. They are only governed by a system that creates the illusion of transport, movement, freedom. The only thing that truly happens is that the tap forward/tap back provided by hyperlinks establishes instead a paradoxical successivity that remains in place. It is paradoxical because the content source is structured as lack and the target source is structured as fullness, yet once clicked, the back button only reverses the problem: source becomes potential new target. In this way, there is no exit properly speaking, only a frenetic clicking standstill, the hallmark of capitalism.[6]

The duping performed by our little pointing finger shows that the contents of curators and their audiences is effectively always predigested. With hyperlinks, we are always on well-trodden paths, the linkage of contents preestablished and predetermined. The hyperlink or the hyphen is effectively always the sign of a departure that is also the sign of a departure already taken. This constant stepping onto someone else's path reveals that with hyperlinks, we are always already caught in a double bind: a self-incurred tutelage and an emancipation from tutelage, neither of which is able to win over the other. In other words, the supposed salvation of the Internet is our enslavement. Fascism and freedom are here cousins. The reason for this double bind is that the other/Other (cf. "Angels") has effectively been denied. Emancipation supposedly leads only to further emancipation, with no positive and alluring alternative. Gruber describes this double bind by referring to the child: "The adult defines the 'child' as non-emancipated so as to be in a better position to impose upon him a preconceived model of 'emancipation,' one from which he himself has not been emancipated. He thus bears his own 'wound of childhood' and then bears it upon the child who comes after him."[7] By clicking, hovering, or tapping, we do the same. We keep ourselves in a childhood state as adults. The double bind knows no letting go because it gives us the illusion of growth when none in fact takes place.

Stuck in this double bind (self-incurred tutelage/emancipation from tutelage), we click on without moving. In doing so, we do nothing else but obey the fable of Western modernity, one that has no prescription except itself. On this, Lyotard is famously crystal clear: "This fable has the very emancipated virtue of not prescribing anything to the one who hears it, and so does not need to be believed. It eliminates the horizon of a call. Man simply has to go on wanting to be emancipated in order for this fable to be validated."[8] The little pointing finger is indeed not prescriptive, except as an invitation never fulfilled. Nothing forces us to believe that something more interesting could be lurking in further contents, yet we continue to click, tap, hover. Clicking, hovering, or tapping only calls for more thus abolishing the very possibility of change. Our horizon is foreclosed by the false openness of our browsers and the seductively tempting pointing finger. The fable will not let go as long as we continue to follow it. The revolution will not happen if we continue to surf and this, even if—and especially because—2.5 quintillion bytes of data are created every day worldwide.

The question then is, of course, how do we escape this double bind, this paralyzing fable? Gruber points to the importance of the blank underneath or above the hyphen—or, in our case, underneath, around, and in between the letters or symbol forming the hyperlink. He writes:

> There is no hyphen . . . without the "blank" supporting it. . . . What is meant by "blank"? "Support," certainly, as well as "absence" or "omission," depending upon the passage cited, the question thus becoming in what way the "blank" differs from the "trait" that is (super)imprinted upon it. But "blank" or "white" also suggests "innocence" that the white-support seems to procure insofar as it lets itself be taken by the trait, insofar as it lets the trait take its course.[9]

The blank is thus the complement of the hyphen or hyperlink. Without it, there would be no hypertext. But the blank, taken on its own, like the hyperlink taken as such (i.e., without the linked content), is of little interest. What matters is the relation between the two, between blank and hyphen or blank and link. To pay attention to this relation is to stop surfing; it is to finally put an end to the lure of the next page and draw attention to who made this relation of black and white in the first place. In other words, it is to draw attention, perhaps for the first time in a long while, to ourselves as instigators of this fable—that is, to what cannot (yet?) be hyperlinked because we are out of the self-sufficiency of contents, out of these enclosed passages of time. We alone click, tap, hover, because we alone are out of joint from these false passages in time we created; we jar amid the fascism always thrusting us in the passage to the always predigested.

So it is not just a question of clicking, tapping, or hovering thus continuing the merry-go round of the Internet. It is also a question of what relates blank, link, and content, and from that relation of an "us" without content (cf. "Gnoses"). To pay attention to this contentless relation is to escape the dictatorship of ontological questions: What is it that I see here? What more can I discover by clicking there? This dictatorial quiddity traps us in our tutelage double bind and never leaves room for this other question: Who am I hearing (beyond the hyperlink)? A question, which once heard, often becomes: Who are we together? Only mortals who happen to be gods amid earths and skies can answer these questions, and when they do, they will have no content: "Here I am,"

"Here we are," self-secluding immeasurable. These responses will effectively be directions (similar to the pointing in Caravaggio's painting; cf. "Angels") not to the next page but to each other as mortals/gods—that is, to a Future beyond all contents (cf. "Beckoning" and "Obsession"), to a new fourfold as yet unimaginable. Shifting from "what?" to "who?" diminishes the power of the hyperlink and reintroduces an anarchic and anachronic difference in the seamless sea of our preformatted world. Mortals—curators and their audiences—might want to heed this shift of direction because it is the only way out of childhood—that is, out of the nonprescriptive fable we obey every day of our lives.

# Names

**A question of onomatology is addressed. • What are names? • What enjoins their force of generality? • Analyzed are the names of curator Françoise Cahin and that of God. • A name is first an inheritance. • It is on the edge of property. • There can never be a nameless person. • Names renders the subject uncertain. • Names show the insufficiency of language. • They stand for the desert of what cannot be named. • Names are a hyperbole signaling danger. • Curatorial names are gifts punctuating logos.**

Everything that concerns mortals/gods between earths and skies (cf. "Objects," "Angels," "Words," "Ghosts," "Images," "Gnoses," and "Contents") revolves around a question of onomatology: the logic of names (from *ónoma*, "name"). More specifically, everything revolves around a question of anthroponomatology: the logic of mortals/gods' names (from *anthrōpos*, "human being," and *ónoma*, "name"). Let's backtrack a little. We have seen before (cf. "God") that God is effectively just (and more than) a name, an irreplaceable name that expresses as little as triangle or Nature and yet opens itself to (mis)projection and (mis)interpretation. The reason it opens itself in this manner is because as a name, it expresses not only what cannot be expressed but also what cannot be an essence in thought: a quiddity. There will never be an answer to the question "What is God?" and yet we will never get rid of this question. As such, God, this simple name that points to a supposed elsewhere, can only therefore be a relation. It relates us to what can never be remembered or anticipated, an immemorial Past or unhoped-for Future that might never have happened or might not even materialize as such (cf. "Angels" and "Conclusion"). When it comes to God, it is always a question of onomatology because no logos can truly take place without this haunting empty name lurking about, and this even in the most stringent of atheist or agnostic contexts imaginable.

If God's name is ineliminable, then in turn mortals/gods' names are inescapable, especially when it comes to culture and the curatorial in particular. Like for any practice, curating is awash with them. I will name here, in no particular order, a few celebrities that any contemporary art world–going person would be familiar with: Koyo Kouoh, Catherine David, Maria Lind, Carolyn Christov-Bakargiev, Nancy Adajania, Nancy Spector, Naomi Beckwith, Dorothy Canning Miller, and Lowery Stokes Sims. The fact that some of them are good curators while others are terrible is of no importance. What matters above all is that they are household names. They stand for particular exhibitions, projects, or biennales and for particular points of view about nearly everything, including the state of contemporary art, particular theories about cultures, current events in the world, and socioeconomic and political issues. Through their projects and speeches, curators populate the art world with names—names of mortals who also happen to be gods. Everything indeed revolves around a question of onomatology because no logos can take place without names.

If this question of onomatology is indeed all-pervasive, then it is necessary to address it, if not comprehensively then at least in its most salient aspects. The question will here be formulated in this broken-down way: if names indeed punctuate contemporary culture and curating in particular, what enjoins their force of generality? Why do we obsess (cf. "Obsession") so much about them? And if we obsess so much about them, how do they compare with the name God? In other words, is there a parallel between, say, the household name Françoise Cachin, who was a famous French curator, and the name God? This last question does not imply that God was a curator but rather that the name Françoise Cachin and the name God have something in common. What? In order to address these thorny onomatological questions, I will thread together a few passages on the topic of names in Jacques Derrida's book *On the Name*, and specifically his essay "Sauf le nom (Post-Scriptum)" on Angelus Silesius's collection of poetry *The Cherubinean Wanderer*. This threading will show not only that we can never escape onomatological questions but also that the curatorial is made up of gods and that these gods retain their godliness, however faintly, by simply bearing mortals' names.

Names. Obviously, a name must first and foremost be understood as an inheritance. People have ancestors' names. Through them, they live in their stead. This is the meaning of the word *surname*. It stands for a "family name" and usually comes after the first name or baptismal name—that is, the forename. As such, a surname is always a repetition, and this is precisely what makes it a "proper" name, a name that the repetition has confirmed as proper—hence the use of the prefix *sur*-, derived from Latin *super*—that is, what comes above all as a name, what is unquestionable as this name. But things do not always go in one direction. Inversely, through names, ancestors also call into question their name bearers' lives. The name Françoise Cachin, for example, refers to a woman who lived between 1936 and 2011, yet her surname also refers, as is well known, to her paternal grandfather, Marcel Cachin, who was the founder of the French Communist Party and its newspaper, *L'Humanité*. As such, Cachin doesn't quite belong to Françoise. Names are thus marks of an inheritance, but they are also marks of a lineage that is always lost in time, thus turning these names into improprieties: what can never belong to someone properly.[1]

As such, a name is really what is on the edge of properness, property, and particularity—neither that of Françoise Cachin, nor that of her ascendants or descendants, strictly speaking. Of course, one could argue that with her forename, Françoise owned Cachin temporarily between birth and death, but this argument is necessarily flawed because the name Cachin would also have been that of other members of her family, thus invalidating her entitlement to full ownership—and this without mentioning unrelated patronymic bearers. In this way, it is the lexical ambiguity of the name—or its undeconstructible character—that prevents the possibility of thinking a properness, property, or particularity to names. In other words, there cannot be any proprietorial adjudication as to what truly belongs to this or that name bearer strictly speaking. With a name, a person therefore always lives over this edge of properness, never on firm ground, never seated as a sovereign owner of a name, not even the queen of the United Kingdom, Canada, Australia, and New Zealand, head of the Commonwealth and of twelve other countries, Mrs. Windsor, ex–Mrs. Saxe-Coburg-Gotha. However much she is a sovereign, however much her ascendants stretch out into a distant past, she will never own the surname given to her by Winston Churchill. There can be no sovereignty on the edges of names, not even for queens.

One of the most peculiar aspects of names is this: there can never be a nameless person. Although bearers of names can live without names, we simply cannot imagine one without it. This impossibility of imagining a nameless person creates an uncertainty between subject and name: is a name indicative of a life or a person? The curator Françoise Cachin lived in Paris during the second half of the twentieth century, yet it is not clear whether saying this refers to the authority on French Impressionist and post-Impressionist art, a curator at the Centre Pompidou in Paris, and a director of French museums at the Ministry of Culture (presiding over thirty-four national museums and more than a thousand local collections) or to the woman who took an average of sixteen breaths per minute for seventy-five years. A name effectively indicates an uncertainty. Derrida goes even further when he writes that a name in fact dislocates the subject: "[A name] takes place after a subject's taking place, in a slight, discreet, but powerful movement of dislocation, on the unstable and divided edge of what is called language."[2] A name not only creates an uncertainty but also dislocates what it cannot pin down. Françoise Cachin breathed, moved, loved, gave birth, and died, yet all this took place before her own name—that is, before her own name dislocated all these events, rendering them comprehensible as Françoise Cachin.

Such a peculiar aspect shows that names—those names that inhabit any sphere of activity among mortals/gods, including those of the curatorial—are effectively nothing other than events that remain at once *in* language because a name is a recognizable representation using letters of the alphabet and *on* language because it is unable to characterize properly that which it represents. As Derrida says, "The event remains at once in and on language . . . within and at the surface (a surface open, exposed, immediately over-flowed, outside of itself)."[3] The name thus shows the insufficiency of language as to what it is said to be pointing at. Such insufficiency translates and betrays the absence of a common measure between on the one hand the knowledge conveyed by a name and on the other a certain heterogeneity allergic to both naming and knowledge. A name provides no common measure, only vexation, and this however much one recognizes a curator such as Françoise Cachin as the personification or even the embodiment, for example, of the movement against the Louvre's decision to establish an outpost—dubbed by her as the "Las Vegas in the sands"—in Abu Dhabi. Names endlessly denounce the poverty of language.

So what is a name for? If it is on the edge of properness, property, and particularity, if it dislocates what we understand by life, if it is in and on language, and if we cannot live without one, then what is its point? Surely there must be some kind of reason for what cannot be possessed, what dislocates, what is indispensable. The most commonplace explanation for names is that they stand for what cannot be named. This "what cannot be named" has often been metaphorically interpreted as a desert—that is, as the one place emptied of all language, existence qua existence. This is not an ordinary desert. It is neither objective nor earthly; it comes under no geography, geometry, or geophysics; it does not harbor the nucleus of existence as if a mysterious object abandoned in the middle of a desert. The desert that the name points to is, as Derrida says, to be "found in us, whence the equivocal necessity of at once recognizing it and getting rid of it."[4] The name Françoise Cachin then points to this nonlocatable and nonspatial desert that manifested itself through each and every one of her breaths on earth. But can the name Françoise Cachin really point to a desert, her desert, this absolute absence of language? Can it point to existence as such?

A less commonplace response to the question "what is a name for?" might help address this problem. This response states that a name does not point to a desert because it is effectively a hyperbole. Hyperbole is often used in casual speech as an intensifier, such as saying, "This bag weighs a ton." Hyperbole of this type makes the point that the speaker finds the bag to be extremely heavy, although it is nothing like a literal ton. As such, hyperbole conveys or relays an emotion (annoyance at having to carry this bag, for example). To say that a name is a hyperbole is not to suggest that a name is an emotion but that, because it is on the edge of properness and language, it refers to something that is in excess of language. It stands for a movement that always transports us beyond language. As a movement, it signals an open possibility: Françoise Cachin, curator, director, granddaughter of Neo-Impressionist painter Paul Signac, and so on. Its event is at once revealing and producing; it is at once a postscript to an event already past and a prolegomenon for more. A name is thus a hyperbole because it announces what happened and what is to come, even if whom it refers to has been dead for a while. The naming of Françoise Cachin in this chapter, for example, would not have been possible otherwise.

Now it would be wrong to imagine that because a name is a movement that transports beyond language, it is automatically stained with metaphysical connotations: "a name points to the other in me," for example. A name is a hyperbole not because it reaches toward the other of the name or toward the radically Other of whomever bears it, but because a name is always in danger. It is in danger of being misspelled, misheard, misprinted, misreported, misnamed, forgotten, lost. As such, a name is never safe, secure, guarded, protected. As Derrida says, "The name itself seems . . . no longer safe. . . . The name itself seems sometimes to be no longer there, saved [*sauf*, 'safe']."[5] In this way, there is no shelter for a name; it is always what is exposed to danger. Going back to the name Françoise Cachin, one could say that this was the name behind the creation of the Musée d'Orsay, but it was also the name of a daughter, a mother, a wife—of a whole range of references that are always already in danger of being lost when the focus changes. In this way, a name is a hyperbole, a movement not toward some higher or external reality but toward the beyond of any form of totalization. A name is effectively what is always unsheltered, exposed, at risk.

It is thus a movement of transcendence without transcendental realm. The name rests in and on the edge of language, dislocating the subject that bears it without leading it to some hypothetical elsewhere. As such, what matters in a name is not the target, object, or end result of the movement (the other of language, for example) but the movement itself. The movement of a name is effectively a gift, not in the sense of a little parcel involved in an economic exchange but in the sense of a donation exempt of return. This gift is indeed neither of being (through birth, for example) nor of knowing (as an inheritance, for example); it is a gift of what can and cannot fall into the category of being or that of knowing. Derrida again is very clear on this: "If the name never belongs originarily and rigorously to s/he who receives it, it also no longer belongs from the very first moment to s/he who gives it. . . . The gift of the name gives that which it does not have."[6] In this way, these small bundles of letters that we call names, these strange referents without properness or propriety, fall in the category of neither existence or knowledge; they are simply gifts "dissociating being and knowing, and existence and knowledge"[7] and open to danger.

The crucial thing for us is that this dissociation between being and knowing, existence and knowledge, is precisely what levels us with God (cf. "God"). We said at the start that God is just (and more than) a name that expresses as little as triangle or Nature and yet never ceases to express and reexpress, thus necessarily opening itself to (mis)projection and (mis)interpretation. The names of mortals know the same fate. They are irreplaceable, yet they express and reexpress themselves across generations, thus highlighting a gift that knows neither where it comes from nor where it is going. Perched on the fracture between being and knowing, existence and knowledge, names—the name of Françoise Cachin, for example—can only therefore be those of gods because they alone can indeed move beyond language, give without return. Derrida says so himself: "This fracture between existence and knowledge is as valid for me as for God."[8] This similarity between the name of God and that of mortals does not equate or equalize finite and divine beings or godly and mortal knowledge; it only highlights their mutual givenness.[9] The name of God or those of mortals/gods structure and punctuate logos—or, in what concerns us here, the curatorial—simply because they give notwithstanding ancestors or descendants, and despite what these names stand for. Realizing this leveling exposes not only the power of onomatology between earths and skies but also the unheeded traces of gods in our midst.

# DEEDS AND ENDS

# Saving

**Saved! 100 Years of the National Art Collections Fund. • What does *saving* mean? • Is the museum the only destination for art? • Art is put under arrest. • There is no arguing against a protectionist and populist agenda. • Saving needs to be rethought. • Heidegger says that "I am" is to dwell. • To dwell is to protect, save. • Such dwelling is part of earths, skies, and divinities. • But what does *save* actually mean? • Saving means allowing someone or something to dwell. • What for? For what is unhoped for. • Without hoped-for economic returns, saving maintains the work of strife.**

Between October 23, 2003, and January 18, 2004, the Hayward Gallery in London held an exhibition titled Saved! 100 Years of the National Art Collections Fund. The aim of this exhibition was to celebrate the centenary of the NACF[1] with a spectacular exhibition of around four hundred masterpieces that span nearly four thousand years of art history, from classical antiquity to the present day. The exhibition included many of the world's best-known works bought with the NACF's assistance, such as sculptures by Canova, Epstein, and Kapoor; paintings by Velazquez, Rembrandt, Picasso, Holbein, and Riley; drawings by Cezanne and Michelangelo; and photographs by Wall and Cameron, to name only a few. The exhibition was curated by Richard Verdi, with Michael Craig-Martin as special advisor and Piers Gough as architect. Saved! was one of the United Kingdom's must-see exhibitions of 2003. On November 13 of that year, I took part in a panel discussion at the Hayward on the theme of Heritage and the Moment of Modernism. The aim of the discussion was to explore the difficult intertwinement among modernism, heritage, and colonialism. Part of my talk at the time was to reflect on this idea of "saving" works of art for a nation. What does this word mean?

At the time my response was that the use of the word *saving* was meant to confirm the eighteenth-century ideology—still prevalent today—that works of art are always, in the end, destined for the museum. In this context, *saving* meant consolidating the museum as the final and only destination for all works of art. This idea of equating saving with final destination was borrowed from philosopher, historian, and archeologist Antoine-Chrysostome Quatremère de Quincy's famous 1815 book, *Considérations morales sur la destination des ouvrages de l'art.*[2] Quatremère de Quincy's book was a reaction not only against Napoleon's looting of works of art during his European conquests but also against the idea of creating museums altogether. He thought that museums represented the end of art. He conceived this end in two different ways: first as a spatial finality (i.e., this is their final resting place), and second as a temporal finality (i.e., this the only future for works of art). These spatial and temporal ends—embodied not only metaphorically but also physically by the museum—echo this other ideology from the eighteenth century, Hegel's teleological understanding of the destination of history across the ages: absolute knowledge. The museum stood for the place where this destination was the most guaranteed to eventually materialize. In this way, the word *saved* implied, as I saw it then, the consolidation of the museum as the only possible safe haven for works of art, their hallowed teleological end point. With the museum—and the help in this case of the NACF—art was therefore saved both spatially (in one location) and temporally (until absolute knowledge).

My response was also intended to indirectly imply that the word *saving* meant not only securing museums as the only possible destination of works of art but also suspension or arrest. Following a Foucauldian line of thought, I argued that since the turn of the last century, works of art have effectively been progressively but decisively taken into custody; they have been given over to the custodians of nations, these museum directors and curators, whose one major aim in life is to safe keep a nation's cultural heritage for future generations. In this way, works of art in museums are effectively always under house arrest with no possibility of ever being freed, except for the occasional release on temporary license, short-term paroles to be part of an exhibition or event, for example. By adhering to the principle that saving means consolidating the automatic destination of all works of art, the NACF thereby also adhered to the idea of their permanent detention. The exhibition Saved! thus traced not only the history of the apprehension of works of art in the United Kingdom but also of the many attempts at preventing art from straying or wandering in other galleries in Europe, America, or—God forbid—a developing country. As such, the NACF participated in nothing other than the great ordering and incarcerating project of the Enlightenment, including its violent colonial avatars.

Now, whether saved or detained, there is no point arguing against this populist, institutional, and nationalist agenda. The NACF operates on the basis of a deliberate confusion between a democratic ideal (free access to all) and a protectionist agenda (possessed and controlled by the U.K. government)—a confusion that only serves to consolidate institutions in their powers. There is no way to either clarify the confusion or propose an alternative. This is not a defeatist realization. This populist, institutional, and nationalist agenda indeed needs to be fought back, but not with placards, petitions, boycotts, court cases, or demonstrations. As is well known, these achieve little (the British Museum's Elgin Marbles or the Benin Bronzes are still on display under lock and key). What can be done instead is to rethink the term *saving* and give it a new and unexpected resonance. The aim is to show that *saving* basically concerns not works of art alone but mortals/gods too. In other words, no reflection on saving works of art can take place without a reflection on saving mortals—that is, as we have seen, gods (cf. "Mortals" and "Gods"). In order to address this issue, it is unfortunately necessary to read a few passages from Heidegger's famous text, "Building, Dwelling, Thinking." I say unfortunately not only because it is a difficult text but also because it requires shifting away from historical, cultural, and political narratives about museums and their agendas to a more complex set of narratives—the only ones, I hope to show, able to debunk the conventional meanings attached to the word *saving* and their attendant ideologies.

Let's start where one must always start with Heidegger's famous text: what does *ich bin* mean? Heidegger's text is, as is well known, not so much about architecture but about being. The central question is indeed that of the "I am." Heidegger is quick to answer that it means "to dwell." As he says, "What then does *ich bin* mean? The old word *bauen*, to which the *bin* belongs, answers: *ich bin, du bist* (I dwell, you dwell). The way in which you are, and I am, the manner in which we humans are on the earth, is *Buan*, dwelling. To be a human being means to be on the earth as a mortal. It means to dwell."[3] The question of the "I am" is therefore a question of how "I dwell" on earth. This juxtaposition between "I am" and "I dwell" is what allows Heidegger to give "being" a sense of spatiality, not just as a geographical place on earth but as a set of sense-making spatial moves that make the "I" what it is. In this way, for Heidegger, "I am" is a spatial event, the result of a concatenation of sense-making movements that determines a dwelling. Now as soon as there is a spatial event, there is also inevitably a temporal event. As such, saying "I am" also means "I dwell" temporally—that is, not just in time but also as someone on earth inescapably destined to death. "I am" is then also a setting into presencing—that is, into being capable of death as death. Dwelling thus encompasses both the spatial and temporal dimensions of being, understood not as a unit in space and time but as a set of sense-making movements with death as the sole structuring horizon.

The crucial thing about "I am" as "dwelling" is the fact that the movements in question also indicate a sense of protection, caring, saving. As Heidegger writes, "The old word *bauen*, which says that man is insofar as he dwells, this word *bauen* however also means at the same time to cherish and protect, to preserve and care for, specifically to till the soil, to cultivate the vine. Such building only takes care—it tends the growth that ripens into its fruit of its own accord."[4] There can therefore be no "I am" without a gesture of care toward that which makes its home on earth. That is, there can be no dwelling on earth without protection of the dwelling itself, "I am." The two go hand in hand. Heidegger goes as far as saying, "The fundamental character of dwelling is this sparing and preserving. It pervades dwelling in its whole range. That range reveals itself to us as soon as we reflect that human being consists in dwelling and, indeed, dwelling in the sense of the stay of mortals on the earth."[5] "I am" is thus a spatial and temporal event that means "to dwell" in the sense of protecting, caring, saving. There would be no "I" without this saving, thus helping "it" remain spatially and temporally in dwelling.

Inevitably, when one mentions space and time, one necessarily also mentions earths and skies in the plural (cf. "Earths" and "Skies"). The "I am" dwells wherever my senses make me feel at home without this "home" being automatically defined geographically as a specific place on planet earth. "I am" dwells on earths, "blossoming and fruiting, spreading out in rock and water, rising up into plant and animal,"[6] which also means dwelling under the skies—that is, under "the course of the changing moon, the wandering glitter of the stars, the year's seasons and their changes, the light and dusk of day, the gloom and glow of night, the clemency and inclemency of the weather, the drifting clouds and blue depth of the ether."[7] But this is not just a question of earths and skies, which, let's recall, is not exclusively idyllic or bucolic (cf. "Earths"). "I am"—that is, dwelling—also happens because of beckoning messengers, these gods who not only "are" but who also obsess us by never letting themselves be seen, by always withdrawing into their own concealment (cf. "Mortals," "Gods," "Beckoning," and "Obsession"). "I am" thus means "to dwell": to spare, protect, preserve, save a whole set of spatial and temporal moves that take place on earths and under the skies, with constantly self-secluding but beckoning gods.

But if "I am" means "to dwell" and if "to dwell" means "to save," then what does "to save" actually mean? The trajectory of the argument is clear enough, but the last term requires clarification, especially because there is currently little evidence that mankind is remotely interested in preserving or saving itself on earth. How can one understand being as saving if there is no evidence that this is what it actually does? What kind of saving is at stake here? In order to address this difficult question, it is necessary to rethink the meaning of the word *saving*. Heidegger helps us to see that "to save" is not to "snatch something from a danger. To save really means to set something free into its own presencing. To save the earth is more than to exploit it or even wear it out. Saving the earth does not master the earth and does not subjugate it, which is merely one step from spoliation."[8] With this redefinition, saving acquires a completely new dimension. Saving has nothing to do with keeping someone or something from harm, danger, or in good health ("God save the queen," for example). Saving means to allow someone or something to simply dwell—that is, to set out into presencing between earths and skies, to face the beckoning gods, and to obsess over them. In this way, saving therefore consists not just in protecting from harm but also, and above all, in letting someone or something "be" their own nature.

This is all very well, but what has this got to do with works of art saved for a nation? What does this understanding of "I am" as dwelling and therefore as saving have to do with precious objects that need saving and therefore protection? This is where we need a shift in perception. The issue is no longer that of a subject dealing with an object, but of a polylogicality (cf. "Introduction") that needs to be perceived, appreciated, and understood all at once. As we have seen (cf. "Objects"), works of art are just events of matter that express or reexpress the surge of earths into and against skies (cf. "Strife"). As such, they are not so dissimilar to mortals who busy themselves initiating their own nature between earths and skies, these gods to whom they are an outpouring/poured gift. This is not a straightforward comparison between mortals/gods and artworks or artifacts, and this is not an amalgamation of subjects and objects under a generic expression, such as "event of matter." This is, on the contrary, an awakening to the fact that a polylogicality is what is always at stake when it comes to saving both subjects and objects. A polylogicality disrupts forever any subject–object relation or "mortal saviors" versus "fragile art" because such a relation cannot be understood without also taking into consideration earths, skies, and gods. What needs saving is not just an art object (or a curated image) but a whole constellation.

Once this shift in perception has taken place and the complexity of what is stake has been taken in consideration, then the role of these gods should not be underestimated. The gods not only fracture planes and axes, devices and cyphers, and the entire arsenal of archic and telic representations and their inevitable epochal stampings but also call into question the reasons for saving—that is, the reasons for dwelling—which are nothing other, as we have seen, than "I am." What do we save for? If saving is not about keeping someone or something—a work of art, for example—from harm or danger in perpetuity or until absolute knowledge, if saving means allowing mortals and their artworks to live out their own nature, then again, what do we save for? These questions could also be formulated in this way: what are we saving ourselves for? If there is no longer a paradise to be regained, a proletarian state to be reached, or an eternity to be attained, then what is all our work as mortals/gods in the strife earths/skies for?

We save because, as Heidegger says, we "await the divinities as divinities. In hope [we] hold up to the divinities what is *unhoped for*"[9]—the most difficult thought imaginable. To hold up to the gods what is unhoped for is to be aware of something recognizable that is also, curiously, without content, outside of all conceptuality.[10] This does not mean that the hold cannot be explained. This simply means that what is held is both within and beyond calculative reason. The gods would not hold such an alluring power if this were not the case. Does this then mean that if we, mortals, are gods, do we then save for our own sake, for humanity's sake? Saving for humanity's sake is not what is at stake here. The unhoped for brought by the gods evades such facile reduction, marring it with an extraordinary lack in predictability, which is precisely what is worth saving. In other words, I save art and save myself in order to remain in dwelling, in the fourfold, in the renewal of the folds—with all its complex requirements, the environment being one of them. This strange awaiting the divinities as divinities, this unhoped for, is thus the "what for" of the saving, something which, no doubt, will infuriate all those who want a clear answer to the question "why am I for?" or "why am I saving this artwork for?"

In this way, if we take into consideration this unhoped for, then there can be no hoped-for economic, historical, or cultural return for saving works of art. If works of art are understood as precious objects unrelated to the subjects that look after them, then their future is indeed exclusively in the hands of a hoped-for economic return: the wealth, power, or prestige of a nation, for example. This is the NACF's aim when saving. This is the NACF's hope. If, on the contrary, saving works of art cannot be understood independently of saving mortals—that is, from dwelling—then the importance of this hoped-for economic return becomes problematic, if not redundant. Would anyone save a mortal in a museum for eternity? Would anyone raise money to safeguard mortals in perpetuity?[11] The questions are nearly absurd precisely because, as we have seen (cf. "Introduction"), there is no price tag on mortals/gods. By leveling the event of matter known as works of art with that other event of matter called mortals/gods, then saving becomes this gesture of maintaining the strife between earths and skies while holding up to the divinities what is unhoped for, what can know no economic return—not even the hypothetical absolute knowledge stealthily inscribed in these busy and fashionable mausoleums that we today call museums.

We save therefore because we hold up to the divinities what is unhoped for. Once again, this is not a mystical or spiritual argument, a kind of coveted prayer that all will be well with ourselves and these works of art. To save in this new sense is to take care irrespective of any value (financial, artistic, historical, geographical, cultural, etc.) because what counts is not mere preserving for a hypothetical future but rather the saving of that which dwells between earths and skies, in the hands of these unruly gods: mortals and their works of art. This does not mean abandoning all forms of economic return (closing down all museums, getting rid of all art funds, and throwing away all works of art) but lessening the importance of these returns—that is, removing the artificial values attached to these works in order to level them amid the polylogicality to what has no value properly speaking (cf. "Introduction"): mortals/gods. The earths or the skies have the same value as a newborn. Leonardo da Vinci's masterpiece *Salvator Mundi* has no other value.[12]

# Caring

**What does *to care* mean? • Virgil thinks it means burdensome worries. • Seneca argues it means solicitude aiming at human improvement. • Hyginus suggests it means what weighs down or lifts up and always escorts mortals. • Herder claims it means a double movement toward perfection. • Goethe intimates it means punishing salvation. • Finally, Heidegger contends it means caring for things and caring for possibilities as the structure of being. • Care involves gods in the work of strife maintaining itself as strife. • For curators, care means culturally exposing strife.**

No self-respecting curator can avoid the theme of care.[1] The reason is simple: etymologically, the verb *to curate* originates from the Latin verb *cūro*, "care," "concern," "looking after." The scholarship on curating is thereby filled with references to the history of the word *curating*: the Roman use of the word (an administrative officer whose duties were caring for sanitation), religious interpretations in the Middle Ages (a priest whose duties was to care after the souls of his flock), botanical references in the seventeenth century (someone looking after gardens), and finally its first official use with regard to artworks at the time of the invention of museums (the first public exhibition in the Louvre, for example, in 1795, was described as "an abundant flowerbed that has been planted with great care"[2]). Contemporary curators also rush to confirm these etymological and historical references in order to justify their work, from Harald Szeemann's original despondent remark ("After all, the word curator already contains the concept of care"[3]) all the way to recent pleas by Anthony Huberman to reinvent curating as an emotional form of care and not as a form of control and self-promotion.[4] It looks as if no self-respecting curator can indeed today avoid this fundamental reference.

But if curating means care, what does care actually mean? What is really at stake when care is evoked to explain curating? My argument will be that curating is not just caring for artworks or audiences but exposing a tense double movement: one that weighs us down and one that draws us upward, thus reflecting the strife between earths and skies (cf. "Strife"). In other words, care is not the provision of what is necessary for the health, welfare, maintenance, and protection of someone or something; it is the considerate and concerted participation in the double work of strife. In order to make sense of this, I will read a few short extracts of texts that will help articulate the exposure of this double movement. As before, because space is limited, there will be no detailed contextualization of these texts. Their choice is self-evident in any reading on the topic of care.[5] These key passages aim to structure the shape of the answer to the question at hand: what is really at stake when care is evoked to explain curating?

Let me begin with what is perhaps the least familiar connotation for the word *care*: burdensome trouble. Care is something that annoyingly weighs us down; it means worries, troubles, or anxieties, as when one says a person is "burdened with cares." Perhaps the most famous reference for this specific connotation is a passage in book 6 of Virgil's *Aeneid*. The story goes like this: as soon as the Trojan hero, Aeneas, arrives at Cumae, an ancient city of Magna Graecia, he visits the cave of the Cumaean sibyl, a prophetess, to ask her the way to the Underworld (Hades) in order to see his beloved deceased father, Anchise, again. The sibyl leads him to the entrance of the Underworld. But the entrance is populated by strange symbolic embodiments for human ills such as Hunger, War, and Discord, as well as some vengeful Cares. Virgil writes: "Just before the entrance, even within the very jaws of Hell, Grief and avenging Cares have set their bed; there pale Diseases dwell, sad Age, and Fear, and Hunger, temptress to sin, and loathly Want, shapes terrible to view."[6] As this passage shows, the Cares stand for the sorrows and troubles of life at the gates of death. In order to pass beyond them and enter Hades, Aeneas decides to fight them, but the sibyl tells him that a sword will have no effect on their shifting forms. Grief, Age, Fear, Hunger, and Cares cannot be fought head-on or ignored.[7] They need patience. Cares are thereby clearly understood as what burdens mortals in their journey to the Underworld, where eventually Charon will ferry them across the river Styx. In other words, and in what concerns us here, care is a worrisome problem for all mortals facing their demise.

A more familiar interpretation of the word *care* is obviously that of attentive conscientiousness or devotion. Roman Stoic philosopher, statesman, and dramatist Seneca shows that care is really a power that enables mortals to lift themselves up toward the good. In a letter to the procurator of Sicily, he reflects on the fact that the good can only be found in beings with reasoning powers:

> There are four natures that we should mention here: of the tree, animal, man, and God. The last two, having reasoning power, are of the same nature, distinct only by virtue of the immortality of the one and the mortality of the other. Of one of these, then—to wit God—it is Nature that perfects the Good; of the other—to wit man—care and study do so. All other things are perfect only in their particular nature, and not truly perfect, since they lack reason.[8]

Seneca highlights here the classic difference between the good in God and mortals. While the good is perfected in God, it still needs to be perfected in humans, and the only way of doing this is through study and care. In this Stoic view, care means solicitude, attentiveness, conscientiousness, and devotion; these are the key tasks to achieve adequate human development. In what concerns us here, Seneca's care is an uplifting process of improvement toward human perfection.

The intertwinement of these two connotations of care (what weighs down and what lifts up) is most clearly exposed in Hyginus's fable.[9] Gaius Julius Hyginus was a Latin author and superintendent of the Palatine library. His fable is part of some three hundred brief celestial genealogies. The fable of Cura goes like this:

> When Cura was crossing a certain river, she saw some clay mud. She took it up thoughtfully and began to fashion a man. While she was pondering on what she had done, Jupiter came up; Cura asked him to give it life, and Jupiter readily granted this. When Cura wanted to give it her name, Jupiter forbade it, and said that his name should be given it. But while they were disputing about the name, Tellus [earth] arose and said that it should have her name, since she had given her own body. They took Saturn for judge; he decided for them: Jupiter, since you gave him life take his soul after death; since Tellus offered her body, let her receive his body; since Cura first fashioned him, let her possess him as long as he lives, but since there is controversy

> about his name, let him be called homo, since he seems to be made from humus.[10]

The dual connotation of the word *care* comes across in the relationship between homo and Cura. Saturn's decision renders homo entirely dependent on Cura for his whole life. Homo is not free. He is burdened to live all his life with his creator by his side. Inversely, Cura gets to keep her creation throughout his lifetime. She will look after him, lead him, care for him. There is no getting out of this double connotation of care: burdened and helped by Care.

This double connotation is made clear in the poem "The Child of Care," by German poet and philosopher Johann Herder. The poem is a Christian rewriting of Hyginus's fable with Care, this time the daughter of a monotheist God. After the angels of Justice and Peace warn the Almighty that creating man can only lead to cruelty, war, and deceit, Care protests and says:

> "Create him, Father! an image of thyself—a cherished object of Thy goodness. When all Thy servants have forsaken him, then will I seek him, and will stand fondly by him, and will turn even his faults to good. His frail heart will I fill with compassion, and will incline it to commiserate the weaker. When he wanders from Peace and Truth . . . then shall even the consequences of his error lead him back, chastened and improved." The Father of the human race created Man—a son of Care—a son of that Love which can never forsake him, but which ever seeks to make him better.[11]

As the poem shows, homo is in the hands of Care because no other divinity can look after him. Again, there is no escaping Care; she is the one who will guide him on the path to perfection. With Herder's poem, what weighs us down is again what draws us upward. The double connotation of care remains, but this time it is transformed into a guiding principle.

The manner in which this guiding takes place is never better explained than in Goethe's *Faust*. The theme develops in this way: although committed to the pursuit of reason, Faust also wants to be carefree—that is, free of the disturbing anxieties of care as burdensome weight. In order to achieve this state, he famously enters into a pact with Mephistopheles. In the final act of the drama, when Faust breaks away from the devil, Care makes her appearance as a graying witch calling herself "Evermore the dread companion":

> Though no human ear can hear me,
> Yet the echoing heart must fear me;
> In an ever-changed disguise
> All men's lives I tyrannize.
> On the roads and on the sea
> Anxiously they ride with me;
> Never looked for, always there,
> Cursed and flattered. I am Care:
> Have I never crossed your path?[12]

Such disregard for Care is met with severe punishment: Care blinds Faust for the darkness and ambiguity of his soul, thus turning the tide of care. It moves from burdensome weight in life to the uplifting and positive solicitude for people on earth. The overall lesson of Faust's relationship with Care is therefore this: what worries and weighs you down needs to be transformed into a concern for people. It is Faust's moral salvation.

What seems to transpire from all these tales is that care is a fundamental characteristic of mortals; it is part of their lives not so much as a moral gesture but as a structuring tension (weighing down, drawing upward) at the heart of being itself. In order to make sense of this tension, it is now necessary to turn to our last author, Martin Heidegger. For Heidegger, care has the double meaning of worry and solicitude. These two meanings represent two conflicting and yet fundamental aspects of the event of being. The most important aspect of Heidegger's argument is that both worry and solicitude occur at the same time in a tense temporal relation. In this way, unlike previous interpretations, there is not a moment of worry and then a moment of solicitude. The two take place at once.

Heidegger begins with worrisome care *(Sorge)*. For him, the reason we are structured as worrisome care is because we are always already busying and struggling for things: "Care has the formal structure of being-ahead-of-itself-in-already-being-involved-in something. This being-ahead implies a structure whereby care is always a being about something, specifically such that Dasein in concern, in every performance, in every provision and production of something in particular, is at the same time concerned for its Dasein. This being-ahead-of-itself signifies precisely that care or Dasein in care has thrust its own being ahead as existential facticity."[13] In busying ourselves, we put ourselves ahead in things. In doing so, we reveal ourselves as worrisome care. We care about things because we worry that we are nothing other than a being destined to death.

Yet care also bears the meaning of solicitude or caring for *(Fürsorge)*: tending to, nurturing, caring for possibilities. Again, this second meaning cannot be extracted, replaced, or made independent from the previous one; the two go together. Heidegger writes: "The Dasein which I myself am in each instance is defined in its being by my being able to say of it, I am, that is, I can. Only because this entity as Dasein is defined by the 'I can,' can it procure possibilities in the sense of opportunities, means, and the like, and to care for them. Every concern and every entity which is defined by care implies a priori the mode of being of the 'I can.'"[14] So it is not all doom and gloom. We are also possibilities. We also lift ourselves up from the worry that our involvement into things leads to, and in doing so we care for possibilities. With this twofold nature, we thus acknowledge a deep ambiguity amid mortals because worrisome care is also solicitous care, a tension that can never be resolved because it is the way of being destined to death.

Now that we have seen the importance of care not only in mythological (Virgil, Seneca), ontic (Herder, Goethe), and to some degree ontological terms (Heidegger) as a tense movement that weighs us down or draws us upward, it is necessary to think of it in relation to the structure put forward in this book. There is indeed something missing here. While Heidegger's structure of care is essentially a way of describing how Dasein cares for itself, there is no sense of what happens to this care, this worry (involvement into things) and solicitude (care for possibilities). In order to address this, it is necessary to avoid philosophies of difference or of the Other because they invariably reinforce the dichotomy same/other as well as the autism of being,[15] and to return to the issue of gods, this dimension of mortals that prevents them from understanding themselves as self-contained entities resolutely destined to death.

We have already seen (cf. "Gods") that mortals cannot be understood on their own, that they are always already not in an intersubjective structure, but in a way whereby mortals are gods and gods are mortals without either of them being able to fully embody one or the other separately. This structure revolves around a question of lack and excess. The gods are the counterpoint of mortals, for they have it all and yet their absolute wealth is an excess of lack, making mortals need. It is in this renewed configuration that care, understood as this tense double movement, is most clearly exposed. Mortals worry. They are burdened with cares, but they also are concerned for possibilities. Both of these indistinguishable tensing movements are effectively directed to the gods, these mortals who obsess them (cf. "Obsession") and who also, in reverse, so to speak, beckon them (cf. "Beckoning") with their surplus—that is, with the fact that there is more Future even if there is no indication as to what this Future looks like, or even if it will take place at all. That is, worrisome care and solicitude are also concerns addressed to the gods, these mortals over and beyond their existential facticity.

This double address (worrisome care/solicitude both directed toward things, possibilities, and gods) gives us the answer to our question: what is at stake when care is evoked to explain curating? Because I direct myself toward things, possibilities, and gods/mortals, my burdensome worry and my solicitude only aim to maintain the strife as strife. We have seen that what maintains the strife as strife is work (cf. "Strife"). Care is an aspect of work understood in that sense. However, this work involves no trading aiming to achieve a result—getting rid of worry to have peace or expecting a return from being solicitous, for example. Care is indeed outside of all forms of economic exchange. Care is simply what produces a change—not in order to achieve something but in order to continue with change: turning earths into skies among mortals/gods. As such, care exposes the work of carefully maintaining the strife as strife. Care is its visible manifestation. This manifestation knows no development, progress, or goals. In this way, there is no "good" toward which care directs itself, as in Seneca; there is no moral improvement, as in Herder; there is no redemption, as in Goethe; there is no stopping short at the other, as in early Heidegger. The burdensome weight and upward movement of care is how the strife between earths and skies is maintained among mortals, these gods.

If curating is caring, then curating needs to take on board the whole range of meaning of the word *caring* and not just focus on a banal "looking after artworks" or an equally banal "responding benevolently to the other, the audience, the public." Curating as caring means exposing the way the strife maintains itself as strife—that is, the way earths self-seclude themselves and the skies challenge all forms of measuring. This means nothing other than exhibiting the way mortals embody gods, the way they both self-seclude themselves (earths) and measure themselves against what is immeasurable (skies), and in so doing create their own particular destinal trajectories. This does not mean exposing more artworks, creating more projects, frantically involving more things, but on the contrary exposing what makes all these so important to mortals who also happen to be gods. This is not much. This is not something that can be quantified with surveys or statistics. This is not something that can be ticked in funding applications. Curating as caring means exposing the very conditions (cf. "Introduction") under which we simply create and view curatorial projects in the first place: to reassure ourselves culturally that the strife maintains itself as strife.

# Preparing

**All curators are failures. • Curators prepare. • What does "preparing a project" mean? • A commonplace response is success/failure. • Foucault proposes an alternative interpretation of preparation. • *Paraskeue* means "preparing for the unknown." • Foucault suggests equipping for whatever circumstance may arise. • The sage/athlete is never caught unawares. • How? Through exercises in rational discourses. • Can rationality really prepare for the unknown? • Allison suggests that *paraskeue* is not necessarily rational. • Allison discusses fear and love. • One can embrace the unknown at the edge of reason. • Curators become skilled in the work of gods.**

All curators are failures. They are failures inasmuch as they all have at least one failed project among their ever-expanding portfolio of successful projects. There is no escaping this. All curators have at one point or another disappointed artists, fans, funding bodies, venues, followers, galleries, museums, subscribers, and colleagues. As such, they all knowingly, secretly, unconsciously, or inadvertently incarnate at one point the very first curator in the modern sense of the term: Le Comte d'Angiviller. If the first state museum is the Louvre, then the first curator that could claim such a title is Charles-Claude de Flahaut, Comte de la Billarderie d'Angiviller, King Louis XVI's director general of royal buildings. D'Angiviller is not only the first curator but also the first to fail on a grand scale. No one can possibly compete with d'Angiviller's level of failure. He prepared an exhibition for thirteen years (between 1779 and 1792), establishing in the process what is arguably the foundations of curators' work today: a scientific method of viewing art (optimizing the architectural presentation of galleries), an ordered method for the display of art (on a line, according to size, and with the viewer unable to touch the works), an official reading of art history (an evolutionary reading with the end of art as absolute beauty), and an official selection of timeless masterpieces (thus distinguishing museums from art dealers, or, as he called them, "moneychangers"). All this preparatory work toward the first public opening of the Louvre led to nothing: D'Angiviller fled abroad at the first signs of the French Revolution.[1] D'Angiviller is the archetypal failed curator.

The possibility of failure shows that curating is for a large part preparing. Even if it is a tiny show or an online project, curators spend their time preparing. They often prepare several shows at the same time. Preparation work includes conceiving a project; writing a proposal, a funding application, and a brief to artists; securing a space; organizing the display and the catalog; liaising with the media; advertising the show; socializing; securing deals; cajoling editors and reviewers; reassuring funders; and so on. There is no end to the list of things that curators need to do in order to prepare for their shows. Like for any cultural event, preparation is the only action or process that gets something done, that leads the way for an event or undertaking. There is no escaping this preliminary action or process. But what does preparing for a project actually mean? Besides the aims and ambitions of the project, the commonplace response is invariably "to be successful, to avoid failure." Curators work hard preparing their projects in order to avoid becoming the next Comte d'Angiviller. Such a clichéd response necessarily reduces the meaning of preparing to simply two outcomes: positive or negative, with many shades in between. As such, the meaning of the word *preparing* is reduced to an economy: return in the shape of prestige and power or shame and humiliation, again with many subtle variations in between. Is there no other way of thinking this preparation? Is there a way of thinking this work of preparation without ending up with this inevitable economic alternative?

In what follows, I would like to evade this reductive interpretation in the meaning of the word *preparation* in order to put forward a new interpretation of the word, one that does not imply an economic return (success/failure) but a renewed approach to the Future. The reading that will be performed in order to devise this new meaning is at once faithful and deviant. It is faithful inasmuch as it subscribes fully to some of the ideas of the author investigated. It is deviant inasmuch as this investigation will necessarily also deviate from this author's work in order to fulfill the framework of this very book. The author in question is Michel Foucault, and the main text investigated is *The Hermeneutics of the Subject*, his late lectures at the College de France during the academic year 1981–82. Considering the limited scope of this chapter, the only thing that can be done here is to violently but carefully extract one particular passage: his lengthy analysis of the Greek word for "preparation" (*paraskeue*) and give this word a new twist.[2] In doing so, the aim is not to hark back to a forgotten sense of the word *preparation* but on the contrary to make the word *preparation* resonate in such a way that it evades the economic alternative in question.

Although the Greek word is now co-opted by religion (as the work of making oneself ready for the Sabbath), the word *paraskeue* means preparing the individual for a Future of unforeseen events (cf. "Beckoning" and "Angels"). In other words, *paraskeue* means preparing for what cannot be identified in the present. First introduced by Herodotus,[3] the term *paraskeue* is a compound of *para-*, "besides" or "near," and *-skeuos*, "instrument." As such, *paraskeue* is what is beside or near an instrument, what nearly becomes instrument, or more precisely instrumentalized. Unlike the English word *preparation*, *paraskeue* has no fixed aim (like an exhibition or online feed); it is an open-ended work destined to increase the capacity to respond to events whose form, time, and impact cannot be known or calculated in advance. This work is therefore not practiced relative to a law or rule (an economic return, for example) but relative to the unforeseen events of life. Let's read Foucault's interpretation of this term.

Foucault defines *paraskeue* as making ready—not in order to gain knowledge but in order to prepare for the new. He writes: "*Paraskeue* is the equipping, the preparation of the subject and the soul so that they will be properly, necessarily, and sufficiently armed for whatever circumstance of life may arise."[4] The crucial aspect of this interpretation is the focus on the Future. This emphasis on an open Future ("for whatever circumstance of life may arise") is further confirmed later on in Foucault's text when he says, "*Paraskeue* involves preparing the individual for the future, for a future of unforeseen events whose general nature may be familiar to us, but which we cannot know whether and when they will occur."[5]

In line with Herodotus and Demetrius the Cynic, Foucault uses the metaphor of the sage as an athlete who prepares not for one event, but for whatever may come. He writes:

> The good athlete appears as one who practices. But practices what? Not, he says, every possible move. It is definitely not a matter of deploying all the possibilities open to us. It does not even involve achieving some feat in one or other area that will enable us to triumph over others. It involves preparing ourselves for what we may come up against, for only those events we may encounter, [but] not in such a way as to outdo others, or even to surpass ourselves.[6]

This is an unusual sage/athlete inasmuch as he or she does not train in order to achieve a goal (winning a competition, prize, medal, or accolade) but in order to ensure the vicissitudes of the morrow will be met less anxiously, on a more stable footing. Now inevitably this could mean to improve or strengthen oneself in order to be masterful or expertly skilled. But Foucault is adamant that *paraskeue* does not mean working toward gaining a skill or mastery, but not letting the unexpected take the sage/athlete unawares. He writes: "[*Paraskeue*] does not involve doing better than others, nor even surpassing oneself, but it involves . . . being stronger than, or not weaker than, whatever may occur. . . . The *paraskeue* will be nothing other than the set of necessary and sufficient moves [or] practices, which will enable us to be stronger than anything that may happen in our life."[7]

So what is the sage/athlete really preparing for? What does being "stronger than . . . whatever may occur" mean? Foucault is quick to reply that, unlike later interpretations of the word *paraskeue*, the ancient sage/athlete simply prepares for unforeseen events. As he says, using the example of athletic wrestling:

> The art of wrestling consists simply in being ready and on guard, in remaining steady, that is to say, not being thrown, not being weaker than all the blows coming either from circumstances or from others. I think this is very important. . . . The athlete of ancient spirituality . . . has to be ready for a struggle in which his adversary is anything coming to him from the external world: the event. The ancient athlete is an athlete of the event.[8]

In this way *paraskeue* means preparing in order to be stronger than the event—that is, stronger than whatever comes without specifying the degree of strength necessary to achieve such a control over the unknown. Indeed, because the future is unknown, preparing for it cannot take any specific path, yet the sage/athlete must prepare for it.

In order to prepare for such an unusual aim—an aim that is not one, strictly speaking—Foucault then gives us the manner in which this is to be achieved. A sage/athlete who prepares in the sense of *paraskeue* needs to basically improve his or her discourse (logoi). In order to do so, the athlete/sage needs to embed in his or her mind a set of phrases "through daily exercises, by writing them."[9] These logoi or phrases are not any discourses whatsoever. They must be not only "justified by reason"[10] (that is, they need to be "true and constitute acceptable principles of behaviour"[11]) but also be "persuasive."[12] The outcome of this memorization exercise is to consolidate the athlete/sage in the way he or she deals with the vicissitudes that time throws up in life. Foucault writes: "It is as if it were these *logoi* themselves, gradually becoming as one with [the athlete's] own reason, freedom, and will, were speaking for him: not only telling him what he should do, but also actually doing what he should do, as dictated by necessary rationality. . . . This is the *paraskeue*."[13] *Paraskeue* is basically a way of transforming oneself through repeated exercises of rational discourses in order to face whatever may come in the future, thus making one stronger than any future event whatsoever. This extraordinary view is precisely what leads Foucault to famously and most masterly conclude that "*paraskeue* is the element of transformation of *logos* into *ethos*."[14]

But can Foucault really say this? Can *paraskeue* be understood as preparing for the unknown? That is, can exercising rational discourses (logoi) in order to calmly face the Future truly master all future events? Would these logoi exercises not lead precisely to the opposite, an increase in discursivity and therefore in anxiety about the Future? What Foucault is not attentive to here is perhaps this question of time. How can anyone who prepares through these rational practices end up being stronger than everything the Future can come up with? Foucault has perhaps forgotten here Emmanuel Levinas's famous argument that it is impossible to be "stronger than time."[15] The reason is pretty evident: if the prepared "I" becomes stronger than all Future time, then this "I" appropriates everything that does not yet belong to it, including the unknown Future. *Paraskeue* would then mean the mastery of the self over time, including, to push the argument further, mastery over entropy and old age—that which cannot be rationally averted. Because it is limited to logoi, Foucault's *paraskeue* is thus a delusion. Logoi cannot master anything because the sage/athlete using it cannot overcome the law of absolute heterogeneity that structures time itself (cf. "Law"[16]). To assert the opposite is simply to reinforce the irrational idea that the sage/athlete can control what he or she has not yet faced.

How can one then rethink this *paraskeue* in a way that is less riveted to these logoi and therefore to a mastery of reason over time? If Foucault gives us a fundamental alternative to the meaning of preparation, one not structured exclusively through a mechanism of return (success/failure), then how can one conceive of it not in the problematic way he proposes (being rationally stronger than the event and therefore time), but in a way that comes with the event—that is, in a way that accompanies time and its unpredictable law? In order to answer this question, it is necessary to pay closer attention to the way *paraskeue* was used in ancient Greece. There is no space here to perform a full exegesis of this term among the many fragments of countless Greek authors. Philologist June W. Allison provides us with the clearest analysis of this term not only in the work of fifth-century Athenian historian Thucydides but also in a number of other writers of roughly the same period.[17] The outcome of Allison's thorough analyses shows that the term *paraskeue* was understood in a context for which preparation was not necessarily a practice ruled by logoi. Let's look at two examples that help us see beyond the limits of Foucault's own interpretation of *paraskeue*.

In her book on Thucydides, Allison reads two crucial passages from the famous general's *History of the Peloponnesian War*. The passages refer to fear and love. Instead of understanding fear as the likelihood of something unwelcome happening and a potential cause for panic, Thucydides sees it instead as a major component of *paraskeue*: it is that which leads the one who prepares to do "the unexpected, 'being prepared,' and anticipating the enemy, an enemy who is not aware that the preparation comes from fear."[18] As such, fear arms the one who prepares not by inducing a sudden uncontrollable anxiety but on the contrary by bestowing him or her with an ability to tackle the unexpected, embrace that which cannot be seen as coming. The same occurs with love. As Allison says, "*Eros* is capable of accomplishing feats which defy reason."[19] The philologist gives the example of Pericles's advice to his army to become lovers of the city, *philopolis*. Such an example shows that like fear, love can also play a part in *paraskeue* in the way it turns an anxiety about the unknown into a doting fortitude that nothing can stop.

With these examples, Allison allows us to see that *paraskeue* is not necessarily structured by logoi. *Paraskeue* does not just involve rational discourses and therefore potential benefit or deficit, success or failure. It involves a whole range of emotions and discourses that both address and embrace the Future with poise and renewed resolve. Such a complementary approach shows that the Future is not an empty placeholder that needs to be filled but rather an integral aspect of *paraskeue*. It basically recognizes that a dread of or a love for the Future can be turned into an advantage, a stimuli for preparedness. The one who practices *paraskeue* is thus free from all those troubles that unhinge the mind; he or she neither hopes for nor covets anything, being simply satisfied with a kind of preparation that is open-ended, that confidently embraces the Future—that is, what is radically unknown. This does not mean reducing the Future to nothingness and living satisfied with being in the present, a kind of mindfulness of each instant, for example. This simply means feeling and knowing that the Future also manifests itself through the work of *paraskeue*, and therefore through each and every one involved in it.

In this way, unlike the English term *preparation*, which is rigidly confined to the rational actions and processes of working toward and realizing an event, *paraskeue* reveals a multidimensional approach that partially defies rationality and therefore economic logoi in order to let what cannot be anticipated take its rightful place in the work to be accomplished. In other words, with *paraskeue*, the task to be accomplished is to transmute what cannot be imagined, with all the emotions and reasonings that come with it, into the stimuli for another Future. To go back to the overall argument of this book, this means simply to reconcile us to the gods that we are. We are not the victims of an unknown Future falling on us; we are also the stimuli for a Future as yet unimaginable. In this way, to practice *paraskeue* is to recognize that I am both mortal and god, not whereby I master the Future and all times to come, the vainglorious boast of personal infallibility as in Foucault, but whereby I am the true stimuli for change on a par with the Future itself. Once again, this does not mean to seek out a god to protect me from whatever may come but to recognize that preparation can only truly be done if that which does not belong to it also takes its rightful place. In other words, prepare in order to bring in what is not strife so as to renew strife itself.

So why is *paraskeue* crucial for curators? If curators spend their time preparing for projects, this preparation cannot therefore limit itself to the successful or unsuccessful realization of an event. Curators who practice *paraskeue* would then understand their work not just as the activity of reaching out for a result in the future but also as the very embodiment of the Future itself: the work of gods. Such curators would then become skilled in the work of gods and mortals alike. Partially liberated from exclusive forms of economic planning, such *paraskeue*-practicing curators would then not just aspire to being stronger than time and therefore great achievers, masters of time well spent, but also embodiments of their own strife—that is, embodiments of events of matter, surges of self-secluding earths into and against immeasurable skies. Exhibitions and online projects would then not only represent cultural economic achievements to be added to a CV but also outpourings/poured gifts, which are nothing other than gods' excesses of the lack of need, participations in and for the fourfold—something that no curator can really afford to ignore if he or she wants to escape a little from the strict confines of economic returns and the fate of Le Comte d'Angiviller.

# Irritating

**The partisan is a specter among curators. • Schmitt notes that in a technological world, partisans become nothing more than irritants. • The partisan has four characteristics: irregular, engaged, versatile, telluric. • The telluric character must be rethought. • Earth is not land but an order. • The partisan's role is to invent a new earth order. • The new order will come from a sentinel (hideout/Dark Web). • It is a place where the risk of disappearance is high. • It is like a stray dog on a motorway. • To avoid such a fate, partisans should embrace the interplay of earths, skies, and gods, without measure. • Curators need to realize their telluric character.**

There is always a persistent specter among contemporary curators: the partisan. All curators aspire to be seen as partisans—not in the sense of being members of an armed group fighting against an occupying force but in the sense of being strong supporters, advocates, and/or defenders of a particular political cause. Curators cannot just busy themselves with culture; they need to be seen as taking sides, involving themselves in complex socioeconomic and political problems, responding to the latest global urgencies, getting familiar with recent political theory, even if they have no expertise on these issues and no training in how to address them. This is especially true of noninstitutional freelance curators aspiring to be international agents; they, unlike politicians tied to their own institutions, are able to focus on the real enemies (globalization, capitalism, neoliberalism, gentrification, patriarchy, extremisms, etc.) and to fight them with participatory exhibitions and projects.[1] Curators who aspire to be partisans are the embodiment of what is truly political, of what rises above mere politics. They are the *zoon politikon* who know unambiguously their friends and allies, and who are the heroic defenders of just causes in a situation where there is no longer any *jus belli*. The partisan-curator radiates the glamour of political autonomy and independence. No curator can resist the spectral draw of the partisan.

Although I define it succinctly above, I use the term *partisan* deliberately because it is vague. As is well known, the term *partisan* derives from the word *partei*, "party" (from Latin *pars, part-*) and refers to the adherence of members of a party to engage in some kind of fighting, warring, or political activity. The term appears as early as 1595 in French army decrees to describe a group of soldiers on horseback or on foot sent out by a general to either investigate or to do damage to an enemy by ruse and speed in advance or in lieu of an army's official invasion or defense. However, from Carl von Clausewitz to Vladimir Lenin, from Johann Ewald to Rolf Schroers, via Mao Zedong and Che Guevara, to name only a few political theorists and politicians who have favored this term,[2] the meaning of this word changes to the point where it becomes confused with other terms: secret agent, saboteur, revolutionary, terrorist, resistance fighter, guerrillero, anarchist, rebel, Blanquist, conspirator, activist, infiltrator, clandestine insurgent, jihadist, hacker, counterterrorist, resistance fighter, dissenter. The meaning of *partisan* therefore changes radically between place and time both with regard to what constitutes the party, group, or front supported and to what the adherence entails. The word *partisan* is thereby excessively and conveniently ambiguous and polysemous, and yet—perhaps because of such ambiguity and polysemy—it haunts the curatorial.

In what follows, I would like to explore this theme of partisan-curators through what they most often do: irritate. As we will see, in an age of rapid technological development, the only thing partisan-curators can do is to irritate their enemy. I use the verb *to irritate* deliberately because it is, according to one of the most prominent theorists on partisanship, Carl Schmitt, the only real effect that partisans can have in a technologically advanced society. As he says:

> In a thoroughly-organized technical world, the old, feudal-agrarian forms and concepts of combat, war, and enmity disappear. That is obvious. But do combat, war, and enmity thereby also disappear and become nothing more than harmless social conflicts? When the internal, immanent rationality and regularity of the thoroughly organized technological world has been achieved in optimistic opinion, the partisan becomes perhaps nothing more than an irritant.[3]

In such a world, then, gone indeed is the low-tech partisan, best first embodied, as Schmitt reminds us, in the *empecinados* who fought the Napoleonic occupation of Spain in the 1810s. With their MacBook Pros covered in stickers shamefully hiding the ubiquitous Apple logo, the partisans of today operate globally and remotely from the party, group, or front they support, and the effect they produce is indeed that of being mild irritants on the often vague and all-pervading enemy they have identified.[4] How is one to make sense of this strange irritation?

In order to address this—no doubt controversial—idea that whatever their exhibitions or projects, contemporary partisan-curators can only be simple irritants, it is necessary to rethink this extraordinary passage from the low-tech partisan of yesteryear to the high-tech one of today. This passage has often been understood as a technological one. As Derrida remarks in his own reading of Schmitt's famous theory of the partisan: "As a consequence, the speed of motorization, and hence of tele-technical automation, produces a break with autochthony. This rupture cuts the telluric roots characteristic not only of the classical enemy, but of the first form of the partisan guerrilla war."[5] In what follows, I will slightly alter this classic reading of this passage from the low-ground, low-tech partisan tied to the homeland to the high-flying, high-tech partisan without borders or frontlines. The aim is to offer a reappraisal of these telluric roots that the partisan—and the partisan-curator specifically—has supposedly lost in the world's frenzied technological advancements. With this reappraisal, the hope is to demonstrate that if one conceives these telluric roots differently, then there is still hope for partisan work—and curating specifically—to be more than just an irritant.

Let's return to Carl Schmitt's interpretation of the partisan, and more specifically his understanding of the telluric character of the partisan. As is well known, Schmitt identifies four specific characteristics of the partisan: irregularity, political engagement, tactical versatility, and a telluric aspect.[6] Let's quickly survey them one at a time before looking in detail at the last one. Troops in an army have a hierarchical structure, visible symbols (uniforms and flags), weapons, and rules (the Geneva Convention, for example). By contrast, partisans refer to anyone whose warfare challenges or ignores some or all of these structures and rules. This is what makes them irregular. Second, regular soldiers participate in warfare because they are supposed to; it is their job.

In contrast, partisans are called to participate in warfare voluntarily (and not professionally) for specific political reasons. This is what distinguishes them from mere criminal gangs and gives them a political engagement. Third, unlike an army that advances slowly because of the size of men and matériel, partisans are lightly armed and provisioned; they move rapidly from attack to retreat, and they use guile and disguises to achieve their aims. This is what gives them their tactical versatility and speed. These are the first three famous aspects that Schmitt identifies as characteristic of the partisan. But let's now focus with more precision on the last character: its telluric aspect.

Schmitt says that the classical partisan is someone who is essentially tied to his homeland, defending against invaders. He recognizes, however, that partisans lose their telluric character if their actions take on a more global perspective (fighting for human rights, for example) or a more international enemy (fighting against embargoes, financial and corporate takeovers, or oil sponsorship, for example). Whatever their enemy, and whatever the reasons for engaging in partisanship, the question of their telluric character cannot be so easily discarded as a historical peculiarity. In order to make sense of the importance of this fourth characteristic, it is necessary to reflect on the way Schmitt understands the word *earth* (telluric comes from the Latin *tellus*, "earth"). For Schmitt, the earth is essentially, but most crucially, always understood as the origin of all human laws. As he says in *The Nomos of the Earth*, "In mythical language, the earth became known as the mother of law."[7] The earth indeed provides for wealth (through cultivation and exploitation), division (through demarcations and borders), and power (through forms of ownership and human proximity), all of which generate laws. "Law is bound to the earth and relates to the earth. This is what the poet means when he speaks of the infinitely just earth: *justissima tellus*."[8]

The earth is therefore not just the land surface on which an army steps; it is a legal order that regulates wealth, rules, and power as well as their destruction, transgression, and ruin. As such, the earth is an order that constantly changes, mutating into different orders, each time there is a redefinition of any one of its components: wealth (gas overtaking coal, for example), division (world wars, for example), and domination (decolonization and recolonization, for example). Every new age and every new epoch in the coexistence of peoples, empires, and countries is founded on ever-changing legal orders of the earth. Partisans are thereby tied to the earth not just because they defend a geographically identifiable parcel of land but because the legal order of the earth, however it is conceived, has been altered and therefore needs changing. In this way, the *empecinados* fighting against the French army in Spain in the 1810s relate to the order of their earth in exactly the same way as a computer hacker exposing the greed of international banks and politicians in the 2010s. In both cases, the order of the earth has been altered—through invasion or secretive exploitation of offshore tax regimes, for example—and therefore dealt with—either repelled or exposed.

The role of the partisan is therefore to modify a specific legal order of the earth, however this order is defined. As such, the partisan's role is not so much to defend, protect, or destroy a particular wealth (parcels of land), a particular division (specific demarcations or borders), or even a power (ownerships or heritages), but through partisanship to create a new one. Schmitt describes this work of creating a new order of the earth by emphasizing the way the partisan creates new spaces: "In partisan warfare, a new, complicated, and structured sphere of action is created, because the partisan does not fight on an open battlefield and does not fight on the same level of open fronts. He forces his enemy *into another space*."[9] This new space is obviously the underground, the space in which the partisan works undercover or in hiding. In such a space, the partisan opens up the possibility of a new earth order. Whether successful or not, the order of the earth is, in most cases, never the same again.

The telluric character of the partisan cannot therefore be, as Schmitt never tires of repeating, underestimated. Even in situations in which the idea of earth has been dissolved in the crucible of industrial-technical progress, there will always be a tie to the earth. As Schmitt says, summarizing this telluric aspect, "The partisan always has been a part of the true earth; he is the last sentinel of the earth as a not yet completely destroyed element of world history."[10] This last sentinel should not be seen as meaning the place where a partisan keeps watch over the earth but rather as the space—a real or metaphorical underground lair, for example—where the orders of the earth are reshuffled and/or (re)created. Once again, this sentinel can be a physical hideout or the Dark Web. It matters little. The relationship to the earth is not always physical; it can take place in any configuration or constellation that the partisan seeks to protect, defend, or destroy. It also matters little what side he or she is on; in all cases, the aim is to alter the order of the earth in a way that no politician or army could possibly achieve with their monolithic, bureaucratic, and accountable infrastructures.

Inevitably, by putting themselves in such a vulnerable position of creating a new earth order, partisans run the risk of disappearing altogether. Schmitt is aware of this when he foresees the impact of technological progress on the work of the partisan. He uses an unusual image: he compares the partisan to a dog killed on a motorway. In a thoroughly organized technological world, he notes, "The partisan simply disappears of his own accord in the smooth-running fulfilment of technical functional forces, just as a dog disappears on the freeway. In a technologically-focused fantasy, he is neither a philosophical, a moral, nor a juridical problem, and hardly one for the traffic cop."[11] Schmitt's metaphor is clear: if technology takes over entirely, then the work of the partisan is reduced to nothing other than a nuisance on a motorway. The partisan becomes indeed a mild irritant, a stray dog that the techno-driven mass of humanity hits at high speed without making the effort to stop and rescue. Reduced to mere vermin that not even the traffic patrol can be bothered to eliminate, the partisan's crucial role in opening up a new earth order thus disappears in the night of forgetfulness. The motorway continues to carry its techno-driven zombified cargo, and the earth forgets to renew itself. Schmitt's warning is serious, now more than at any point in history.

In order for partisans, and partisan-curators in our case, to be more than simply irritants—that is, mere vermin on the motorway of our technologically driven world—they therefore need to rethink their fundamental telluric character. As we have seen, Schmitt basically refers to the earth as a legal order and the partisan as the sentinel of this legal order's renewal (new wealth, division, and powers resulting from his or her underground work). In a previous chapter (cf. "Earths"), we conceived of a plurality of earths. There is not just one earth but many earths. The plural allows us to think of earth not as a unique entity to be stepped on, invaded, appropriated, and exploited, but as whatever allows for the rising of light, whatever gives itself over to scrutiny. In this way, there is not one event called earth but many mattering events called earths. Read through Schmitt, this means that the orders are also therefore multiple. There is not one earth order that needs to be altered or renewed (as some activists who, for example, naively demand an end to capitalism as the current governing earth order); there are many earths, and therefore many orders that offer themselves up for change.

The crucial issue in this shift from one to many earths is to abandon all spatial and temporal referents. In the plural, the earths are no longer dependent on spatial (land, region, realm, country, nation, etc.) or temporal (history, heritage, tradition, lineage, future prospects, etc.) dimensions. Detached, the earths are then conceived alongside skies, mortals/gods, not as a unity but in the interplay of their taking place. There would be no earths without mortals/gods participating in turning them into and against skies. There would be no skies without earths furnishing them with self-disclosing matter in need of light and measure. There would be no mortals/gods without the strife of earths and skies. In this interdependence, the issues that need addressing (invasions, hegemonies, fraud, control, sovereignty, jurisdiction, influence, authority, domination, etc.) no longer respond to measurable spaces and times—that is, to calculable and therefore questionable orders. This does not mean that orders (borders, limits, frontiers, monopolies, etc.) disappear altogether. It simply means that other dimensions are also in play. By being in play, these other incalculable dimensions lessen the power of all measured spatial and temporal orders and therefore of all ideologies, idealisms, dogmatisms, principles, and beliefs.

The difference between the old model (whereby the partisan fights to defend, restore, destroy, and/or reinvent a new earth order) and the one proposed here (whereby the partisan fights to defend, restore, destroy, and/or reinvent his or her own earths' orders) is stark. In the previous model, the partisan fights heroically against an enemy for a common cause measured spatially and temporally by a chosen party or organization—poverty threshold, climate change maps, social inequality graphs. He operates on an order on the basis of a calculation—concrete, abstract, or ideological.[12] By contrast, the partisan fighting to invent earths orders operates so as to participate as gods in this rising of earths into and against immeasurable skies. This fight needs no party or organization understood as the measured representation of a telluric autochthony because the parties are earths, skies, mortals/gods, dimensions strictly allergic to any kind of measure and yet intrinsic to the taking place of the fight itself. To realize and engage these measureless dimensions is to rekindle with the true telluric character of the partisan, someone who only works to see more strife between earths and skies, something that annoyingly knows no determinable outcome, attainable targets, or achievable objectives.

If this renewed vision of the telluric character of the partisan is possible, then he or she will become more than simply an irritant, more than a stray dog that is killed on the motorway of our technologically driven world. Mortals/gods, these new partisans, will highlight that they are not just vermin but rather all earths and skies, all mortals and gods. These partisans will show not that the technological order must be stopped in order to prevent future senseless killing but that it is secondary to the earths orders—that is, it is secondary to immeasurable skies and the life of mortals/gods. This secondariness does not mean to naively denigrate technology and elevate "life" above all. It simply highlights the danger of the potential disappearance of all earths, skies, mortals, and gods under the spell of the technological order.[13] Without its spell, technology is in fact an ally to what knows no calculation, opening up the Future and creating new earths orders. The new partisanship starts there, in the recognition and affirmation of an incalculable order (the fourfold) over and beyond any other measurable order, including that provided by technology. These new partisans must therefore rekindle with their telluric character; they must renew the skies with and through which they work and thus relight their mortal character, which is nothing other than their very godliness.

The noninstitutional freelance curators who aspire to be international partisans (or activists, saboteurs, dissenters, revolutionaries, resistance fighters, anarchists, hackers, etc.), who haughtily flee politics and, in the best of cases, rise themselves up to a political level and heroically defend real enemies, therefore have a lot of work on their plate. Their exhibitions or online projects do not need to adhere to a specific party line or to the views of a spatially and temporally defined order, as was the case for the classic partisan (low- or high-tech). They simply need to realize their telluric character, their adherence to the surge of earths in their strife with immeasurable skies and the commonality of fellow mortals/gods. It is only from the premise of this telluric renewal that partisan-curators can begin fighting again, knowing that their earths would never darken the skies (thereby rendering them measurable) or prevent mortals from being gods (thereby rendering them replaceable). This is neither a utopian dream (as in "make poverty history" or "another world is possible") nor a nostalgic romantic idealism (as in rekindling with nature, the earth, and the sky). On the contrary, this is the most concrete partisanship imaginable, as no fighting could take place without this telluric renewal amid the fourfold. It is the only one that finally gets rid of the specter of the classic partisan and of parties with always questionable measures and rules.

# Fraternizing

**War characterizes the work of curators. • What happened to fraternity? • Fraternity is dealt with not as a historical ideal but as a concept renewed. • How can curators be more fraternal? • Chalier argues against fraternity as the privileging of the same. • Fraternity occurs across generations. • Fraternity is a moment free of sociability and perpetuation. • It arises from the immemorial. • It occurs right at the inception of language. • "Here I am." • It is the only hope amid wars. • Curators can potentially become mortals/gods on the bank of the "Here I am."**

War characterizes the work of curators. They are always at war. They compete against one another, fighting for scraps of funding, stealing artists and works from each other, wrestling one another to win coveted jobs, locking horns with critics, dealers, and agents, admonishing viewers who do not behave as told, arguing with others about ideas and theories, and cruelly criticizing and vilifying one another despite, of course, a million claims to the contrary.[1] No curator would indeed admit to these vile actions, yet all curators know of, or have witnessed, at least one of these actions at some point in their careers. As in any field of work, the world of curating is always at war—so much so that one wonders what happened not so much to peace but at least to fraternity. Asking such a question does not necessarily assume that there once was a glorious historical past when there was no war and curators came together in fraternal love. Asking such a question does not also imply that liberty and equality have been won and that fraternity still needs to appear on our universal (i.e., French) revolutionary horizon. Understood outside of all fantasist and/or dodgy historical referents, the idea of fraternity still needs to be addressed, not in order to get rid of war—we all know this is impossible—but in order to curb its most threatening aspects.[2] How can curators be more fraternal?

In order to address this no doubt controversial question, I will read a few extracts from a book on fraternity by Catherine Chalier. Chalier is a prominent French Jewish scholar who has received little attention outside of her native country, perhaps because of her extraordinary modesty and for tirelessly avoiding vacuous sound-bite networks. Through this reading, I argue that fraternizing, far from being an attempt to express some kind of masculine kinship, is a much more complex and nuanced gesture that curators should perhaps adopt for themselves, even if everything around them prepares for war. There is still time for fraternity, however much the word is derided and ridiculed for being both delusional and patriarchal. As will become clear, in saying that there is still time for fraternity, I am not suggesting that there is still time for a club of men to rule the world of curating or to bring peace to its constituents. This would be as ridiculous as saying that there is still time for sorority. However strange this might seem, the following arguments will evade at all costs this kind of gendered policing. In the context of this book, the argument instead will be that fraternity is possibly curators' best shot at encouraging not their siblings and friends to come together in an embrace of brotherly love but at participating together, irrespective of gender, in the surge of earths in their self-seclusion and of skies in their immeasurableness, a type of fraternity that, if acted out, can withstand all inceptions of warfare. How is this remotely possible? Let's read some excerpts of Chalier's careful analysis of this term.

Chalier starts her investigation into the theme of fraternity by referencing Charles Baudelaire's poem "To the Reader," his well-known opening to *The Flowers of Evil* of 1857. The last line of the poem famously reads, "My fellow, my brother!"[3] Baudelaire's final sentence points to an irrevocable basic trait among human beings: the brotherhood that ties mankind together. Chalier writes: "Occasionally, when hatred and jealousy have ruined everything, some venture a word of reconciliation toward the other, even if this other is an enemy, with: 'my fellow, my brother!'"[4] Chalier is quick to highlight the impossibility of achieving Baudelaire's commonplace equalizing appeal: "To address the other as a 'fellow' and as a 'brother' is to think fraternity from the premise of an essentialist and identitarian model that posits the addressor as the model subject. This fraternity is thus tributary to the idea of the other as alter-ego, another 'me.'"[5] Understood within an essentialist framework, fraternity is thus impossible to achieve because whomever claims it has to be the same as the claimant, which invalidates the claim. Chalier's starting premise is thus clear: any fraternity that recognizes the other as the same ("being," "genus," "human," "man," for example) rests on a scheme that effectively only purports to defend the hegemonic privilege and eminence of the One.

The clearest expression of this problematic privileging is obviously when the expression "my fellow, my brother!" is addressed to women. As Chalier pointedly asks: "In this context, the place of women within this fraternity poses problems: can a man address himself to a woman as 'my fellow, my brother!'? Can a woman find any solace in acknowledging this address that also negates her?"[6] Chalier's clear and concise reply is as follows: "A fraternity that attempts to define individuals according to specific characteristics—gender, class, race, or sex—can only become hateful toward those that do not belong to it."[7] In this way, if fraternity has any chance of resonating again today, it needs to abandon all types of phallologocentrisms—that is, discourses in which everyone is subsumed under a hegemonic masculine language with supposedly neutral pretensions. This is not an easy task because fraternity is obviously etymologically linked to the concept of brother (from Latin *fraternus*, from *frater*, "brother"), and therefore to the coming together of sibling men only. If this etymology is not rethought, then fraternity can indeed only be left in the dustbin of history with all the other phallologocentric ideas inherited from Christianity and bastardized by the Enlightenment.

But Chalier remains undaunted. In order to avoid such a reductive and dangerous view, she insists that it is necessary to rethink fraternity as the inception of hope for all: "The only way to recognize the other without appropriating everyone under one essence . . . is to rethink the other outside of all determinations such as 'this or that.' This rethinking of fraternity would not depend on a prior definition of the essence of fraternity. It would instead emerge right when the addressor signals to the other that his or her . . . life is the inception of hope for all."[8] Chalier is thus concerned not in homogenizing the concept of fraternity but in identifying the moment when fraternity emerges, when it exposes itself, notwithstanding all essentialist discourses. This unique moment that disturbs all types of essences appears to be when there is the recognition that the other's life becomes, as she says, "the inception of hope for all." What does this mean? What kind of hope is at stake here, and when does it emerge? Is it comparable to the "unhoped for" discussed earlier (cf. "Saving")?

First, Chalier's unexpected answer is to link fraternity not spatially (that is, between siblings or friends at any one time and place) but rather temporally (that is, between generations). To signal to the other that their life is the inception of hope for all is to point out that they hold the hope for all, not because they are optimistic but because they can bring children to the world. This is not a pro-life endorsement. It is simply an acknowledgment that hope takes place not in the next person but in whoever comes next, whoever brings over time a new dimension to the ills of the world. This is where hope really resides. It does not take place in feelings of expectation and desire for a particular thing to happen because these would necessarily imply the egoism of the one hoping. Hope happens, on the contrary, in the unconditional opening of the future provided by the child, however this child is conceived, desired, cherished, or not. Again, this is not a reactionary and paternalist discourse that children must be born at all cost in order to guarantee fraternity. This is simply an acknowledgment of where hope lies: in the future brought on by another generation (cf. "Angels" and "Conclusion").

This unusual move has the merit not only of avoiding all forms of essentialist discourses but also of pointing to a beyond our present horizon in which lies hope. Chalier writes, "To talk of fraternity between generations, is to argue that the men and women of today work for a time in which they will no longer be there. The work of leaving a world in which future generations will be able to live and prosper gives it a dimension that transcends the narrow horizon of the living present because it goes beyond death."[9] This radical move allows Chalier to focus not on a similarity of views, inheritances, or positions (identities, genders, races, politics, or sociocultural affiliations, for example) that can be spatially attributed and/or negotiated, but rather on a fraternal temporal gesture that extends beyond death. As such, it is a fraternity not shared between contemporaries but with others who are coming or still to come. Fraternity thus becomes a reaching out to a not yet that is curiously free from all forms of coexistence, sociability, and even—this is crucial—perpetuation (ensuring our existence after death through filiation, for example).

But Chalier does not stop there. After having identified where hope lies properly—that is, where fraternity has the most chance of being exposed—she highlights that this hope also takes place between mortals in a gesture that makes us fraternize irrespective of brotherhood, sisterhood, parenthood, and the birth of babies. This second gesture is the one directed toward and in response to a call from the immemorial (cf. "Beckoning," "Obsession," and "Intuiting"). She writes:

> Fraternity asks us to think an opening towards the immemorial that, in each one of us, is irreducible to any form of origin determined as either contingent or historical. . . . This opening towards the immemorial is allergic to any form of interest, not even that of being well-disposed towards the other. This opening responds in fact to a call that imposes itself without question. It is there, in this juncture of opening and call that fraternity expresses itself in all its acuity.[10]

There is no doubt that Chalier's language flirts dangerously with metaphysical and even theological connotations. The immemorial can indeed easily be understood in an ontotheological sense whereby what falls outside of all memories, contingencies, and histories is basically God, the alleged origin of all things. But Chalier is not easily seduced by metaphysical or theological talk. To assert that there is an interhuman gesture directed toward and in response to the immemorial and that this fraternal gesture evades both common self-interest or altruism is in fact strategic.

Chalier is indeed aware that this opening to the immemorial can only effectively take place not by referring everything back to an original essence (i.e., "God") but by emphasizing the moment prior to the inception of language, and specifically the moment prior to the inception of homogenizing concepts (being, genus, human, man, woman, artist, curator, etc.). Fraternity, this inception of hope, takes place just before language emerges and imposes its sovereignty. To make a fraternal gesture is thus not to address an individual as if a common genus, and it is not trying to comprehend the other in its essential singularity. Rather, it is to establish a relation structured by hope before all forms of essentializing discourse take over. This does not mean that language and concepts have been eradicated. They can obviously, and no doubt immediately, take over once this initial fraternal moment has passed. However, what counts is the fact that this violent language always occurs afterwards—after the inception of an initial fraternity of hope.

Chalier does not simply want to give the impression that there is such a thing as an emotional feeling of fraternity prior to language. She is very much aware of the dangers of identifying feelings with concepts. She writes, in one of the most startling sentences of her book, that this gesture, directed toward and in response to the immemorial, takes place prior to the moment when "in fraternity—or language—the genus is founded."[11] Why this extraordinary alternative, "in fraternity—or language"? One would imagine that fraternity—as this inception of hope—is precisely what takes place before language and concepts. How could there be an alternative when there should be a sequence, the hope of fraternity and then the violence of language? The answer is simple: fraternity is still language. As such, fraternity still stands for the violence of concepts. When not conceived across generations, it is therefore necessary to think of fraternity not as a concept but in its taking place—that is, right when language (and the language of fraternity in particular) violently initiates itself. This is a much more difficult notion that requires us to think of the immanent inception of language, right when there appears to be no identifiable language yet, not even that of emotions or feelings.

In this way, fraternity is not based on an act of autonomous freedom by a self-governing subject or a desire to measure one's commitment to an idea of fraternity shared among a collectivity, community, association, or group. Not even the most radical societies with strong senses of identity and purpose can generate or foster fraternity. Fraternity stems instead from an immemorial before, from a preoriginary alliance that precedes freedom and desire, commitments, interests, and preferences. It takes place right when these are called for, but it only comes into effect and into view as "an aftermath."[12] This aftermath is what curiously ties fraternity to language. The immemorial does not appear out of nowhere; it is always there at the inception of language. In other words, without language, there would be no fraternity, yet language would not take place if it were not for this preoriginary or immemorial fraternity that allows it to take place. What kind of example would embody this strange instance of fraternity as the inception of hope?

As Chalier says, the most salient example of this fraternity that arises right at the inception of language is the expression "Here I am" (cf. "Angels"). It is the clearest example of this inception of hope besides that provided across generations. Chalier writes: "Forever inchoative, fraternity signifies the hope and promise of a 'Here I am' *(hinneni)* to the other prior to any questioning of identity."[13] Chalier's use of this famous biblical expression is obviously intended to recall the story of the binding of Isaac. However, as Chalier shows, and as we have seen before, this "Here I am" is not addressed to God but to the other.[14] "Here I am" is basically a prereflexive response that can be identified with nothing but the very manifestation that delivers it. It stands for the moment when one presents oneself to the other without prudence, circumspection, or forethought. It is a spontaneous gesture that cannot be memorized and rendered supposedly genuine through repetition.[15] It is obviously most clearly seen in mothers with their children, but Chalier insists that it exceeds this cross-generational relationship. It is also what binds mortals together before all forms of essentializing discourse, before the dictatorship of the relation same/other and of any form of communitarian discourse on what it means to be fraternal.

The fraternal hope thus lies in these types of "Here I am"—these expressions that stem spontaneously not from a commitment to helping others but, crucially, from a time beyond memory. These are fleeting glimpses of hope that are allergic to any kind of codified aspiration, systematized expectation, or legitimized plan, aim, or dream to be fraternal. They take place because they bypass all self-interests, including those of wanting to make the world a better place for our children. Such fleeting moments can only disappoint those who hope that fraternity—Judeo-Christian fraternity in particular—can eradicate all ills in the world. Chalier is not naive. She writes: "Such hope or promise has obviously no chance in eradicating hatred or avoiding fratricides."[16] War and genocide, violence against others, and general self-centeredness will continue to predominate our horizons. However, amid all this brutality, the immemorial stalwartly provokes this fleeting "Here I am" as the only hope for a world where fraternity has effectively vanished. It steadfastly continues to call, occasionally precipitating these moments that reveal our radical unsubstitutability, a disposition that is fundamentally alien to the interests of the ego.

Inevitably, as with the "unhoped for" studied earlier (cf. "Saving"), this inception of hope is equally without return. "Here I am" expects nothing, not even a response. It is expressed fraternally, without assumptions or conjectures. It is a fraternity that evades all forms of economy, including all forms of goodness. "Here I am" possesses or displays no moral or amoral virtue. It occurs without kindness or meanness, a spontaneous expression that has and creates no standards. To think of fraternity as this response to this call from the immemorial is therefore to retain again something recognizable (language) that is also fundamentally without economic calculative conceptuality. It is gratuitous not because it is expressed without good reason (the immemorial triggered it, the call is heard) but because it is freely given, without preconceived thoughts about whomever hears it. In this way it is indeed the expression of a hope vocalized without any hope in mind—unhoped for. What cannot be remembered provokes here through the "Here I am" what cannot be anticipated or planned for, what irks language's relentless economic drive.

A strange and fascinating fraternity brings us back to what matters above all else: the fact that it is at the heart of the fourfold as described in this book, and specifically with these gods that we are. The preoriginary and immemorial hope that Chalier talks about is indeed with these gods that always harbor in themselves the possibility of more, the possibility of a future beyond death—and this not just with babies. Who else could respond to the call of the immemorial? Who else could direct himself or herself toward the unhoped for? Mortals/gods, of course, but not because they are godly, above others, proud possessors of a power or talent given over by what cannot be remembered; simply because they can hear the call, they can respond without forethought, triggering, consciously or not, a Future that can never be anticipated. "Here I am" discloses gods in our midst, hauling up mortals with what they cannot possibly imagine, not because it is surprising, avant-garde, or groundbreaking, but because it joins the surge of earths into and against immeasurable skies, revealing, participating in, and maintaining the work of strife.

Can curators and anyone around them heed this immemorial call and respond with an unhoped-for "Here I am"? To heed such a call does not mean abandoning all attempts at creating fraternal communities—artistic, activist, communal, collective, national—based on the interests of others (cf. "Gnoses"). It simply means being aware that occasionally an ephemeral spark of fraternity flares up unexpectedly amid the usual noisy disharmonies of the world. "It is this spark," as Chalier writes, "that allows mankind to cross over to the riverbank where 'Here I am' is addressed to all. . . . Right at that moment, the spark of the immemorial illuminates human language and gives meaning to the hope of fraternity."[17] By letting the immemorial or the unhoped for play its part, curators, these mortals, then open up to the gods that they are. Again, this is not a religious or metaphysical gesture. To recognize in language that there is such a thing as the immemorial or the unhoped for is already to recognize that we are structured by it through our godly selves—these selves that know no measure. Curators' projects, their talks and arguments, their socializing and networking, their warring gestures, will then be not just expressions of an inevitable reality but also expressions of gods amid the fourfold. Curators can be godly not in the sense of being divine, fraternal, or sisterly but in the way they can cross over to the riverbank of the "Here I am."

# Communing

**The paracuratorial is what brings people together. • How can it be turned into a communion of spirits? • Meister Eickhart and Reiner Schürmann address this. • Mortals/gods see and know. Their act is one. • Their act is not relational. • It is as indistinguishable as mind and thought. • It is the Verb in act. • It reveals mortals to their godliness or the reverse. • Together, they hatch knowledge. • The paracuratorial is the communion of spirits hatching a knowledge unhoped for. • Strife is made flesh.**

Paracuratorial—what an odd term! It could have been the metacuratorial, with an affix meaning with, across, beyond, or after, thus indicating an uncertainty of location or time. But no. It was called the paracuratorial, this unpleasant term, originally used for the first time, in a negative sense, by Jens Hoffmann to describe the activities of curators other than producing exhibitions: conferences, seminars, workshops, off-site projects, performances, launches, speeches.[1] The paracuratorial expands the single activity of exhibition making to encompass, and in some cases make primary, "a range of activities that have traditionally been parenthetical or supplementary to the exhibition proper."[2] With the affix *para-*, the word thereby takes on not only the connotation that something is taking place on the side of an exhibition but also that something is amiss or irregular, thus potentially disturbing what should always be given central stage. The term is much maligned now in the conservative belief that the purity of what is presented in the hallowed halls of exhibitions should never be disturbed by what can be said parenthetically. Yet is it not precisely what happens aside, in parentheses, that matters above all? Is it not precisely what comes alongside exhibitions that makes exhibitions seem so important? In a way, without the paracuratorial, there would hardly be any curatorial—merely halls without discourses, dialogue, or community.

What happens during paracuratorial activities is, perhaps against all odds, what brings people together, what allows them to commune with one another. Viewers, artists, invigilators, speakers, organizers, volunteers, curators, directors, cleaners, caretakers—all talk to each other, agree and disagree, approve and reject, discuss and participate, remaining, in most cases, never indifferent to what has taken place center stage. To suggest that people commune during paracuratorial activities is not an attempt to rescue this much maligned term, give a chance to secondary over so-called primary activities, or give prominence yet again to the so-called educational turn in exhibition making. To suggest that people commune is enough to highlight that an event is taking place notwithstanding its relation to other primary or secondary events. As such, the paracuratorial should still be considered in its own right. However, the question is not so much whether we should consider paracuratorial activities or dismiss them, but what exactly happens during these activities. I would like here to investigate this parenthetical communion not by providing a critical lexicon of how it happens—investigating the role of discursive events appended to exhibitions, for example—or analyzing specific cases of successful or unsuccessful paracuratorial projects, but by looking into this coming together of spirits who share their thoughts and feelings about what has been seen or experienced center stage.

I deliberately use the expression "communion of spirits" to distinguish it from other terms such as meeting, gathering, convening, assembling, or even getting together. The term *communion* deliberately refers to the sharing of intimate thoughts and feelings. It talks not of an economic exchange of information or knowledge, but of a private, shared moment together in which emotions and ideas coalesce indistinguishably. This communion does not mean there is no longer any discord or disagreement, divergence, or even a difference of opinions. A communion of spirits simply refers to the fact that there are moments when mortals bond, when language and feelings cohere, even if these moments always take place amid a war of words (cf. "Fraternizing"). Inevitably, the idea of using this much maligned word *communion* also gives the impression of a religious reference. The challenge in what follows will be to insist on thinking the term *communion* outside of all religious contexts. What does it mean to commune with one another without automatically imagining a religious "God" or context interfering in any way in the process? The task will be even more arduous because, as might be expected, the term *gods* will again be used to denote mortals.

In order to think the paracuratorial as a (rare but not impossible) communion of spirits emptied of all religious references, I would like to read a set of difficult passages by the most intellectual of all Western mystics: Meister Eckhart. In order to help us in this task, I will follow one of his most astute contemporary readers: Reiner Schürmann. With this short reading—only a few extracts of one sermon will be addressed—the aim is not to provide a new exegesis on Meister Eckhart. In what follows, there will be no study, for example, of his overcoming of Christian trinity, his desire to know God through an analogy with His creation, or his attempt to overall create a henology—a philosophy of unity—in lieu of an ontology for mortals. Yet I can only direct the reader to Schürmann's unrivaled set of analyses. Instead, the aim here is simply to think with the help of Eckhart and Schürmann this idea of a communion of spirit, here exemplified in the paracuratorial.

The only place to start with this idea of a communion of spirits is to return again to this no doubt controversial idea—central to this book—that mortals are also gods (cf. "Mortals" and "Gods"). Mortals are gods in the way they break the form of the sensible, in the way they appear to one another from the depth of their earthly self-seclusion into and against immeasurable skies, in the way they foster obsessions and passions, and all this without an almighty God generating, looking in, out, or after, and then decimating the lot. In order to make further sense of this idea of mortals/gods, let's read a few passages from Eckhart's Middle High German sermon, "See What Love." In this sermon, Eckhart famously establishes, following Aristotle and Aquinas, the analogy between man and God. The difficulty here is to retain the import of Eckhart's ideas about mankind and God without automatically falling for conventional interpretations of a Christian God. Overcoming such a difficulty will then reveal how mortals/gods commune with each other. Eckhart writes:

> It should be understood that to know God and to be known by God, to see God and to be seen by God, are one according to the reality of things. In knowing and seeing God, we know and see that He makes us see and know. And just as the air which is illuminated is

> nothing other than illumination—it illumines indeed because it is illuminated—likewise we know because we are known and because He makes us know Him.[3]

At a first reading, this might give the impression of a reciprocal relation between God and man, who both see and know, thus emphasizing both the embodied aspect of God and the inherent spiritual nature of mankind. However, as Schürmann points out, Eckhart does not refer here to a relation between two entities. He explains: "God and man are not considered as two separate beings, one facing the other, but in their act: knowing, seeing. This act, Eckhart says, is indistinguishably human and divine; it is one and the same act for both man and God."[4] In other words, both God and man see and know, and this commonality is what renders them indistinguishable to one another. This means, going back to our secular vocabulary, that whatever mortals see, gods see, and vice versa—and this without a third party butting in.

The difficulty with this idea is obviously that from a commonplace perspective, a mortal cannot be compared with God for the seemingly apparent but difficult-to-prove reason that by definition mortals are finite, and God is infinite. To insist on such a segregation necessarily proceeds from the premise of an ousiology—that is, a search for substances—that thetically separates the entity God from that of mortal. But as we have seen, this is not a relation of two separate entities but instead most simply a common act—here, seeing/knowing. In this way, there is no opposition between a physical creature dying and a spiritual creature that goes on forever; there is instead the act of seeing and knowing in the ambivalent fullness of the act itself—neither strictly mortal nor divine (cf. "Introduction").[5] With this move, Eckhart abolishes the conventional distinction between finite and infinite, revealing it instead to be an indistinguishable occurrence, "the reality of things."

Eckhart deliberately chooses the act of seeing and knowing. As is well known, Western civilization always favors sight over all other senses, to the point where seeing and knowing are effectively synonymous, as the expression "I see" for "I understand" in some European languages testifies. This synonymity between the two acts is perhaps problematic, but it is hardly questionable. Mortals/gods see; therefore, they know. But Eckhart goes further than this arguable indistinguishability. As Schürmann comments: "For Eckhart, we are one with God just as, in the act of knowing, the intellect is one with what it knows."[6] That is, the oneness between man and God is identical to that between a mind and his own thoughts. This oneness can no longer therefore be developed according to the modes of substantial distinction and of predicamental reciprocity. Just as mortals cannot detach themselves from their own thoughts and therefore from what they know, they cannot detach themselves from their godly selves either. The fusion is in both cases unequivocal. Hence Eckhart's quasi-poetic comparison with air and illumination: "The air illumines because it is illuminated," but the air is no longer considered as a substance; it "is nothing other than illumination."[7]

The important thing to remember here is that this union does not create a new or superior entity or identity that would then distinguish itself from both. Mortals and gods remain themselves not because of their union but because of their act. As such, this oneness must be understood precisely as a verb *in act (seeing, knowing)*, or more precisely, to not stray too far from Eckhart's references, as the Verb in the act of becoming flesh.[8] With every thought, mortals manifest themselves, and through seeing and knowing, they embody the Verb in act. With such an acting embodiment, mortals/gods are therefore the driving force of the action implied by this Verb—a driving force that mortals cannot extricate themselves from. As Schürmann writes: "Eckhart in no way teaches a simple identity between the human intellect and God, he teaches the imperative of an identity to be accomplished. Identity is not thought of here according to a nominal scheme, but rather a verbal one."[9] With Eckhart, we therefore no longer have a conventional Christological narrative whereby God sends a message—the Word—to mortals. Instead, we have a Verb bringing itself into existence through the mortal/godly acts of seeing and knowing. By emphasizing the driving force of the Verb, Eckhart thus avoids placing man before God and exposes mortals' manifestation through the acts of seeing and knowing.

The crucial thing about this common exposure of oneness in act or this advent of the Verb is that it does not solve the ambiguity of the union; it simply characterizes it. In order to expose this character and how it reveals the way we commune in spirits—for example, paracuratorially—let's read another crucial passage in Eckhart's sermon: "For [God] to make me know and for me to know are one and the same thing. Hence his knowledge is mine, quite as it is one and the same in the master who teaches in the disciple who is taught. Since his knowledge is mine, and since his substance is his knowledge, his nature, and his being, it follows that his being, his substance, and his nature are mine."[10] This metaphor of the teacher and pupil might give the impression that there is yet again a hierarchy, with a teacher/God above a student/mortal below. But as we now suspect, Eckhart's thinking goes beyond this simple hierarchy and evades it altogether. As Schürmann says:

> To explain that there are two beings [teacher and student], two substances, and that between them words come and go, is still to say absolutely nothing of the teaching itself as an event. . . . In the diligence and the zeal of learning, the face-to-face encounter between teacher and student is abolished. Properly speaking, only the coming forth, the hatching of knowledge "is"; in other words, a process is rather than a duality of substances. An event gathers together the teacher and the public which abolishes the one's superiority and the other's inferiority.[11]

The focus is not therefore on whomever is involved in the lesson but on the process of knowledge itself. Gone is the God-Person, and gone is the Man-Person. "Only the process 'is.'"[12] With this abolition of the face-to-face encounter between teacher and student, Eckhart frees from teaching/learning all dialectical processes for which there is always on one side ignorance and on the other knowledge—and absolute knowledge to boot. Through this freeing, mortals not only reveal their godliness but also the Verb in action, the hatching of knowledge, a mind in act.

If this vocabulary reeks too much of a religious stench, then it is perhaps a question of rethinking the singularity of the denomination *God*—that is, of cleansing mortals of the idea that their godliness is One. As we have seen before (cf. "Introduction"), there is not just one humanity but rather many mortals. Similarly, there cannot be just one God but rather many gods. This does not imply a shift from monotheism to polytheism, only the realization of where and between whom exactly the breaking of the new (this "immemorial," this "unhoped for," to use our vocabulary) takes place. It does not come from on high or from the One (God churning out the Future, for example) but rather appears between mortals amid strife. In this archsecular context devoid of a Most High, the acts that Eckhart talks about (i.e., seeing and knowing) become therefore godly acts (surges of earths into skies) that only mortals can effectively bestow onto each other, and this without any hierarchy whatsoever. The communing of mortals/gods sees and knows, and this without knowledge or know-how about what is seen or known. The crucial thing about these acts is that they cannot be conceived as economic exchanges between two substances or entities for the simple reason that an incalculable more is always already involved in their taking place. As such, these acts can only be conceived as a communion of spirits, a free sharing of thoughts and feelings between mortals, these hatchers of knowledge unhoped for.

If we accept these controversial arguments, then the supposed educational aspects of paracuratorial activities take on a different connotation. There is no longer a hierarchical relation—always structured by a false modesty—between curators and visitors, professors and students, artists and viewers, critics and amateurs. There is also no more curatorial side events understood as economic and participatory exchanges of information between individuals. Instead, we now have a communion of spirits, a begetting of difference and enigma between mortals/gods that curiously allows no religiosity or mysticism, however much the vocabulary might indicate otherwise. This shift toward communion, toward this intimate hatching of knowledge, allows us to perceive these activities as something indeed amiss or irregular, but not in a way whereby this activity would disturb what takes place center stage. The paracuratorial is not quite right, inappropriate, and often out of place simply because it brings in the new, it breaks the form of the sensible. In a nutshell, it reveals mortals to be more than just mortals, gods with the immemorial and the unhoped for at their disposal. To the question what is there properly in the paracuratorial? One can no longer therefore answer with a set of relational determinations and a predicament of false reciprocities. One can only see and know an event—that is, a communion of spirits in which the strife is made flesh.

# Dignifying

**Artists often make outrageous demands. • How ought one respond? • One should respond neither by checking a code of ethics nor by elevating the other. • Another kind of morality is needed. • To dignify. • Nietzsche and Nancy indicate a value beyond all values: life evaluates, truth. • Long live physics! • Life dictates, and so we must be its best disciples: physicists. • Morality takes place not in the obedience to a value but in the accomplishment of physics, its unique value. • Contentless, this value befalls; it happens. • It does so without creating a state or higher rank (dignity), but rather an act. • Curators can use this act; they will be as godly as artists.**

How often have curators been disconcerted by the surprising demands of artists? There is no space here to provide an anecdotal list of outrageous requests in order to prove this point. I am sure many curators can recall artists who have made excessive, unwarranted, questionable, or extravagant demands in the name of their art. I am also sure that many artists can recall a moment when a request was far-fetched, unreasonable, unrealistic, or simply over the top. Even I, as an ex–site-specific curator for a mere ten years, can recall a few eyebrow-raising requests: install a natural lawn in an old geriatric ward, mirror the concrete features of a parking lot ceiling onto the floor, cover all four walls of a room with potpourri, find ten king-size used mattresses with stains, produce a river of shredded steel in a garden, re-create a perfect replica of a 1930s London suburban living room. There is no point debating whether these were justified; in most cases, they were. There is a point, however, in asking how one responds to these requests. What is the most ethical response to something that defies the odds? If the response is not an immediate "I will not dignify this request with an answer," then what could be a dignified response once amazement has subsided?

The verb *to dignify* usually means to either make something seem impressive (a curator has dignified the exhibition with an opening ceremony, for example) or to make someone feel as if he was entitled to a response (a curator has dignified this request with an answer, for example). The interesting aspect of this verb is that it not only ascribes a certain worthiness to the person who dignifies but also endows a further worthiness to the person who is dignified with a response. To some extent, the verb ennobles addressor and cajoles addressee. From the late Latin *dignificare* and its root *dignus*, "worthy," the verb *to dignify* thus attributes worth to both interlocutors. Even when one says, "I will not dignify this request with an answer," one already elevates addressor and addressee inasmuch as it assumes that at least one, if not both, are "better than this." To dignify thereby merits attention, especially if it has the advantage of distracting us away from the noun *dignity*, which immediately connotes a higher state, status, rank, or quality,[1] thus endangering the eminently ethical aspect that the verb seems to possess. But what exactly does *to dignify* mean?

In order to address this issue, I will read a few carefully chosen extracts from an essay on Nietzschean morality by Jean-Luc Nancy. Nancy's text is a fast and furious reading of Nietzsche's attempt to come up with a type of morality that would go "beyond good and evil." In this reading, Nancy suggests overall that when trying to make sense of Nietzsche's morality, it is necessary to think "an altogether other morality, one which . . . would nonetheless still be a morality: that is to say, it would have the imperative and normative aim of relating to a value."[2] His aim is therefore not to assume that because Nietzsche wants to go beyond good and evil, he automatically gets rid of all moral values. On the contrary, to go beyond good and evil is to assert the fact that a morality based on values is still necessary even if the values "good" and "evil" are no longer operative. The question, of course, is what kind of value is at stake here if it is no longer that commonplace couple, good/evil? In what concerns us here specifically, the question then becomes—more modestly, if it is no longer a choice between "this is a good/bad request"—what kind of value is at stake when a curator dignifies a demanding artist with a response.

In order to justify this new reading of Nietzsche's work, expose this "altogether other morality," and explain this value beyond good and evil, Nancy reiterates a few crucial points from an earlier reading of Nietzsche's work, namely that of Martin Heidegger. From Heidegger, he highlights the following three key points:

> [First, this new morality] implies thinking *life* precisely as that which evaluates; and in consequence, the supreme value (the one by which we are to evaluate) is evaluation itself;
>
> it implies recognizing that life evaluates . . . according to life itself as a creation, the incessant creation-evaluation of ever new perspectives . . .
>
> it implies thinking . . . Nietzsche's fundamental evaluation: positing something as true implies always leaving something to be surpassed, and it is through this incessant creative surpassing that the living can attain its full consistency.[3]

Succinctly, this gives us a number of crucial clues in the elaboration of this "altogether other morality." First, life evaluates. The issue is not to find a new arbitrary value but to pay attention to the fact that life itself is a value that gives us the measure of all values. Life is therefore evaluation itself. There is no other value but life evaluating. Second, life is not understood as a condition ("I'm alive"), an existence ("this is my life"), or a finite state ("being alive") but is rather understood as an incessant act of creation-evaluation. If life is to be a value, if it evaluates, then it needs to be an act of creation—not in an artistic sense but in the sense of never remaining the same, of always becoming other. Life evaluates precisely because it constantly creates itself. Finally, what gives value to life is the fact that it is true. It would not be a value if it were not true—that is, self-evident. Again, this truth is not a quality or a state. Because life evaluates, this truth also evaluates; it also participates in the process of creation. The three go together hand in hand, so to speak: life, value, truth—all three participate in the act of creation. Beyond the "true life," life-value-truth is therefore our only value. There are no other.

In his different approach to Nietzsche's morality, Nancy's aim is therefore not to create a new set of arbitrary values but to seek the value in the subject of evaluation. As he writes: "It is not merely a matter of an 'overturning' of moral values, but rather, through a strategy which gets to the bottom of every morality, of assigning *the* value in the very subject of evaluation."[4] The word *subject* should not be understood here to mean subjectivity but rather to mean what matters: the subject of evaluation. Life is what evaluates, and this is what matters. The difficulty with this move resides in not turning the subject (i.e., "what matters") into an objective value that would perdure over time. Because life is creation, this value, this truth, must also create, change. This is not therefore your run-of-the-mill value, something moral, a fixed principle or standard deserving to be held in importance. This is an unusual value that forces us to recognize that nothing in life has value but life itself, and because this life is never the same, this value never ceases to change, surpassing itself every second of time.

The main focus of Nancy's reinterpretation of Nietzschean morals is therefore this strange concept of life as a supreme value that evaluates, and in doing so always surpasses itself. In order to make further sense of this crucial term *life*, Nancy reads paragraph 335 of *The Gay Science*, entitled "Long Live Physics!," in which Nietzsche denounces, as usual, people's petty moral judgments and puts forward instead the idea that we should all become physicists—that is, creators of life values.[5] Nietzsche's new morality should then, in Nancy's reading, be created "by those who make themselves into 'the best disciples' of the 'necessity of life,' by 'physicists' therefore, who . . . are able to recognize the physique . . . of moral judgement and evaluation."[6] If life is indeed the supreme value (i.e., evaluation itself), then the ones who know most about life are basically physicists. They are the best disciples of this unquestionable value called life. To this Nancy adds a crucial characteristic: physicists alone are able to recognize the form of moral judgments. In other words, if life is best studied from the standpoint of physics, and if life is evaluation itself, then physics and physicists are better placed to provide us with moral guidance. Physics should therefore provide our guiding moral principles.

Nancy's aim in emphasizing that Nietzschean morality only comes from physicists should not be understood as if saying, "If you know 'Nature' like a scientist, you will end up being moral." On the contrary, his aim is to highlight a double bind: on the one hand, physics is the regime in which we find moral guidance, and on the other, physics is also the regime that allows us to create our moral guidance. As he writes, Nietzsche's critique of conventional morality "makes us recognize [physics] as . . . the regime of a 'conformity to the law and the necessity of the world,' a conformity of which we must be 'the best disciples'; but it also makes us acknowledge and choose 'physics' as the very space of the creation of new values, for we must also be 'the best inventors' of this legality and of this necessity."[7] This double bind cannot be overcome. If it were, we would elevate physics or ourselves above the other, thus creating an artificial value that would have nothing to do with life and that would revert us back to the petty moral judgments of conventional morality. Nietzsche's new morality is therefore an inextricable double bind: life creates, and we must be the best disciples (i.e., physicists), yet we are also life, thus participating in the creation of new values.

The aim of Nietzsche's new morality is therefore to create values as life creates values. It at once recognizes a supreme value and actively participates in creating it. As Nancy writes: "To create values, in sum, is to create—to re-create—the necessity of the world; it is to identify oneself with the law as with evaluation itself, as with the true physics and physiology of evaluation."[8] The crucial aspect of this recognition of physics and of our role in the creation of values is that it must be devoid of all content. It cannot signify something (righteousness, for example), it cannot be the outcome of a reasoning process (a maxim, for example), it cannot be an enigma (the Other, for example), and it cannot be an incarnation (God the Son, for example). The creative act of being a physicist needs to conform to physics—that is, to life, to what is. As Nancy observes: "This act is rid of all content. It has no other content than 'the necessity and the law of the world.'"[9] This does not reduce everything to a question of form; the shape of the world dictates our values, for example. This simply highlights that there cannot be a thinking of value without such a thinking being also part of that value.

Emphasizing such a type of moral value generates a new type of morality because it is based on a truth that has no equal: life as created—and not as defined—by physicists. The crucial focus on this value that has no content, this morality that has no equal, is that it therefore can only take place in moral judgments—not as a final verdict or outcome, but as the act of judging or evaluating itself. Nancy writes: "[Nietzsche's] extreme act—which in fact reduces everything to an act, to the act of judging, of evaluating, to an 'evaluating' which is absolute and without subject because it is the subject—this same act is nonetheless carried beyond itself."[10] Morality does not take place in the obedience to a value external to the subject; it takes place in the very act of judging, an act that accomplishes physics, an act that creates life itself. Again, the crucial aspect of this argument is that judgment here is not understood as a good or bad conclusion. Because we have done away with the couple good/evil, judging can only be perceived as a decision, and because we make decisions every second of time, we judge, we value, we evaluate.

This is what makes us physicists—creating life, the world, and their necessity.

Not unlike Lyotard's understanding of ethics as the "it happens" (cf. "Images"), Nancy also emphasizes the fact that Nietzsche's "physical" morality is something that effectively befalls the subject. We make decisions; we value, evaluate, judge. All these take place not as a choice between good and evil but because a necessity enjoins us to do so: physics. As Nancy writes: "No one pronounces the [necessity]. . . . [It] is the voice of no one, neither the voice nor the discourse of any consciousness; it is, over and beyond any *verifiable* utterance, that which is imposed as a constraint without having to justify *itself*, without having to authenticate *itself*. It 'befalls' the subject; it happens to him without his being able to master it."[11] This should not be understood as if we are passive victims of a physiological reality. Because we are part of physics, because we create, then this constraint, this unverifiable necessity that befalls the subject, comes as we pass judgment, as we evaluate. This is what enjoins us in the "it happens," in the "Long live physics!"

How is one to characterize this value that Nancy attributes to life, that only physics can make sense of, and that befalls us as we judge? Nancy suggests that it is dignity. Dignity is the only value that escapes all forms of economy. It is the value of life. It is physics' most evidential proof: the dignity of matter or energy, the fact that "it happens" and that "we happen," and this is what enjoins us in our judgments. As Nancy writes: "Dignity, or absolute value, escapes all evaluation."[12] In this way, the value of Nietzschean morals is no longer "*a* value"; it no longer stems from an evaluation of this or that; it does not hold itself to be good or evil; it simply is, as the value that cannot be valued being the other of all relative values (cf. "Introduction"). The curious thing about dignity, this supreme value that exceeds all relative values, is that it is entirely in the hands of unconscious ends. There is no telos or ideal here. Dignity does not know where it is going; like matter, it simply expresses and reexpresses itself (cf. "Matter"); it happens without "why" or "for what." This does not mean it is blind or stupid. To be in the hands of unconscious ends is to precisely let go of all conventional morality, all aims and objectives, all ghosts haunting us as if from above (cf. "Ghosts"). To be in the service of unconscious ends is to embody dignity properly, and when that happens, as Nietzsche poignantly says, in a passage quoted in Nancy's essay, "Man can excuse his existence."[13]

However, as we said right at the start, dignity is not good enough. It comes across as a higher state, status, rank, or quality, and as such undermines what Nancy is really attempting to pinpoint here: life as evaluation, physics as creation. Nancy remains far too Kantian in his Heideggerian reading of Nietzsche. Let's indeed recall Kant's famous own words: "In the realm of ends everything has either a price or a dignity. What has a price is such that something else can also be put in its place as its equivalent; by contrast, that which is elevated above all price, and admits of no equivalent, has a dignity."[14] To pinpoint dignity as the character of the value of life is inevitably to retain a horizon—an end—and therefore to return us to conventional morality (people aspiring to some dignity, for example). In order to avoid this tiresome aim, it is necessary to turn Nancy's idea into a verbal action: to dignify. As a verbal action, we as physicists—that is, we as life creators—can then embody this act that is nothing other than a supreme value carrying itself beyond itself. But this embodiment can only take place if we allow ourselves to befall as the value befalls us. To dignify is to carry ourselves over as value in the service of unconscious ends—hardly a matter for the high-ranking judge. This is something that we can all do: *to dignify.*

Considering all this within the context of this book, we can then add that it is only mortals who also happen to be gods who can truly embody this kind of Nietzschean/Nancyan act, because it is only they who are able to escape all relative valuations—not in an attempt to do without good and evil and the whole arsenal of moral economies, but in a manner that reflects life as evaluation. Why would that be the case? Simply because mortals (cf. "Mortals") are open to acts that are in the hands of unconscious ends—that is, in the hands of gods (cf. "Gods"). They are an outpouring/poured gift. As such, to dignify is to act as a mortal who happens to be a god, not in the sense of being superior or an Übermensch but in the sense of never being able to be other than this tension between mortality and its questioning, between what is true and what remains to be discovered, between what conforms to physics and what remains to be created. This act is therefore not only the most difficult of all verbal actions but also the only one worth accomplishing, not because it is saintly or divine but because its worth, its value, is life itself. Mortals who happen to be gods are physicists; that is, they are the most capable at excusing their existence.

If Nancy's reading of Nietzsche tells us anything at all, it is that it is necessary to dignify each other not in order to abide to an already established form of dignity but in order to be eminent physicists (that is, life creators), surpassing ourselves as we pass judgments. The dignified response to a demanding artist, or to anyone with unexpected requests or stipulations, is therefore not to adhere to a rule of conduct but to recognize in them the physicists that we all are: physicists evaluating in the service of unconscious ends. Once again, this does not mean creating a clique of supermen and superwomen scientists with higher moral values. Rather, it means attributing the other—the artist in our case—with a worth that exceeds all values: that of being creators, not just in an artistic sense but in a way that enjoins life. Seeing them as physicists is therefore to ascribe a certain worthiness to the person who dignifies and to endow a further worthiness to the person who is dignified with a response, which means nothing other than recognizing each other as mortals/gods, and this even if the demand is unacceptable. Curators aspiring to respond as ethically as possible to artists' difficult requests now have a value that is nothing other than their very own mortal/godly surge between earths and skies. Such a unique value is the only one that can determine how to ethically respond to artists who make extravagant requests.

# Midwifing

**Curating is woolly. • This woolliness can be turned into a powerful tool. • Plato/Kofman. • Mistakenly, Plato places philosophy at the apex of knowledge and arts at the bottom. • Kofman addresses this issue by focusing on dialectics. • She describes a quasi-divine tool to get mortals out of trouble. • Plato's old "science of being" links pure and impure techniques together. • It is not a tool available to all or applicable in all situations. • Such work requires midwifing abilities. • Knowledge always needs to be invented. • Life and death are at stake. • Curating can become a midwifery.**

Curating is woolly. It is woolly because it relies on many things for it to take place. It relies on circumstantial approaches to art (artists, artworks, sounds, or images accessible to the curator), some chunks of visual history (usually the period or context known to the curator), some theory (whatever is found online or remembered from universities' core courses), a plethora of adjacent disciplines quickly read (philosophy, politics, economy, psychology, geography, sociology, etc.), and a whole gamut of personal, situational, and parochial knowledges, emotions, and know-how. I already hinted at this in a previous book, saying: "We often complain that it is impossible to limit the field of the curatorial because it always actively engages more than one discipline (art and architecture or art and anthropology, for example)."[1] At the time, my response was to abrogate all disciplines in order to focus on the curatorial act of thinking itself, an act that knows no disciplinary limit. I would like to come back to the famous woolliness of curating. But this time, I would like to give this woolliness its respectability, not by singularizing and elevating it in any disciplinary hierarchy but by emphasizing its power. Curating is woolly and curators are woolly practitioners, but such facts can be turned into a fundamental power that, if played well, can overcome all disciplinary divisions. Inevitably, the adjective *well* in the previous sentence is what matters most.

In order to reveal the power of woolly curating, it is necessary to go back to the birth of disciplinary hierarchy as established by Plato. Fear not; my aim is not to do an archaeology and then trace a very long history leading us to some kind of explanation for the current woolliness of curating. On the contrary, my aim is to rethink the problem through a contemporary reading of Plato. This rethinking will reveal that the woolliness of curating is not a flaw but a power: the midwife power of thinking and acting by using a concert of practices. The contemporary reader of Plato investigated here is perhaps one of the most profound and daring philosophers of the twentieth century, someone who is unfortunately rarely read today. This philosopher is Sarah Kofman, and the essay read here is "Comment s'en sortir?," a formidable exploration of the power that can be extracted from this line of thinking that we find in Plato. Let's proceed slowly and cautiously. Revealing the potential power of woolly curating is no easy feat. It requires not only determination and patience but also careful detours into forgotten worlds when and where distinctions were discretely first made. Thinking and acting in a concert of practices does not come quickly—doing so well even more so.

The clearest account of the problem at hand comes with Plato's decision to define philosophy as the only science worthy of its name. Kofman reads this unfair decision by contrasting the arts understood broadly (*techne*[2]) against philosophy understood not as *doxa* (opinion) but as *episteme* (knowledge). Plato's decision is therefore to condemn the arts as an oblique, unscientific, imprecise, and skewed human form of knowledge, and to determine philosophy as the only science worthy of its name. Kofman writes: "Plato is famous for having cast a shadow on art: not only the way art grasps the world, but also its practical modalities. In particular, he condemns its oblique processes, its approximations and lack of certainties. Against art, he pitches the only science worthy of its name: precise and rigorous, namely, philosophy *(episteme)*, which is by nature contemplative."[3] The dice are cast. There is no going back. Anything that is not philosophy basically lacks rigor and is evasive, imprecise, and open to unjustified emotions and contingencies. It does not take long to see that the idea of the woolliness of curating effectively starts with Plato's dangerous discrimination.

But it does not stop there. Plato's condemnation also installs a hierarchy between disciplines that even to this day can hardly be shaken: philosophy comes first, then the social sciences, and then the arts and humanities. Kofman explains: "Positioned right at the apex of all forms of knowledge, philosophy would have decided between truth and fiction, skewed and straight reasoning, and determined which human achievements depend on uncertain knowledge and which rely on exactness, thus dismissing with a sovereign gesture most arts, including rhetoric and sophistry. And all this without hesitation. Plato's condemnation of everything that depends on conjectural thinking is clear. Such conclusion is classic and remains unquestionable."[4] There is no point in debating the details of the hierarchy (what comes near philosophy or is the least philosophical, for example). The damage is done. Ambivalence, conjectural thinking, skewed reasoning, and a general inability to distinguish between fact and fiction constitute the hallmarks of the arts. It is not surprising that artists and curators today always pitch practice against theory and experiment against science; it is their last-ditch attempt to rescue their work from Plato's fateful, hurtful ranking.

However, Plato's condemnation needs to be articulated with much more discernment. In order to do so, Kofman insists that for Plato, it is actually not philosophy per se *(episteme)* that is situated at the apex of knowledge but more specifically dialectics. *Dialectics* is a difficult term that is often misunderstood. This confusion is because philosophers (Kant and Hegel, but others too) use the term to mean different things. In ancient Greece, the term *dialectics* is understood as a tool to overcome obstacles. This tool is thought to have been given by the god Prometheus to help mortals overcome problems in life, thus giving them an ersatz of divinity that Zeus prevented them from possessing. Dialectics is therefore a practical tool that maintains mortals in a quasi-divine state. Kofman writes: "Dialectics is far too beautiful and far too divine a path for human thought. Although human beings never manage to overcome their own limits, dialectics let them remember their own mortal condition thus allowing them to repeat and invent themselves, always the same, always other."[5] Dialectics is therefore what Plato is trying to rescue. It is the only thing that is semidivine in mortals; it is a way of remembering, repeating, and inventing stratagems to get mortals out of trouble without, in the process, ever becoming properly divine.

Kofman's insistence on reading dialectics and not philosophy per se in Plato's condemnation is crucial. It highlights not a discipline but a way of thinking that surprisingly values conjecture, intermediary positions, and discernment without aiming at bringing anything to a close. She writes: "Prometheus' dialectics gives mortals the ability to avoid summarizing quickly or slowly everything into 'one,' preventing them from positing indefiniteness immediately after this 'one' has been reached, allowing them to fashion intermediary positions between 'one' and the multiple and to number them in a precise manner. This respect for intermediaries is precisely what distinguishes dialectics from eristic [the practice of winning an argument rather than reaching the truth]."[6] The thinking project that Plato defends in his condemnation of the arts is therefore not what is now known as an institutional discipline (philosophy) but rather a quasi-divine work to get us out of aporia by encouraging recollection, repetition, and inventiveness. In this way, contrary to how the term *dialectics* is understood today (pitching thesis against antithesis to reach synthesis, for example), Prometheus's gift is really the process of avoiding end results, steering clear of quick conclusions, evading swift and unwarranted synthesis, all in the hope of continuing the quasi-divine work.

Such a crucial focus allows Plato to return to a much older definition of dialectics, which he explores in *The Republic*, namely, "dialectics as the science of being."[7] This return to an old definition of dialectics enables Plato to concentrate not on the accuracy of dialectics against the inaccuracy of the arts but on the way the former deals with what has no ground: the being of mortals. The idea here is not to single out ontology as the only science but to find out what is most capable of addressing aporetic topics such as the being of mortals. As Kofman writes: "Plato focuses not on the accuracy of dialectics' instruments, but on its actual object: the fact that it is able to be most precise, meticulous, true, consistent, and pure: 'How else could we make sense of what precisely has 'no firmness?'"[8] What is elevated, therefore, is not an accurate science or a disciplinary apparatus but a Promethean tool that not only avoids conclusions and is allergic to winning arguments but that also, and above all, treats ungraspable topics such as the being of mortals not as a solid and identifiable "one" but as "a play of differences."[9] Plato's unfair condemnation can now be read under a completely different light—not as a dismissal but as an attempt to find a way of articulating difficult or impossible issues (for example, what makes us mortal) without resting on winning arguments, convictions, or faith.

In what concerns us, the crucial aspect of Plato's return to a repressed definition of dialectics as the science of being is an attempt to think so-called pure and impure techniques together, to bring them in concert in order to maximize their Promethean potentials. There are no more hierarchies and no more exclusions; there is only dialectics, not as an elevated institutional science above others but as what addresses the most difficult topics in the most accurate way. Kofman writes: "After having declared the superiority of dialectics . . . Plato recuperates everything that he originally condemned, repressed, or at least, devalued: 'he opens the doors' and 'lets out' even the vilest of all techniques, the most empirical ones, the most utilitarian ones: a human life, worthy of its name is a mixed life allying the purest of sciences with the most impure of techniques."[10] This is not a reversal of situation. Nor is Plato contradicting himself. He simply highlights that in order to help mortals deal with difficult issues, they need all the tools they can get, from the most precise forms of knowledge *(episteme)* to the least precise of all techniques (the arts).

The question, of course, is this: what do we want? If we simply want to create further abstract thoughts that have no practical knowledge, then dialectics is not right. If we only want to create beauty without a thought for self or others, then dialectics is not right either. However, if one truly addresses the most difficult problems—that is, broadly speaking, our mortal condition with all its sociocultural and political implications—then dialectics is the requisite quasi-divine tool. As Kofman points out, giving examples of this mix of pure and impure arts and sciences, "Of course, all this is valid only if one really wants to find a way home and avoid at all costs aporia: 'Should we then *throw in the mix* this impure, weak *techné* with its false rules and false practice? It seems as if we have no choice if we wish to find our way *(odon)* home.' 'Should we also include music, even if we said that it is full of conjectures *(stochaseos)*, imitations, and lacks purity? This seems inevitable, if we want our life to measure itself up as a unique life.'"[11] Prometheus's tool is therefore not useful for any odd task. It is the tool par excellence that allows mortals to think their most finite sense for themselves—that is, as Prometheus's children: both mortal and divine.

How is one to go about this difficult path *(poros)* that helps us address the most difficult issues *(aporia)* in life, that leads us to a science of being that is not just reductive to the one? How does one practice dialectics without falling immediately into easy *doxa*? Kofman points to a difficult path, one that requires measure and proportion. She refers to the path always taken by the midwife and that Socrates takes on as the only possible way to overcome aporia. She writes: "Railing against those who criticize him for abandoning men in the middle of aporia, Socrates puts forward in the *Theaetetus*, the fertile work of giving birth to spirits: the work of the midwife whose duty is to awaken birth and alleviate the pains of child-birth."[12] Highjacking the work of the midwife for his own ends is not a way of dismissing the work and labor of women. The work of the midwife is not simply relegated here to that of a nurse (typically a woman) who is trained to assist women in childbirth. Rather, it concerns anyone who helps to create or develop something out of a difficult situation. A midwife is basically a supreme dialectician inasmuch as he or she is primarily concerned with the science of being—that is, with the science of bringing bodies and/or spirits to light.

This supreme dialectician, this practitioner who works not to win arguments but to help others with birthing, has no single knowledge at her disposal. Midwifery is not something that requires one supreme science or art; rather, it demands a concert of practices to see that a child and/or spirit is brought forth into the world. Kofman writes: "Not unlike nurses who are trained to assist women in childbirth, Socrates uses drugs and magical incantations to help men extricate themselves from a problem, creating a passage, a *poros* for the child that will bring them to light. The work of the midwife indeed requires no knowledge. It is a task whose practitioner knows that they do not know—the only advantage over those who think they know and who give birth to pseudo-knowledge."[13] This knowing that they do not know is not humility; it is a way of emphasizing that no skill, competence, expertise, or mastery, and therefore no science, can deal with what in childbirth is unexpected. Everything always needs to be invented. For the midwife, every situation is a new one that no previous body of knowledge can address. In this way, the work of midwives—be they men or women—is free of all disciplinary apparatuses.

Again, this does not mean that this tool can be used in all circumstances. Dialectics, this quasi-divine *poros* to get mortals out of aporia, has one crucial criterion: it needs to take place at the brink of life or death. The midwife's responsibility is indeed that of bringing a child into the world. Socrates's responsibility is to bring a spirit into his or her own. In both cases, the task is not a common one. It takes place right at the edge of life and death, right when a life or a spirit is about to be lost. As Kofman points out: "The midwife has a practical intelligence that aims at reaching a goal with the help of an intuitive outlook: knowing when labour should start and determine whether the child deserves to live or die."[14] To determine whether to let a child live or die is not an easy task, and it is not an everyday occurrence. Dialectics implies a conjectural knowledge on what bears the highest of responsibilities, one that concerns a matter of life or death. Hence the fact that such a science of being can be neither elevated above others nor singled out as either a science or an art. It is the workings of life par excellence, the unique *episteme/techne* that allows one to create life or let it veer it into nothingness. The stakes of dialectics are high.

Free from disciplinary hierarchies, unconstrained by the hierarchical distinction science/arts, the repressed science of being, this midwifery, this supreme dialectical tool, therefore requires a quasi-intuitive approach, a way of using what one feels to be true even without, at times, conscious reasoning (cf. "Intuiting"). As Kofman concludes:

> For Plato, an intuitive outlook, an easy-going attitude, and a keenness of thought are the qualities of a genuine natural philosophy (cf. *Charmides* 16a and *Republic* IV). These qualities are met by the midwife of spirits, whose work, from start to finish, in its diverse roles, its means and its goals, and the talents it employs is the same as those of the midwife who delivers babies. Not unlike a midwife's intuitive outlook, Socrates is able to know when to start working, where lies aporetic suffering, and the time at which a spirit is about to give birth.[15]

This intuitive work does not mean that anyone with some wits for themselves can be a midwife of babies and/or spirits. This intuitive work requires experience and learned patience. It is a path that establishes itself at the confluence of science and art—that is, between an oblique, unscientific, imprecise, and skewed human form of knowledge and a precise, rigorous, rational, and systematic approach.

Could Socrates's midwifing be a way of rethinking the power of woolly curating? The detours that Kofman has taken us in her reading of Plato all end up with a single realization: there are no superior disciplines. No single art can address the most difficult of all aporias, namely bringing a child and/or spirit into the world. In order to address what matters above all else, in order to truly embody the old science of being (that is, not ontology as the science of the one but as the science/art of the play of differences), it is necessary to engage in a concert of practices that rely on both accurate and artistic practices that no academy could possibly channel into a curriculum destined to create know-how or expertise. Curating can become a midwifery; it can become the science of being if it is done not in order to come up with pseudoknowledge but as if lives were at stake. Of all practices, curating can become a tool that relies at once on conjectural knowledge and on the highest of all disciplines, the most stringent of all practices, the only one for which mortals can finally recognize themselves as gods. This is the only way curating can lose its supposed woolliness and acquire the respectability it deserves as the one practice that can potentially overcome the ideology that supposedly stemmed from Plato whereby the arts are not worthy of the name science.

# Intuiting

**Curators are intuitive people. • What does a curatorial intuition mean? • It is not a guessing but the act of contemplating what is immemorial or unhoped for. • It describes a relation with what defies finite reason. • Spinoza. Jaquet. • How is one to addresses the immemorial, what is unhoped for, or the eternal—what is out of space and time? • Two visions dominate: *sub duratione* and *sub specie aeternitatis.* • Chords, rectangles, and circles provide a fractured vision at the edge of space and time. • It is necessary to intuit (the vision at the edge of space and time). • It is never an experience. • Curators should let the immemorial or what is unhoped for play its part.**

Here is another truism among contemporary curators: they all work intuitively, and intuition is a key component in their busy lives. Forget expertise, abandon all forms of scholarliness, neglect theories, leave behind all disciplinary rigor. The zeitgeist of the times is one entirely approached intuitively and most often quickly, as if the pace of modern life permits no other approach. In their frenzied jetsetting and trend-setting work, curators are in touch with what is hot; they know who the coolest artists are, what the right topics are, and when to address them. Funding bodies, museum directors, and a whole plethora of creative industry bosses need to listen to curators because they have the right intuition; they are in touch with everything that is of importance in today's obsessively repetitive world. This is particularly true of content curators who sift through endless material in order to bring you what matters above all else. This is also true of curator-academics who not only know but also fall prey to the hottest theory, articulating the world as if they alone can sum it all up in one word, like "contemporaneity" or "the Anthropocene." There is no end to this claim that curators are in touch with their intuition. Let's simply check out two recent curatorial accounts, one European, one American, to give us a hint of this all-important intuitive approach.

The first curatorial account of this predictable intuition comes from Serbian independent curator Lara Pan, who is based in Brussels. Founder of the New Art Project, Pan has curated several exhibitions, such as Pandora's Sound Box at Performa (2009) and Torre at the Guggenheim Foundation in Venice (2009). In an interview with *Artpulse*, Pan says:

> Intuition is my favourite "weapon." . . . In group exhibitions I try to respect each individual work as an original contribution to the theme. All works together should trigger a particular atmosphere and make the exhibition concept clear. The latter is in the first instance the product of my intuition. But I do not understand intuition as something irrational, or even magical. It is the synthesis of any kind of life experience and knowledge. . . . In the end, I can say that I like to work hand in hand with my intuition, keeping my eyes wide open to the future.[1]

The second account of intuition comes from Carolyn Bell Farrell, executive director of the MacLaren Art Centre, a regional public art gallery serving the residents of Barrie in the county of Simcoe, Ontario. Bell Farrell writes:

> The contemporary curator is engaged with interpreting the traces of artistic activity. Be it reason, conjecture, deduction, luck or intuition, "divining" aptly describes one approach to this process of reading between the lines of artistic practice. The activity brings to mind the curators as seers who read and translate the signs of culture and the patterns of artistic phenomena. . . . In my experience, anticipation, intuition, and chance all play important roles in reading artworks. . . . Curatorial intuition necessitates a degree of faith in an unseen order.[2]

So what does a curatorial intuition mean? An intuition is usually defined as the ability to understand something instinctively, without the need for conscious reasoning. At bottom, an intuition refers to nature, to a natural pattern of behavior that is reminiscent of animals and their response to certain stimuli—the homing instinct, for example. As such, an intuition is a way of acting or thinking that supposedly evades the artifices of reason and keeps people—and curators specifically—in touch with their natural selves. Someone who relies on intuition therefore has an inherent propensity or skill for being at one with nature, intuitively making the most of his or her chances. There is nothing more annoying than this definition of intuition. It is an essentialist and reductive way of approaching a fundamental human act. An intuition should really, and most simply, be understood on the premise of its Latin root (from late Latin verb *intueri*, from *in-*, "upon," and *tueri*, "to contemplate"), that is, as "a task of contemplating." In what follows, I would like to take up this Latin root and focus on the verb instead of the noun and simply say curators could intuit; that is, they could work by intuitive moves, by contemplative moves. The difficulty with this unusual approach to intuition is that it is often considered impossible because no one can work on a feeling or hunch, and no one can fine-tune one's guesswork. How does one work on an intuition, for example? However, this difficulty can easily be circumnavigated if one clearly redefines the premise of what *to intuit* means, thus giving this verb—and subsequently the noun—a better chance than that currently given by curators.

In what follows, to intuit will be considered as the task of contemplating what I have called throughout this book the immemorial or the unhoped for—that is, what no longer or not yet constitutes an event of matter, what is not strife (cf. "Matter" and "Strife"). At first sight, this might seem utterly removed from the work of curators. Why should they, or anyone else for that matter, contemplate the immemorial or the unhoped for? What has this got to do with selecting, arranging, and sharing culture? How is it going to get curators closer to their cherished zeitgeist? The task of intuiting is not for curators who want a quick fix. As I will endeavor to show, the immemorial or the unhoped for is never clearly evident, never quite accountable or even manageable, and to intuit is never determinable as a favorite weapon or a divining process, for example. The task to be accomplished implies, as we will see, a conscious contemplative reasoning of letting the immemorial or unhoped for play its part. Curators could intuit in order to carry out their task; that is, they should contemplate what is immemorial or unhoped for as they work. How ought one go about this?

First, I have approached the topic of the immemorial or the unhoped for a number of times so far in this book (cf. "Beckoning," "Obsession," and "Fraternizing"). In all instances, the aim was to highlight a relation with what appears to defy reason, what seems to fall out of our contemporary present. As such, the question was therefore always a question of intuition, of a relation with what cannot enter into any form of economy, of what stubbornly refuses to provide us with a return in this or another life. How should we relate to this teasing coming from this past or future beyond all economies? How should we relate to what stings us every second of time and never lets go? How should we relate to what seems to disappear into oblivion or appear out of nowhere? In all cases, the answer is most simply, as we will see, we could intuit. With the immemorial or the unhoped for in mind, the issue is therefore no longer one of having a hunch about this or that artist or hot topic, but of working out a way of relating to—that is, of intuiting—what defies rationality while remaining on the riverbanks of our rational living present.

Because what is at stake here is something that no religion or science, including philosophy, can make sense of, because it defies even the most astute of metaphysics, we can therefore only assume that what is immemorial or unhoped for refers to what seemingly knows no space and time. We intuit what appears to evade space and time. In order to make sense of this, it is necessary to come back to a philosopher who has attempted to think this odd evasion of time-space that defies our memories and projections. This philosopher is Spinoza (cf. "Matter"). However, in order to make sense of this topic without falling under the dangerous spell of Spinozism—that is, of a whole set of endless debates on the celebrated Sephardic philosopher—I will let the following arguments be guided by a specialist of Spinoza's understanding of space and time. The reason it is necessary to read this specialist is because only such a person is able to make sense of what Spinoza tries to say when he himself addresses, sometimes confusedly or evasively, the issue of what knows no space and time. Spinoza is also useful here because alongside his understanding of what evades space and time, he also puts forward, alongside *doxa* and *episteme*, a third type of knowledge, which he calls, intuition. His take on intuition will therefore also be our guiding tool in order to make sense of what is immemorial or unhoped for, this relation that defies both religion and science.

The specialist in question is Chantal Jaquet, a contemporary philosopher whose work focuses quite remarkably on the way the body deals with space and time. The specific topic that Jaquet develops in great detail in her first book on Spinoza is his famous expression, *sub specie aeternitatis*. The reason we need to explore this strange expression is because, as we will see, it is one of the few attempts in Western philosophy to think this relation with what precisely evades space and time, and as such can only be intuited. Looking briefly into the meaning of this specific term will help us make further sense not only of what we call the immemorial or the unhoped for but also of the verb *to intuit*, this singular approach to what teases us as if from nowhere. The structure of this chapter will be as follows: we will begin by uncovering the way Jaquet translates Spinoza's famous expression, *sub specie aeternitatis*. This will illuminate the way we contemplate what defies space and time—and in what concerns us here, the immemorial or the unhoped for.[3] We will then move onto what matters most here, namely how to intuit. In order to make sense of it, we will quickly survey the way Spinoza defines intuition. This will, I hope, give us the way we should work by intuitive moves and how this is a crucial component of curating.

Let's begin with a simple—yet at this stage inevitably problematic—hypothesis. There are two ways of seeing things: from inside and from outside of space and time. The former refers to an apprehension of things and beings that is finite. This is our common understanding of the apprehension of matter: from a finite standpoint. The latter refers to an apprehension of things and beings that is not contingent on finitude and is therefore hypothetically, for now, eternal. To say that what is outside of space and time is eternal must not be confused with saying that it is immortal or infinite. These terms refer to durations that can be counted: *x* number of days in an immortal life and counting, for example. The term *eternal*, by contrast, refers not to something that lasts or exists for an exceedingly long period of time but rather to something that effectively has neither beginning nor end, and consequently does not appear to exist in space and time. So this is our first hypothesis, which Jaquet puts forward as an introduction to her attempted translation of Spinoza's famous sentence: "The idea behind *sub specie aeternitatis* only makes sense in the context of a philosophy that acknowledges the fact that it is really possible to think things both in time and outside of time."[4]

The key issue with this hypothesis is the fact that it cannot be seen as if occurring in two different places. This is a difficult issue because our vocabulary always spatializes and temporalizes everything. What is outside of space and time is also inevitably in space and time, and vice versa. The two take place at once without what is inside space and time being able to make sense of what seemingly appears outside of them. In this way, there are eternal and durational aspects to things and beings, with the two being impossible to distinguish. This is what Jaquet insists on when she says that the two come together: "The structure of Part V [of Spinoza's *Ethics*] shows that what is *sub specie aeternitatis* comes together with what is *sub duratione*; this is the double-structure of things: being both durational and eternal."[5] Again, this coming together is obviously skewed, inasmuch as from a finite perspective, it is necessarily and exclusively one sided; that is, the durational is unable to elucidate the eternal. This does not make any metaphysical assumption that there is an elsewhere or elsewhen called "the eternal," only that what happens to things and beings is necessarily skewed, split in their spatiotemporal and nonspatiotemporal determinations.

Free from any temporal and spatial situated referent, what is *sub specie aeternitatis* must nonetheless be understood as somewhat taking place, but in a situation whereby this taking place is not entirely impinged on space and time. In order to think this through, Jaquet refers to the scholium of proposition 29 of Spinoza's *Ethics*, in which Spinoza attempts to prove the fact that some things do not necessarily take place in space and time. Let's read this famous scholium:

> Should anyone want an example for a clearer understanding of this matter, I can think of none at all that would adequately explicate the point with which I am here dealing, for it has no parallel. Still, I shall try to illustrate it as best as I can. The nature of a circle is such that the rectangles formed from the segments of its intersecting chords are equal. Hence an infinite number of equal rectangles are contained in a circle, but none of them can be said to exist except insofar as the circle exists, nor again can the idea of any one of these rectangles be said to exist except insofar as it is comprehended in the idea of the circle.[6]

The idea here is simple: a circle exists in space and time. Inside it, necessary but invisible intersecting chords form equally necessary but invisible rectangles. As such, unlike the circle, the chords and rectangles do not actually exist in space and time. They are dependent on the circle to exist, but they "are" not "there," empirically speaking. This does not necessarily involve the imagination and therefore a finite space and time perspective. A *sub specie aeternitatis* apperception starts from the necessity of the rectangles contained within the circle, not from assumptions or projections derived from the circle. Chords are necessary for there to be a circle.

As Spinoza's scholium shows, everything hinges on a question of double contemplation: *sub duratione* (from the premise of a spatial and temporal perspective) and *sub specie aeternitatis* (from no specific spatial or temporal perspective). Jaquet explains this double contemplation by referring to Spinoza's understanding of knowledge: "contemplation as rational thought *and* as intuitive thought."[7] Spinoza's synoptic vision thus involves both an adequate set of ideas about the properties of things (i.e., knowledge of the second kind, in Spinoza's taxonomy[8]) and another set that takes place without any form of rationality (i.e., knowledge of the third kind, intuition), with the two operating at the indecision of what is in and out of space and time. This indecision with regards to contemplation reflects the indecision between inside and outside of space and time. This double contemplation is not strictly ocularcentric; it involves not one faculty alone. By referring to contemplation, Jaquet clearly emphasizes that this synoptic vision is in fact an apperception that essentially gives the ability to see without necessarily being uniquely reduced to one sense alone (cf. "Communing").

To justify this unusual approach, Jaquet refers to Spinoza's well-known example of an intuition: "For example, three numbers are given; 1, 2, 3, everybody can see that the fourth proportional is 6, and all the more clearly because we infer in one single intuition the fourth number from the ratio *we see* the first number bears to the second."[9] An intuition is therefore a type of contemplation that takes place in space and time—numbers are human finite determinations—about something that is not empirically present on paper, namely, the ratio the first bears to the second, and so on. This type of contemplation takes place *sub specie aeternitatis*; that is, it takes place from the standpoint of what is finite (what is inferred) and from the viewpoint of what defies this finite inference (what is intuitively seen beyond what is inferred). The two take place at once. Jaquet thus concludes with her own definition of Spinoza's famous expression, *sub specie aeternitatis*:

> Considering that this third kind of knowledge is a synoptic vision, it is therefore clear that the expression *specie* in what concerns us, refers to a way of seeing, and must thereby be linked to the verb *specio*,

> which means "to see." This leads us to suggest that a correct translation for *sub specie aeternitatis* is therefore, from an eternal viewpoint [*sous un regard d'éternité*]. To contemplate things *sub specie aeternitatis* is therefore to see them with an eternal eye.[10]

But is it really possible to intuit—that is, to contemplate—from an eternal viewpoint? Is this not a ridiculous claim, the lucky outcome of a warped use of language? Are all viewpoints not necessarily finite? Is something "seen" from what is "inferred" not necessarily taken from a finite perspective? Jaquet equally asks: "Is to suggest an eternal viewpoint not to fall for a distasteful type of divine anthropomorphism?"[11] But she is also quick to reply magisterially: "If Spinoza does not hesitate to say that God contemplates himself, he cannot rescind from speaking of an eternal viewpoint since human understanding is also divine understanding. It is also necessary to recall here that this idea does not engage substance, but thought's eternal immediacy."[12] The shift here is crucial. If there is no outside of space and time, and if there is only a fractured taking place of space and time (finite and eternal), then what occurs in space and time also occurs, now, in the immediacy of this contemplation, outside of all spatial and temporal considerations. These types of viewpoints thus can only concur at once, however much this will infuriate those who only consider that which is plainly evident here, now, from this one and only finite perspective.

How can we, mere mortals, contemplate—that is, adopt—this finite standpoint and eternal viewpoint? How can we undertake this work of intuition? Any response must be clear: it cannot be an experience as such. An eternal viewpoint cannot be felt or experimented with the senses alone. Neither the eyes nor any other sense can give us an eternal viewpoint because all senses begin and end with the finite body. The same goes for memory and imagination. As such, it is clear that, as Jaquet says, "the type of experience or feeling in question here does not concern the body and the senses because if it did, it would only give us a sense of immortality or of an unlimited duration. To contemplate from an eternal viewpoint, mankind needs to be affected by the intellect through demonstrations."[13] The crucial word here is *affected*. Right at the moment of reasoning, right when the intellect plays its part, that which is not in space and time (the eternal) affects us. This is what to intuit actually means: to be affected by an eternal viewpoint, through neither the senses nor rationality alone but in their very finite and eternal taking place. In other words, right when one acts, rationally, through the intellect, from this very finite perspective, one can only also be affected by what falls out of space and time. To intuit is therefore to act using this more accurate synoptic vision, one that can only take place at the cusp of experience.

If the idea that we can operate from both an eternal viewpoint (i.e., *sub specie aeternitatis*) and a durational standpoint (i.e., *sub duratione*) is valid, then is it at all possible to train our intuition in such a way as to help us in our everyday work? The answer is inevitably, here again, no, because what is outside of space and time is not something that can be grasped and forced into an economy. At the start of this chapter, we hinted at the fact that to intuit cannot be determinable as "a favorite weapon or a divining process." To intuit implies a conscious reasoning and a letting go of all conscious reasoning. This does not mean play a half-dumb game. This means letting ourselves be rationally affected by this eternal viewpoint, this vision that affords us a perspective that is not simply finite and rational. Going back to the vocabulary we have used throughout this book, this can also be said thus: to intuit means to rationally contemplate what is immemorial or unhoped for in a situation where finite rationality is never enough. Right at the cusp of space and time, the task cannot be tamed or trained. It can only be synoptic inasmuch as what is memorable and hoped for is always marred by what is immemorable and unhoped for.

Curators might thus want to consider the idea of intuiting in order to carry out their tasks; that is, they might want to contemplate what evades all spatial and temporal considerations: what is immemorial, unhoped for, or what Spinoza calls the eternal. This does not mean being attentive every second of time as to what might fall out of time. Being a sentry on the lookout for the eternal is exactly the opposite of what is required here, precisely because what is sought cannot be found as if a shadow in the distance. When it comes to working intuitively, the task is rather to work in concert with the twofold nature of everything that takes place in life, and specifically here in gallery or online settings: both in and out of space and time. To intuit is to never take what is self-evidently present here and now as the only reality worth dealing with and to acknowledge that something of it is not necessarily finite but most simply eternal, and this affects us in our own synoptic apprehension of reality. Recognizing this doubling is the only way to rationally and intuitively expose and work with finite thought's eternal immediacy.

This "to intuit" is obviously not an easy task. Spinoza himself acknowledges that it is a difficult task.[14] To give what appears outside of space and time a role to play—that is, to let ourselves be affected by what defies rationality—is without doubt rebarbative, going against intuition understood in the conventional sense (i.e., a hunch). Again, it requires not "faith in an unseen order" but a willingness to partially abandon our finite ratiocinations in order to let ourselves be taken with the happenstance of space and time as it unfolds itself in its own twofoldedness. For curators, this no longer means to let themselves be guided by their instincts to determine who are the coolest artists, the right topics, the appropriate theories, the equitable politics, and so on, but to actively let what is immemorial or unhoped for play its part—that is, letting what defies space and time to participate in the immediacy of each and every spatial and temporal determination, in every one of their curatorial acts. To let what is immemorial or unhoped for—to let the eternal—play a part is to act not just like finite and rational animals but like gods that we also are.

# Dispensing

**Curators and viewers cannot avoid trolls. • Can these trolls really be called gods? • They "are" mortals and so play their part as gods amid earths and skies. • But how can a community establish itself on the basis of such enmity? • Blanchot discusses communities. • Communities may be against the "same." • A radical irreducibility occurs. • It is nothing other but death. • It is in the shape of an undecided injunction/interrogation: Don't die!—Will you die? • The impossibility of community is addressed. • Sacrifice. • Friendship. • My death equals god. • Gods always provide. • Curators can stop trolls in their tracks.**

Trolls.[1] Curators will invariably encounter trolls at one point in their careers. No, they will not encounter ugly cave-dwelling creatures. Rather, they will encounter annoying people who deliberately post provocative messages to a newsgroup or message board with the intention of causing maximum disruption and argument. This affects most of all the content curator: who has not been annoyed by the reductive, racist, multiphobic, and gratuitous attacks posted by trolls on curated sites, blogs, or forums? Who has not been dismayed by the surreal intensity of people's prejudices toward others? Who has not been appalled by the aggressive use of language to denigrate, deprecate, and defame? I doubt if there are content curators out there who would reply negatively to these questions. The same is true, albeit to a lesser degree, of gallery or museum curators. The posts often take the shape of small paper notes and can usually be found on noticeboards in the last room of an exhibition, where an institution, in its pretense of listening to the public, encourages audiences to respond to what has been exhibited. Who there has not been amazed by the unfounded vitriol, sarcasm, derision, and mockery evident in some notes? Trolls are everywhere. They no longer live in caves. They are out in the open, making the world a darker place.

Yet if one thing in the preceding chapters managed to strike a chord, then the question beckons: how on earths could these banal, trite, and irritating comments, remarks, and observations come from mortals who also happen to be gods? Surely trolls do not deserve such a twofold appellation. Surely they are only mortals, and as such deserve to disappear as quickly as their comments are disabled or removed. Unfortunately, they might only repeat clichés, platitudes, stock phrases, and fictions, and they might only foreclose the future by forcing others to repeat over and over again the same counterarguments, banalities, and truisms; they still "are," and as such, they make us think more than we can, however impossible this might seem at first. This does not mean to imply another banal thought, namely, "Trolls are human beings after all, and as such, they deserve as much respect as the next person." To convey such banality is as vapid as the trolls' comments. On the contrary, this means that amid all the brutality, barbarity, and even savagery, the fundamental dimensions—mortals/gods—never cease to play themselves out. We might not like trolls, but they are "us" amid earths and skies.

The question then is therefore not how they can do what they do, but what constitutes this "us" made up on one side of trolls and on the other of moralists. Can this "us" still constitute a community of mortals/gods? In order to address these questions, I will perform an oblique reading of a few passages taken from the first chapter of Maurice Blanchot's difficult book, *The Unavowable Community*. Referencing this work in a book on curating and ethics is, I admit, a bit of a cliché. Although fashion has moved on, there was a time when no self-respecting curator could utter a sentence without mentioning the idea of community. Endless texts and numerous exhibitions[2] were created on curating in relation to this idea, ruthlessly borrowed from a handful of books on this theme.[3] My aim is neither to return to these discussions nor to debate the pros and cons of this history. The oblique reading of Blanchot's famous text is instead intended to point at an activity that takes place among communities (virtual or real): dispensing. We come together not in a unison of voices or a communion of spirits (the trolls remind us of this), not because of an ideal, rule, norm, criterion, model, principle, or law (all of which, as before, are negotiable and thereby eminently questionable), but because of a radical and thereby unnegotiable dispensing that involves nothing less than our mortal/godly selves. So how do we make sense of a community that even trolls partake in?

Let's begin with Blanchot's clear remark that among the many types of community, one must be able to conceive of at least one that attempts to not reduce everybody to the same. He writes: "If the relation of man with man ceases to be that of the Same with the Same, but rather introduces the Other as irreducible . . . then a completely different relationship imposes itself."[4] Let's not stumble yet on that dreaded capitalized word "Other." Let's just assume for now that Blanchot refers here to a type of community for which assimilation to one unique identity (the Same) makes no sense. As we have seen before (cf. "Fraternizing"), this is a difficult first thought because the ideology of equality—one that establishes the same status, rights, or opportunities for all—remains not only unquestionable but also inalienable. We are all interchangeable alter egos in front of the law; we claim and defend nothing less: the Same. Blanchot is not asking us to leave this aside, only to consider something even more fundamental and archaic: the fact that beyond our equality of rights, there is a radical dissymmetry between us that constitutes what can be called a community. What is this dissymmetry, this irreducible Other?

Blanchot replies that this irreducible Other is something eminently close and yet radically ungraspable: death. Communities come together because of the sting of death in each being (cf. "Mortals"). Death is the only radicality that truly brings a community together:

> What, then, calls me into question most radically? Not my relation to myself as finite or as the consciousness of being before death or for death, but my presence for another who absents himself by dying. To remain present in the proximity of another who by dying removes himself definitely, to take upon myself another's death as the only death that concerns me, this is what puts me beside myself, this is the only separation that can open me, in its very impossibility to the Openness of a community.[5]

Blanchot's community therefore comes together not because of a common fear of death per se but because each member of this community witnesses the other dying. It is the scandal of others absenting themselves that forces us to be beside ourselves, to cry out our need to come together.

The curious thing about this community that comes together in the scandal of others absenting themselves is that the scandal itself pivots around an undecided injunction and question about death. As Blanchot says, "Don't die now; let there be no now in which to die. 'Don't,' the ultimate word, the injunction that becomes complaint, the stammering: 'Don't die!—Will you die?'"[6] No encounter, no meeting—whether in corporate boardrooms, factories, cozy homes, busy streets, lurid digs, dark backrooms, or peaceful fields—can take place without this strange and mostly unheard injunction/question encapsulating this radical Other, this death at the heart of the community: "Don't die!—Will you die?" A community is therefore not a group of people having a particular characteristic in common or unified by common interests. Rather, a community is structured by this stammering but radical injunction/question: "Don't die!—Will you die?" This is what gives birth to a community: a stammering supplication/interrogation to any fellow mortal, anyone sharing (and therefore still part of) the strife together. This injunction/question never lets go, and this is what brings us together over and beyond anything we might have, or aspire to have, in common.

It is thus a community of death, which is nothing other than the impossibility of community itself. This is perhaps one of the most paradoxical aspects of Blanchot's understanding of community. If what brings us together is nothing other than a radical injunction/question "Don't die!—Will you die?," one that triggers the birth of our sense of community, then what brings us together is nothing other than the very impossibility of community itself. Why? Simply because the relentless zeal of death renders it impossible. As Blanchot says, "If the community is revealed by the death of the other person, it is because death is itself the true community of mortal beings: their impossible communion."[7] We come together on the basis that there cannot be any coming together. We cry out, we contest, we urge, yet all these cries, contestations, and implorations mark the fact that we cannot effectively come together. Death forces us into a community but in doing so also highlights the impossibility of community itself. In other words, no community can take place without inscribing at its heart its own impossibility.

What is the point of thinking such a community? Surely what matters above all is what we have in common, what we share, discuss, make, and curate together. This is where we need to acknowledge that Blanchot's community is not a union of bodies and/or spirits but rather the mutual recognition that it is impossible to substitute each other's death. "My death" is unlike any other's; I cannot take over the other's death. As such, it serves no purpose except that of highlighting our absolute irreplaceability (cf. "Obsession"). Blanchot sums it up in one formidable sentence: "Mortal substitution is what replaces communion."[8] Nothing here is owned individually or in a group, and nothing here is understood as a union of bodies and/or spirits. Everything points instead to a communion between what suffers no union, what is allergic to any kind of trade or exchange. We are together; we constitute a community on the basis of what we can neither give away nor appropriate.

Obviously the difficulty in thinking this type of community is to represent it. The only way to think this strange form of community is, following Blanchot, to qualify it as a community of sacrifice. Sacrifice is obviously not understood here in the conventional act of slaughtering an animal or person, or surrendering a possession as an offering. It is understood in the sense of an active involvement of death in the community. This is a difficult leap that must be made if one is to fully understand Blanchot's extraordinary take on community. This leap is made clear when one thinks through what happens in a sacrifice: someone succumbs to death. As such, and however it takes place, he or she is the victim not only of the person conducting the sacrifice, but above all of time. Their finitude is exposed here in the most violent and crudest way. It is the exposure of the absolute priority of time over everything, the fact that it always wins, however long we live. In this way, and more mundanely, sacrifice does not involve, as the cliché goes, a "putting death to work in order to reaffirm life" (better harvest, for example); it involves instead exposing time's cruel priority over all of us. Sacrifice reveals to the community the work of time on the banal altar of our daily lives.

In this way, the undecided injunction/question "Don't die!—Will you die?" basically involves time not as some indefinite and continued sets of durations regarded as a whole (past, present, and future) but as that which dispenses not only death but also, and above all, the continuous sting of death in life. Sacrifice reveals this provision; it enacts the moment when time bluntly manifests itself, when it brings an end to a mortal's life. Through sacrifice, through this clear and evidential provision of time, a community founds itself. As Blanchot writes: "Sacrifice . . . founds the community by . . . handing it over to time the dispenser, time that does not allow the community nor those who give themselves to it, any form of presence, thereby sending them back to a solitude which, far from protecting them, disperses them or dissipates itself without their finding themselves again or together."[9] Sacrifice reveals the absolute dependence on "time the dispenser," thus highlighting the impossibility of community—an impossibility that paradoxically founds community as such.

Contrary to what is usually argued,[10] this is not a sterile and useless understanding of community. On the contrary, by revealing how time plays its part, we create a community. The emphasis is not therefore on the horror of sacrifice, its fundamental absurdity, or the fact that it goes against all enlightened and reasoned projects, but on its ability to reveal how ultimately it brings us together. Everything indeed hinges on what death provides or gives: nothing. The only thing that happens when our time is up is that time retains the upper hand. Time thus marks the ungraspable secret that ties the community together. As Blanchot says, "This nothing to give offers and withdraws itself like the whim of the absolute which goes out of itself by giving rise to something other than itself, in the shape of an absence. An absence which, in a limited way, applies to the community whose only clearly ungraspable secret it would be."[11] This emphasis on time that dispenses does not show the failure of community. Rather, it shows that by exposing time, a community exposes itself to itself, and in doing so, it gathers itself like no other union possibly could.

Blanchot's journey shows that in order to make sense of the idea of community, it is necessary to abandon all commonplace or received ideas about community and go all the way to its most basic traits: an absolute irreplaceability, the giving over of lives to time the great dispenser, sacrifice as the revelation of how a community is formed. Now, inevitably, one can only be disappointed by such a journey. What indeed can be done in a situation in which time is the only dispenser? What is left for a community exclusively tied to time the great dispenser? Blanchot ends his article with what Georges Bataille understood as the only thing capable of counteracting sacrifice: ecstasy, the exultation of existence, the heightening of life against the great dispenser. Yet Blanchot is quick to remark that even ecstasy does not work: "One can write the word 'ecstasy' only by putting it carefully between quotation marks, because nobody can know what it is about, and above all, whether it ever took place: going beyond knowledge, implying unknowledge, it refuses to be stated other than through random words that cannot guarantee it. Its decisive aspect is that the one who experiences it is no longer there when he experiences it, is thus no longer there to experience it."[12] Exit Bataille.

So if there cannot even be a community of ecstatic individuals, what then can be done against time the dispenser? Blanchot, as is well known, ends up by pointing to friendship. He writes: "It is in life itself that the absence of someone else has to be met. It is with that absence . . . that friendship is brought into play and lost at each moment, a relation without relation or without relation other than the incommensurable."[13] But can one truly replace a community of ecstatic individuals with friendship? Is *friendship* not yet another word that also needs to be put between quotation marks because nobody can know if it actually really takes place? Is it not the same as ecstasy, with the one who experiences friendship no longer there when he or she experiences it? The problem with either Bataille's or Blanchot's "solution" is that time the dispenser is purely understood as a negative. Ecstasy and friendship are, for them, the reverse of time—hence Blanchot's remark that friendship is always lost at each moment. In a way, both Blanchot and Bataille remain far too Hegelian inasmuch as they both try to "look the negative in the face, tarrying with it."[14] Their "solutions" inevitably point to a blank (ecstasy, friendship), the symbol of an irreplaceability that cannot be exchanged, serves no purpose, and ultimately fails to create what they long for: a community.

So what is one to do? Perhaps it is a question of siding with time without altogether assuming being superior or the counterweight to time. In other words, it is perhaps a question of making time ours inasmuch as it is also that which holds us captive. How to be time while time casts the final blow? Considering the fact that in this book we understand our irreplaceability ("my death") as one god in the inalienable structure of mortals (cf. "Mortals," "Gods," and "Beckoning"), can this irreplaceability, this "godliness," not help us think through the very problem that Blanchot and Bataille leave us? If this irreplaceability that we ourselves are is effectively god understood not as supreme divinity but as what in mortals not only stings us (death) but also gives us future, then a community is not simply a meeting of lonely individuals who can only cry out, "Don't die!—Will you die?" It is a meeting of mortals/gods who, while witnessing each other die, liberally also free the possible for the Future (cf. "Beckoning," "Obsession," "Intuiting," and "Conclusion"). However much we are in the hands of time, we are also time—that is, we are an excess of time, an exuberance of time that renders possible the possible, frees the possibility of the possible. Time is ours. Time, we dispense.

This also means that Blanchot's community of the sacrifice is more than what he thinks; it is also a community of dispensers, unique givers of time that are able to counterbalance their sacrifice, the inalienable death of the other in the hands of time the great dispenser. Communities arise at the intersection of the two: sacrifice and dispensability. However, this can only truly take place if there is the recognition that it is a community of mortals who also happen to be gods. Recognizing this no doubt difficult fact shows that communities occur not just as impossibility, not just in the ordeal of sacrifice, but also as possibility, in the wealth of dispensability. The sharing of the community is not therefore solely based on what is radically impossible ("my death"/the death of the other) but also on something that, even if it always withdraws itself, still gives rise to something other: possibility itself. This is not a sublating mechanism at the heart of communities; it is most simply the recognition of how time takes place and the way we use it for ourselves, come together, love and hate in equal measure. Mortals/gods indeed both absent themselves (sacrifice) and provide (dispense); they always think more than they can, even at the cusp of death, even when there is nothing left to say.

So both trolls and moralists constitute a community after all, even if the former never cease to attack it with banal, trite, racist, and multiphobic comments and the latter equally try to repair it with counterarguments and sound retorts. Amid all this aggressiveness and retaliation, amid all this unfairness and right-mindedness, these mortals who also happen to be gods never cease to play themselves out amid earths and skies. The question is thus neither to hope to create a community of sacrificial and ecstatic individuals nor to form a delusory bond of friendship, the remnants of long-lost communistic ideals based on the endless tarrying of the negative. Rather, it is of embodying the communities that we are, allowing them not just to meet time the provider but also to dispense time, to succumb as the unexpected rises up in us as if from nowhere. Recognizing such a new conception of community strengthens the bond between mortals, these gods, because it opens up the possibility of a thought of community beyond a mere communion of interests, a thought of community free of the ordeal of mere opinions and impulsive emotions.

Of course, this does not guarantee the disappearance of trolls or their ilk. But this allows for a new type of communitarian activism. The trolls' words need to be debunked with what they could not rationally predict or anticipate. It is precisely with the gods' unexpected dispensation—that is, with the generosity of a thought that trolls cannot see coming—that this community can buttress itself against its own impossibility, against the fact that it can only come together through its members' absolute irreplaceability. This is what our dispensing is all about. It is not about an economic sharing of information (art, images, and captions, for example) but about stopping trolls in their tracks with what they cannot imagine. This does not mean startling them for the sake of provocation but of catching them unawares, freeing the possible for them with the sole aim of maintaining the strife at work. This is a much more difficult task than merely capturing someone unexpectedly; this implies letting mortals' godly sides shine through, revealing the creativity of a future together that the trolls cannot even begin to imagine.

## CONCLUSION

# Irony and Progeny

If mortals happen to be gods, if curators, these mortals/gods, can rely in the surge of earths into and against skies on angels, ghosts, and intangible obligations, and if their midwifing actions imply the involvement of the immemorial or what is unhoped for (i.e., what is not strife), then what overall course of action is thus opened? In other words, what kind of ethics does this lead to? The answer to this final question will necessarily intertwine the three issues at stake here, namely ethics, curating, and the polylogicality of the fourfold. The aim in answering this final question is not to bring everything to a close (cf. "Introduction") but to highlight the fact that understanding ourselves through the metonymy of the fourfold generates a different kind of ethics, one that can potentially alter the way moral agency is usually understood. But before proceeding with this answer, let me first recap the attempt of this book. So far, I have presented curating as ethics in the following way.

First, I started with a few key principles in order to lay some kind of foundation to the project, even if these are, as for any foundation, necessarily shaky. They are as follows. Everywhere is *matter* arising from *dark matter.* By arising, matter expresses and reexpresses itself and thus understands itself. This process cannot take place without a strange acausal *law* of absolute heterogeneity that unsettles all assurances of the same (a final expression, for example). With this law governing reexpression, matter sunders the *strife* of earths and skies, this event of not nothing. Amid this event, *mortals*—that is, *gods*—partake in the strife, the fourfold in act. On the one hand, as it were, mortals have nothing except how they rise from self-secluding earths into and against the skies. On the other hand, and unlike mortals, gods have everything. But this having everything is an excess that makes mortals always want more. Mortals *obsess* over gods because they always make them think more than they can. Inversely, gods need mortals, for otherwise they would not be able to *beckon* each other—that is, free the possible for the future, their own excess. There is no way we can think of mortals without thinking gods at the same time. In all this, *God*, capitalized and in the singular, is just a name, the reexpression of an omnipotence that points to a supposed elsewhere, and in doing so tirelessly disrupts the very idea of omnipotence itself. And none of the above would happen were it not for the *absolute*, this hyper-chaos, the truth of things.

Second, I circumscribed the event of matter known as "the curatorial" and the way its ethical aspects can be understood as arising from these simple foundations. This circumscription can be understood as follows. The event of matter known as "the curatorial" can be seen to start with the *earths*, these self-seclusions that present themselves to and against the skies. The *skies* are what allow the earths to measure themselves up and against what is immeasurable. Partaking in the strife earths/skies are mortals, these gods, who also self-seclude and measure themselves up against the heavens. Amid their many self-seclusions and measurements, mortals/gods expose strife overreaching itself as strife through *objects*. The curatorial properly deploys itself in this overreaching, this endless play of self-seclusion and measurements, the life of objects. Curators, these mortals/gods, also expose the strife through *words* and *images*. Ethically, these are structured by obligations: the obligation of "being just" for words and of the "it happens" for images. Curators deal with these types of visual and written ethics by fits and starts. Amid these fits and starts, and pointing toward what might be right and wrong, are *angels*, simple mortals who happen to be gods. But not all rests on angels and obligations. Moral principles also exist as *ghosts* haunting the strife by their constant withdrawal. There would be no morality without these ghosts. If obligations, angels, and ghosts are heeded, then *gnoses* are produced. When online, these gnoses appear not in the *contents* available or the merry-go-round of hyperlinks, but in the revelation of mortals' godly selves; a revelation that takes place through *names*, dangerous gifts punctuating language.

Third and last, in order to highlight how some curating gestures could be made ethical through all of the above, I explored a number of actions. The first of these curating actions is that of *saving*—that is, allowing someone or something to dwell in order to maintain the strife between earths, skies, mortals, and gods. *Caring* is also another action of curators. They care only inasmuch as they maintain the strife over and beyond any caring act toward artists, artworks, or audiences. Curators also *prepare*. In this context, they prepare exhibitions only if they attune themselves to their godly dimensions and those constituting the strife. Amid all these preparations, some curators aspire to be *irritating* partisans, but they can only be so if they embrace their telluric and godly dimensions. The same is true when curators attempt to *fraternize* with others; by embracing the strife, they create something unique and strange: a complicity for nothing. They might also *commune* with one another, mortals/gods together. They could also potentially *dignify*—that is, reveal the other of value in each and every one of their acts: life. They could equally become *midwives* birthing knowledge at the edge of reason. And they could also *intuit*—that is, allow themselves to arise with the strife. But no other action could possibly compete with that of *dispensing*, especially if it aims to create the impossibility of community itself amid the strife.

Even with such a telegraphic recap, the question still beckons: What overall ethics amid earths and skies does this lead to? Let's begin with a necessary, and no doubt problematic, remark. Considering that the subject of this ethics is no longer understood (cf. "Introduction") as a monologic interrelated or dynamic entity (*mitdasein*, interesse, becoming, etc.) but rather is fractured as mortals/gods amid earths and skies (the fourfold), are we then dealing here with a type of ethics that collapses in on itself because it stands for time itself? In other words, if human agency is necessarily fourfold and none of the dimensions can be taken as a single moral agent on its own, then is time the only real agent? What other ethics could this partial evasion of all traditionally stable ontic horizons (a sovereign subject, an accountable identity, or a responsible citizen, for example) lead to if not an impossible ethics as the time of the strife itself? One more time, just to insist on this point: can fourfolding the conventional interrelatedness of ethics—an interrelatedness that clearly always weighs the good and the bad as well as the adjudication of blame and exonerations—cancel out all forms of morality to leave us only with an exposure of time playing by four?

Time is indeed here of the essence. It is what governs every single thing exposed in this book, from matter arising out of dark matter all the way to the manner we midwife what seemingly falls out of time, and from the law of absolute heterogeneity that prevents sameness all the way to the unbearable sting that afflicts mortals/gods. By strifing, the fourfold is time. Similarly, time is the fourfold, neither properly mortal nor divine, neither entirely earthly nor celestial. This particular time is, of course, an ontico-ontological time; it is simply a speck of vague rationality in hyper-chaotic Time that, for some reason or other, continues to express and reexpress itself with a before, a now, and a tomorrow—dimensions that make sense for us, here and now, amid the strife. The ontic-ontological aspect of this time that structures us must not be forgotten. As soon as there is an event of matter, as soon as there is a sundering, and therefore as soon as there is strife, there is the indeterminacy of a temporal fourfolding that hyper-chaos Time can destroy for no apparent reason—or on the contrary for a very good reason—in the blink of an eye.

Let's explore this issue further in order to grasp what is truly at stake in this exposure of fourfold time and the canceling out of conventional monologic morality. The most curious aspect of this ontic-ontological time that we are—the time of the fourfold—is that it is curiously and annoyingly eminently ironic. This is not time's ultimate truth, only a curious aspect, a peculiar characteristic. Our time is indeed an ironist inasmuch as it always hinders and scorns all pretentions, from any attempt at expression (immediately thwarted by reexpression) all the way to our desperate efforts to persevere in "being" amid the polylogicality of the fourfold. But this is not an ironic backlash from elsewhere. It happens right at the heart of things: when the law of absolute heterogeneity (cf. "Law") structures all reexpression, whatever its nature, purpose, or advancement. As such, time ironizes every time, saying, for example: "However much you persevere in being, you will die," "However much you try to make sense of things, you will never fully get it," or "However much you try to be good, you will never properly succeed." Time indeed ironizes everything that bothers to reexpress itself—that is, everything in the strife earths/skies, mortals/gods.

But how is one to really make sense of our time's ironic thwarting of all fourfold efforts, including the setting up of an ethics as such? *Irony* is a much more difficult word than one imagines it to be,[1] and it must not be confused with other terms, such as *cynicism*.[2] Irony is at once a contrariness (the humor lies in the fact that the reality is the opposite of what one thinks or says) and a simulation, as its etymology indicates (from the Greek *eirōneia,* "simulated ignorance"). It is therefore a movement that goes against the current but pretends otherwise. For example, when our ontic-ontological time is ironic—and he[3] is ironic all the time—it pretends to be a flow: it runs with duration, glides with mortals' lives, sweeps their history, moves them inside enduring gravitational wells, drags them slowly around the long whirling of galaxies. But in fact our time does the exact opposite: it interrupts duration, puts an end to mortals' lives, ends histories, and derails all temporal courses, even those whose end can be predicted in advance. Time as an indefinite continued flow is time's wryly amusing—if not tragic—trick on us all.

This is not something that takes place at some abstract, general, or scientific level of understanding alone. On the contrary, this is something that is above all uniquely ours: if we are time, then we are irony; we create it as much as time ironically imposes itself on us.[4] We would not be affected by chance, the law of thermodynamics, or causality if we could not ironically affect the same: casting reversals of fortunes in one throw of the dice, defying the odds by living longer than expected in life-threatening situations, or creating new causal chains of events, for example. If I can put it thus, our lives take place with time falling upon us as we fall with it—and this without even trying to be ironic.[5] There can be no special occasion, not even a solemn and serious moment, without it, not because irony strikes at all times but paradoxically because irony is what allows us to go through these occasions, what makes us survive them. We ironize even when—and especially when—we cry with laughter or sadness. We ironize even by sleeping. There would be no strife without this irony of time, which is also paradoxically the irony of the strife itself, of our event, matter (reexpressing itself in fourfold fashion, so to speak), because of the law of absolute heterogeneity.

So when it comes to mortals, the issue appears to be a simple one: if time's irony thwarts all of our attempts (ethical, but also political, cultural, social, etc.) and all of our attempts are ultimately ironic, then it is no longer a question of fighting against it in the vague hope that it will cease to ironize our fate. Rather, it is a question of making a chorus with it—that is, of making a kind of vocal ensemble with this supreme irony that governs our lives. In other words, because nothing can be done against our own fourfold irony, it is then necessary to let the fourfold play along with it. This chorus with irony is not a rare, unusual, or incongruous action. On the contrary, it is something that mortals in fact do often without realizing it. When referring to genocide, for example, the eminently ethical but hackneyed phrase "never again" is enough evidence of this effort to create a chorus with time's irony. We inadvertently ironize as time ironizes, however much we lament, mean well, and pray that indeed a genocide will not happen again, with renewed enthusiasm: "yes, once more!" Tuning into the irony of time is our way of addressing the ironic blight that afflicts us every second of time, including all of our vain efforts to counteract it.

But can this tuning into the irony of time really hold any true ethical transformative power? Is there no way of better influencing our dimensions—mortals/gods, earths/skies—as they are caught up in irony? Can the ethics of the fourfold not do more than ironically play itself out with time? If we restrict ourselves to the topic of this book, namely curating as ethics, then the questions become these: Can curators who wish to be more ethical not do more than unwittingly ironize with time? Can curators effect with their projects a more reliable impact on their moral predicaments than their seemingly nonironic cries to end the supreme work of irony? The recurring use of the question format is intended here not to widen the scope until it becomes meaningless but to highlight, over and beyond the predicaments themselves, what is truly at stake when it comes to an ethics—not its telos (a beautiful existence, salvation, or a just and fairer world, for example) but its very taking place, the way mortals, these gods, play with their own time, curb its nonnegotiable irony.

The ethical problem is this: if we accept the fact that we are time and irony and that siding with time's irony is, for all intents and purposes, our only option, then it is clear that there can be no more values we can cling to. In perfect unison with time's irony, one can indeed no longer say that such and such behavior is good or bad, just or unjust, because in such a situation, the verb *is* no longer cuts a divide between values. Everything becomes ironic, even the taking place of the good as such. Against time's irony, one indeed needs the weighty force brought on by the supposedly nonironic ontological ax of the third person singular present of the verb *to be* ("is") to determine any conventional interrelated ethics: she "is" good, this "is" bad, for example. The problem becomes even more acute in a fourfold situation, for which this ontological ax no longer operates with such steadfast zeal. Who can indeed be judge if ironic gods abound? Who is ethical if mortals can always think more than they can, thus ironizing all efforts? Who amid the four can claim to be nonironic if all four, including earths and skies, equally ironize at different speeds and scales? The force of irony, which is at the heart of the godliness of mortals and of the fourfold overall, indeed thwarts all conventional moral efforts and determinations, and this even after the ontological ax has been if not buried then rendered less operative.

Time's irony and our tuning into its game leaves us stuck without transformative power, without any ability to pull the good over the bad and work the strife so that it transforms itself toward what can be seen or perceived (for good or bad) as better. Worse still, even if we persist in chiming with time's irony, we can only be left stranded in a catatonic state, a mock repose, a pretend calmness—the irony of all ironies. Is catatonia not indeed the last stage of an ironist's life, of the one who only sees supreme irony everywhere and in everything? To form a chorus with time's irony is ultimately to catatonize ourselves, like Bataille and Blanchot (cf. "Dispensing") when they reduce our fourfold dimensions to a monologic self and then conflate it with an equally reductive monologic march of time, all in the vain hope that something positive or different will come out of it. And if this were not enough, it is also to cling onto a principle of reason (our ever-enduring irony riveted at the heart of monologic time) so as to reassure ourselves that there is indeed nothing left but the blasé realization of ironic time, performing it as it performs us. Ultimately nothing can be more self-defeating and self-foreclosing than reducing our fourfoldedness to a moral monologic self singing along to a monologic apperception of time's irony.

Can our constellation, these fractured dimensions explored here, not then point in another direction? Can mortals, these gods, with their unpredictability, not curb time's nonnegotiable irony, the strife's ever enduring irony? In other words, can catatonia—or, to push the point further, ataraxia—be sidelined when making a chorus with time's irony, thus giving the polylogicality in question here—mortals/gods, earths/skies—if not a transformative power as such then at least a slightly weightier ethical direction? This is perhaps where we face the extraordinary potential of the fourfold after so many previous mono-ontico-onto-logical ethical projects that rest either on the strict economies of sovereign interrelationality (utilitarian ethics based on an equality of rights, for example) or the uneconomic schemes of philosophies of difference (the radically Other holding the same at gunpoint, for example). Of course, Heidegger is here again useless inasmuch as this topic radically exceeds everything that he envisages when attempting to extricate himself from the confines of his *mitdasein*. So how can the fourfold give a weightier ethical direction to our singing along to time's ironic tune?

The answer is perhaps as simple as saying that in addition to being ironic, time also provides (cf. "Dispensing"). The expression "time provides" should not, again, be understood as if an external element mysteriously but generously gives us "more time." To say that "time provides" is to emphasize the contrary movement to irony. While time mocks our efforts to be, playfully repeats tragic histories, chuckles at our choral efforts, it also provides for more—the law of absolute heterogeneity never ceasing to also encourage reexpression. The crucial issue here is that this provision does not mean that we are also suddenly stronger than time and its tireless ironic posturing. We will always be beaten by time. But beyond such irremediable defeat, beyond the recurrently nagging irony that sours our lives, we—that is, time—through the same law of absolute heterogeneity, also provide. We, as time, provide, not just through economic negotiations, but also, and most importantly, through progeny. As we have seen before (cf. "Angels"), this progeny must always be understood at two different levels. On the one hand, yes, we indeed provide more time by having children, thus extending us beyond our mortality. On the other hand, and this is what matters above all here, we also provide more time by midwifing a beyond in which we no longer matter. We are indeed able to midwife a time that cannot be envisaged as providing us with a return. How is one to make sense of this overall secondary counteracting gesture, and how can it help us think our fourfold ethical transformative power?

Progeny, from the Latin *pro-*, "forward," and *gignere*, "to beget," is indeed a relation to a future that cannot be anticipated. It brings about a time that I cannot envisage. It fosters a future without another "me," a time that has no interest in "me." Levinas, of course, addresses this in the most remarkable way when he writes: "In [progeny],[6] the 'I' transcends the world of light . . . in order to go further than light, to go *elsewhere*."[7] By referencing light, Levinas's target is obviously the autism of Western philosophy whereby everything, including the subject, bathes under a Platonic sun without shade. Progeny casts a shadow; it intervenes with a time that cannot be made sense of, that frustratingly no light can shine on. Progeny jeopardizes the mathematical time of the physicist, disturbs the monologic time of the philosopher by pointing to an elsewhere that nothing can ever clarify or reduce, let alone conceptualize. This elsewhere is obviously not a destination that can be determined in advance. Progeny is most simply "the renewal of the possible in the inevitable senescence of the subject"[8]—that is, what provokes the possible in the taking place of the always dying subject, and this with good reason or without any reason whatsoever. Progeny rebuts time's irony, casting it in the fourfold's shadow.

Mortals/gods, earths/skies indeed midwife another time unrelated to that stamped and afflicted by irony. Among our dimensions, as we have seen, the gods are obviously the ones most clearly providing for progeny beyond death (cf. "Beckoning"). They provide us with not an anticipatable or predictable future but with what frees the possible for the future (cf. "Introduction"). Futural, the gods beckon, thus elbowing time's irony. Once again, this should not be understood as if the gods were pregnant with some extra future that they shell out to anyone willing to hear them.[9] The elbowing of time's irony is just an annoying but fortunate discontinuity in time's ironic path that is also, reassuringly, a forgiveness. Again, Levinas: "This triumph of the time of [progeny] over the becoming of the mortal and aging being, is a pardon, the very work of time."[10] We might be the victim of time's irony, but it also forgives through our divine progeny. This forgiveness has nothing to do with fault. Time does not end up giving us more time or children in order to compensate for taking our lives. A forgiveness is an inversion of time's irony and as such is equally constitutive of time itself—hence Levinas's statement that it is the "very work of time." With divine progeny, time delivers us from both our self-autonomy and our cherished ax ("is") always hung high—by a single hair—over our heads. Through the gods—that is, through mortals' outpouring—a glimmer of nonironic time thus becomes discernible.

The double play of irony and progeny is thus the game of our time, ironizing our efforts to be, begetting more efforts. This is not an unsublatable or undeconstructible paradox that leaves us stranded between two contradictory currents. It is on the contrary, and most importantly, the sign that ensures, behind the blatant ironic failure of the goodness of today, that there can still be the good after all. In the rebuttal against time's irony, our divine progeny indeed disposes of a time in which the good can still take place. The good here is obviously not something that is economically desirable, something that will provide a return—

for example, "By recycling, I do my bit for the future of my children" or "Through procreation, I ensure a cared-for retirement." The good here is not—and here I go against Levinas—sheltered in some always singular height ("the Most High") mysteriously guaranteeing its future arrival. Rather, the good here is, as we have seen (cf. "Dignifying"), the other of all values: "life"[11]—that is, the overreaching of strife, the surge of earths into and against skies amid mortals, these gods. The life that comes with divine progeny is indeed the only value with any true moral weight because it is the only thing that always becomes other to itself. It stands for the fact that the strife can still overreach itself as strife, the earths can still surge into and against the skies amid mortals and gods, and this with renewed vigor or extreme languor, ironic calm, or prodigal excitement. The begotten fourfold life is indeed the only ironic value that divine progeny can sign off as good precisely because it surprises itself every second of time alongside and against time's persistent disenchantment.

The only drawback—ironic, of course—is that this sign can never be captured, appropriated, traded, or used so as to foster a moral code, principle, or inalienable maxim, like "The begetting fourfold 'life' gives us bountiful goodness." Rather, the life begotten by the gods of the fourfold, this efficacious goodness, is precisely what frees us from any form of economy, and in so doing gives justice its always veiled working principle. Is it not this strange unuttered good that features in no moral code precisely what drives people to always save children first and impels judges with their judgments—for the sake of the good in the life lost by murder, for example? Untradeable and useless, the efficacious goodness provided by the begotten fourfold life can never therefore promise a just or fairer world. It cannot even resolve here and now the infinite number of urgent moral issues facing normative ethics today. The slipperiness of this good—that is, of the begotten life—simply never allows it. The only usefulness it can be seen to have is perhaps to justify all midwifery godly efforts (cf. "Deeds and Ends") turned toward the immemorial or unhoped for (what is not strife), and this even if no babies are hoped for. The begotten fourfold life has indeed no other ethical use than its taking place.

Untradeable, this good, this begotten life, prodigally given by mortals, these gods, exposes a potentially new kind of ethics. To be ethical in this new context is indeed, most simply, to unfold the four, to rise as and with self-secluding earths into and against immeasurable skies, and to beckon and respond in ways as yet unimaginable, all in order to maintain the folds in play. This is not something that can be done single-handedly. On the contrary, this is the concerted effort of earths and skies, mortals and gods—to create a future that defies death and irony, exactly in the same way as when a child is begotten. In this new context, ethics can therefore no longer take place in the obedience to a value extrinsic to the fourfold (universal human rights, absolute justice, a priori moral laws, imaginary peace, perfect equality, God, for example) but in the unfolding of new fourfold life, the only prodigality strong enough to withstand—without altogether eradicating it—the ironic folding up of all efforts at the same time.[12] With this begotten life prodigally given by mortals, these gods, the folds remain in play, earths and skies teasingly interacting with each other, and this even if there is barely any life left. Defying the supreme irony of time through divine prodigality is mortals' only ethical aperture in this somber world in which goodness is so seldom heard.

In this new multidimensional ethics, the important thing is that the moral subject can no longer be identified with any precision. This new ethics indeed takes place as earths, skies, mortals, and gods break into four, a strife in which not one dimension can be blamed or exonerated, rendered pious or evil. To go back to an earlier reference, can we say, for example, that the earths should be considered on an equal footing with the perpetrators of a genocide? In conventional interrelational ethics, the idea would be as absurd as the suggestion that nature should also take on the responsibility for mass killing. When considered as part of the fourfold, however, this idea suddenly no longer looks absurd, for there would have been no genocide without the surge of earths into and against immeasurable skies and without mortals, these gods, imposing an irrational murderous logic *or* inventing rational and logical stratagems to save lives. Fourfolding ethical predicaments indeed reveal a much more complex set of conditions than the reductive ones tirelessly used to pitch individual logics (and lives) against one another. The begotten life that comes with a new fourfold invariably dispenses four new folds for which neither "never again" nor "yes, once more!" means much—not because the ringing of the four matters above the cries of victims or perpetrators but because their murderous or peaceable logics survive with less zeal or resolve. The begotten good prodigally birthed by a new fourfold always rises beyond not only all warring logos but also all reductive apperceptions of moral or immoral subjects. Is history not enough proof of this when past logics always appear baffling to more contemporary eyes?

With this new ethics, the objective is therefore neither to focus yet again on new and inevitably flawed moral logics against evil ones, nor to let ourselves be seduced by haunting but always unsound rational prescriptions. The objective is to allow the fourfold to resonate beyond the fall of both logical peaceful axes and warring machetes. If such resonance is allowed to be heard, then the work to be accomplished becomes clearer: let's indeed hear and tune ourselves to our currently exploited earths, rekindling with our own self-seclusion. Let's hear and tune ourselves to our choking skies, relighting ourselves with our own immeasurability. Let's hear and tune ourselves to the anxious and depressed cries of our present-day godless mortals, finally handing them over their godliness. In hearing and tuning ourselves to them together, in fourfoldedness, the good, this new fourfold, can only remain the winner, the godly trump card against the ravaging paths of irony and of its many avatars, including, in a supreme irony, all forms of moral rectitude and ethical upstanding. No logic, not even the most malevolent or sagacious, and no piety, not even the holiest or most dutiful, can upstage or eclipse a newborn fourfold—unless, of course, nothing is indeed worth rescuing and the strife of earths, skies, mortals and gods is ready for hyper-chaos Time.

What has all this got to do with curating? All and everything. If curating has the pretension of articulating the cultural world, then it cannot do without paying attention to what, on the horizon of its many incarnations, evades its grasp. Afflicted by time's irony, curating, like any other human activity, can only see its many earthly sparks flare up into and against the skies, only to disappear in the pit of forgetfulness. Time will always vanquish curating, subjugating its ego-driven enterprises to the darkness of the immemorial. Yet at the same time curating can also reach, besides its inevitable demise, toward a beyond in which it no longer matters—that is, a future without return, an unhoped-for future. This does not mean that curators should make babies. It simply means that curators can acknowledge their progenial selves—that is, their godly selves, and therefore their fourfolding ability to chide time's irony. This is curating's transformative power, its ethical potential: the acknowledgment of the work of time—not just time's ironic slaps and whacks, but also, and above all, the givenness of fourfold life. With such acknowledgment, curating can then choose what value matters most: whether any one of the endlessly debated values inherited by custom and history—curatorial codes of ethics, for example (cf. "Ghosts")—and/or the one provided by life, this value that not only holds curators together amid the strife but also disposes of a progenial time in which the good can still take place. At last, something not for funding.

To realize this transformative power is nothing other than to reveal all those involved in curating as divine fourfold finite players. Because of its unruliness, because of its lack of discipline, and above all because of its gathering potential (it saves, cares, etc.; cf. "Deeds and Ends"), curating is best placed to embody this mortal divinization amid earths and skies. Curating can be more than just encouraging or exacerbating relationality, and it can be more than just giving audiences yet another infotaining experience. It can divinize mortals and thus reveal our intrinsic fourfoldedness. Again, this does not mean making mortals more than they are but encouraging them to think more than they themselves can. There is no minimal knowledge to be had. Any curator can midwife this good—that is, a new fourfold—with and alongside time's irony. In this way, and to personalize the idea, "I curate" not to show, relate, or convince (aesthetically, socially, politically, culturally, etc.) but to divinize together with the fourfold, thus fostering a time without me, a new life over and beyond today's real and pressing needs. This does not constitute a new praxis for a future time to come but an everyday midwifing gesture that can potentially be undertaken by the millions of people around the world who curate their own lives and/or the many images, objects, products, and ideas they trade or share.

But this new transformative power is not just about divinizing fourfold players in the act of curating. This mortal divinization obviously also takes place *with* earths and skies, in fourfoldedness. Beyond progenially midwifing a new life as gods, curators also can embody and expose the earths that bring them up against and into luminous skies. Across the world, curating exposes the innumerable cultural products of human life that, if looked at globally, always appear thrown together in some kind of repetitive profusion. In such excessive abundance, artworks, images, sounds, and/or texts are always pitched against each other—"this life/work is better aesthetically or politically than this one," for example. If against such easy pitching of subjects and/or objects curators can, as they go about their business, let the fourfoldedness that brings them together and apart shine through for the first time, then they can indeed show more than they can. They can reveal that such an overwhelming worldly exposition of surreal magnitude also includes the earthly skies that led to their exposure, this rich seam of life that animates them with every touch, visit, glance, pass, click, or hover. The curatorial can be ethically reborn there, in this dispensing of earthly and celestial reexpressions that, at last, ignores autonomous authorial gestures, sidelines imperious logics, and embraces its very own fourfoldedness—the very event of our time.

# ACKNOWLEDGMENTS

I thank Grant Farred for his unfaltering support, radiant knowledge, generosity, and above all his care and patience. I also thank Jorella Andrews for fascinating conversations about Him and that holy trinity, Sasha Burkhanova-Khabadze for sharing knowledge, Bridget Crone for defying me to always return to practice, Karen Hellekson for being such a careful reader, Adnan Madani for such a straight stalwart friendship, Dimitri Mouton for putting up with me with such grace and dignity, Dinu-Gabriel Munteanu for making me think outside the box, Alice Ongaro for crossing old bridges, John Paul Ricco for all your encouragements and for making me feel that I am not alone in the world, Mirjami Schuppert for thought-provoking conversations about curating, Jon Shaw for never giving up on me, Malin Stahl for your generosity, and Simon Streather for coming up with the right words. I also thank all my MA students for their generous and constructive criticism as well as my colleagues in the Department of Visual Cultures, Goldsmiths College, University of London, for their support and feedback.

# NOTES

## Introduction

1. For a detailed account of this reflection, especially with regards to the academic settings of curating, see Martinon, "Edging Disciplines," and Martinon, ed., *Curatorial.*

2. On this topic, see, e.g., Balzer, *Curationism.*

3. I am grateful to my then student Takeshi Shiomitsu for this astute use of language. See Shiomitsu, "Curation as a Practice."

4. Michael Bhaskar defines curating in even more general terms as the "acts of selecting, refining, and arranging to add value [in order to] help us overcome [information] overload." Bhaskar, *Curation*, 7–8. Bhaskar adds a note at the end of his dazzling but problematic book saying that the term *value* should be taken in its broadest sense—that is, as both an "addition of capital" and an "addition of knowledge." Bhaskar, *Curation*, 314–15. This uncertainty with regard to the value added by curating unfortunately does not help. It only confuses the issue, leaving us stranded in a capitalist dead end of "more" without any discernment between profit and epistemic enhancement—hence my choice of limiting the scope of curating to that of culture and my attempt to rethink this added value not as a loose capitalist interchangeable term but precisely as the other of all value: life. As the arguments in this book attempt to show, it is by focusing on this other value that curating can have a chance to rescue itself from Bhaskar's problematic conflation.

5. On the topic of the expansion of curating outside of the reified art world, see, e.g., Krysa, *Curating Immateriality*; Fisher, "Curators and Instagram"; Landow, *Hypertext 3.0.*

6. I understand culture in a relatively narrow sense, namely as the set of values, beliefs, conventions, and/or social practices associated with a particular activity—here, curating. With this definition, my aim is to avoid defining culture from the premise of a predetermined idea of what constitutes a "group of people" (e.g., Western culture, European culture, British culture, black culture, LGBTQ+ culture).

7. To the point where the denomination *curator* is now applied to the most

unethical practice imaginable: driving suicidal teenagers to take their own lives. I am referring here to the little-known—and perhaps unfounded—Blue Whale Challenge, which is a social network phenomenon that started in Russia in 2016, in which a curator assigns a series of tasks to suicidal teenagers that progressively introduce elements of self-harm until they commit suicide. There is no space here to explore this type of curatorial cyberbullying, not only because it exceeds the remit of the notion of culture that, for good or bad, frames this book, but also because it calls for a type of applied ethics to immediately counteract this urgent moral problem, such as that put forward, for example, by the Brazilian project Baleia Rosa (Pink Whale), which instead assigns positive tasks that value life and combat depression.

8. See, e.g., Mayer et al., eds., *Code of Ethics*; Cgercgu Usai, "Charter of Curatorial Values"; Philbrick, "Exhibition Ethics"; Trevelyan, ed., *Code of Ethics for Museums*.

9. See, e.g., Popova, *Curator's Code*.

10. See, e.g., Huberman, "Take Care"; Eleey, "What About Responsibility?"

11. On this topic, see, e.g., Montmann, ed., *Scandalous*; King and Levin, *Ethics and the Visual Arts*; Beshty, *Ethics*.

12. Martinon, *After "Rwanda."*

13. See Nancy, *L'Impératif catégorique*, 114–37.

14. Heidegger's account of the fourfold is scattered through a number of texts that span nearly twenty-five years, from a first mention in his 1949 essay "Insight into That Which Is" all the way to his 1973 seminar in Zärhingen. See Heidegger, *Bremen and Freiburg Lectures* and *Four Seminars*. The best-known account of the fourfold can be found in the essays "Building, Dwelling, Thinking" and "The Thing," in Heidegger, *Poetry, Language, Thought*, 141–60, 161–84. Mention of the fourfold is also made across a number of other publications, including *Contributions to Philosophy* and *Mindfulness*, as well as his readings of Hölderlin (*Elucidations of Hölderlin's Poetry* and *Hölderlin's Hymns*).

15. The use throughout this book of "cf." (short for the Latin term *confer*, "compare") is not intended as a lazy request to the readers to join the dots. Living with a chronic health problem that affects my memory, these were originally intended to help me ensure coherence of the argument throughout the book. I left them behind in the hope that perhaps readers might also find them useful when comparing the topic being discussed in one part of the book with another formulated elsewhere.

16. Just to clarify, the fourfold makes no reference to any four orders turning (clockwise or counterclockwise) continuously in either ancient Asian traditions (Jainism, Hinduism, Buddhism, for example) or in more recent Western genocidal political ideologies. For an inaccurate interpretation of the fourfold in this sense, see Faye, *Heidegger, l'introduction du nazisme dans la philosophie*,

and for an excellent rebuke, see Mattéi, "Emmanuel Faye, l'introduction du fantasme dans la philosophie."

17. Or more precisely, equated ontology and ethics. For this argument, see Raffoul, *Origins of Responsibility*, 220–46.

18. See, e.g., Hodge, *Heidegger and Ethics*; Nancy, "Heidegger's 'Originary Ethics,'" 65–85; Hatab, *Ethics and Finitude*; Lewis, *Heidegger and Place of Ethics*; McNeill, *Time of Life*; Webb, *Heidegger, Ethics.*

19. There is unfortunately no space here to unpack this topic. Suffice to say that monological apperceptions of the subject of ethics dominates the field, whether from a normative or extemporary perspective. Badiou's someone caught in the process of ethical truths or Caputo's responsible body without ethics are two contemporary examples that show how ethics still remains riveted to monological apperceptions that never truly take into consideration the importance of what radically evades or surprises it. See Badiou, *Ethics*; Caputo, *Against Ethics.*

20. Mattéi, *Heidegger et Hölderlin*; Darwiche, *Heidegger*; Mitchell, *Fourfold.* See also Crownfield, "Last God"; Edwards, "The Thinging of the Thing"; Wrathall, "Between the Earth and the Sky."

21. See Schürmann, *Heidegger on Being and Acting* and *Broken Hegemonies.*

22. See Martinon, "Time Unshackled" and "Between Earth and Sky."

23. The pronoun *me* does not refer to an ego as such but rather to a mortal co-original with earth, sky, and gods.

24. The event of being *(Ereignis)* must not be confused with "mortals" or Dasein, both of which refer, at different registers, to one dimension of this very event. The event of being includes mortals, gods, earth, and sky, each participating in this event as expropriating movements. Thinking four expropriating movements at once avoid monological and monotheistic (and therefore historical) interpretations of being. See Heidegger, *Contributions to Philosophy.*

25. I explore this Heideggerian expression in the chapter "Saving."

26. Obviously the four do not end up creating a suprarepresentational structure because each is understood as an expropriating movement. See Heidegger, *Poetry, Language, Thought*, 178.

27. I deliberately leave this other unexplained. The reading of Heidegger's gods that follows should assuage all those who fear that the other has yet again been violently reappropriated in the event of being.

28. The number four has no mystical, magical, religious, or apocalyptic meaning. As many commentators have shown, it is the outcome of the history of being and that of the world as analyzed by Heidegger through and beyond his readings of Hölderlin. For a mystical reading of Heidegger (one that is not followed here), see Caputo, *Mystical Element.* For a further commentary, see Mattéi, *Heidegger et Hölderlin.*

29. As Reiner Schürmann superbly says, with the fourfold, "The 'mortals' find themselves, as it were, marginalized." Schürmann, *Broken Hegemonies*, 211.

30. I leave aside in this introduction the fact that the event of time-space of the fourfold can be created or destroyed at will and for no reason by hyperchaos time. See the chapters "Strife" and "The Absolute."

31. Edwards, "The Thinging of the Thing," 458.

32. Heidegger, *Poetry, Language, Thought*, 147–48.

33. I realize that in saying this, I depart from conventional readings of Heidegger's fourfold, for which the gods are separate entities that somehow arise after the death of God and the advent of modern technology from sacred places; these remnants of religious sites that rekindle us with our true selves. Mortals only truly experience the gods in holy precincts, thus reviving in us a sense for the divine in the world. There are at least two serious problems with this conventional reading. The first is that there is never any explanation for how the gods are supposed to materialize themselves in these places and send messages. For me, this interpretation is still imbued with the idea that although God is dead, He is still somehow somewhere incarnated in these holy places, thus reintroducing through the back door a monotheistic approach to the divine. The second one is that there is an incredible confusion with these analyses between the earth and the gods. Heidegger's sacred places can only be understood as part of earth, yet there is no explanation as to why the earth carries with it, in its many holy sanctums, the messages from the gods. For these reasons, I can only leave aside these conventional readings of Heidegger's gods, preferring to follow Schürmann and to take Heidegger's reading of Nietzsche's death of God seriously—namely as no longer lurking in churches, temples, and mosques. For one brilliant reading of Heidegger's gods through the holiness of sacred places, see Wrathall, "Between the Earth and the Sky."

34. I realize that this might be perceived as a contradiction inasmuch as any mention of the word *gods* necessarily implies a theology. However, the focus here is on the event of being, its worldly taking place and not on any relation provoked or put at rest by the nominal event called God (cf. "God"). With such an exclusively mundane focus, one that does not even amount, because of earths and skies, to an ontotheology, I thereby extricate myself—with difficulty, no doubt—from the discussions on the possibility or impossibility of a new theology, especially within the phenomenological canon, including those emanating from the work of Heidegger himself. I am thinking here specifically of the debates between either Derrida and Marion, or Caputo and Kearney. See Caputo and Scanlon, *God, the Gift, and Postmodernism*; Kearney and Zimmermann, *Reimagining the Sacred*; Bradley, "God *sans* Being."

35. Nancy, *Dis-enclosure*, 11.

36. Using a different vocabulary, one could also say that mortals are essen-

tially meaningful. It is in their nature to bear meaning. In other words, meaning is finitude or finitude is meaning. As such, mortals are meaningful because they are tied to a beyond themselves that they do not own but that they spend their time trying to reach. In bearing meaning, in reaching out toward this unreachable beyond, they are witness to the constant withdrawal of this beyond. This is not a frustrating gesture that never succeeds. On the contrary, it is the realization that the beyond takes place right at the moment meaning occurs. The beyond occurs in the proffering of meaning. What is beyond is effectively only what appears to us as beyond. It is a call or an invitation (cf. "Beckoning" and "Obsession") from "what always withdraws" to participate in this beyond. There would be no meaning if there were no beyond inviting us to consider itself. There would only be death or absolute darkness. This constant play with what appears beyond is what makes mortals gods. Their godly nature is precisely the ordeal of meaningfulness.

37. I only reference here these two absolute values. Others could be found. After all, is the history of Western culture since Nietzsche's proclamation of the death of God not filled with endless attempts to replace Him with a new suprasensory value? Commenting on Nietzsche's madman speech in *Gay Science*, Heidegger famously gives a list of all these values: conscience, reason, progress, happiness of the greatest number, civilization, enterprise. I only focus on two here because of their unique tautological characteristics. See Nietzsche, *Gay Science*, 119–20; Heidegger, *Question Concerning Technology*, 53–114.

38. I develop this theme in Martinon, "Im-mundus."

39. Marx obviously made this point long before me: "A particular kind of commodity acquires the character of general equivalent, because all other commodities make it the material in which they uniformly express their value." Marx, *Capital*, 79.

40. On the way natural disasters are recuperated by the principle of general equivalence, see Nancy, *After Fukushima*.

41. As Deleuze famously remarked. See Deleuze, *Negotiations*, 6.

42. Lacoue-Labarthe and Nancy, *Literary Absolute*, 42.

43. Lacoue-Labarthe and Nancy, *Literary Absolute*, 51 (translation modified).

44. I refer here to an ontico-ontological structure because the constellation at stake here—the fourfold—always hovers hesitantly but deliberately between ontology and the ontic sciences. Cf. "Mortals" and, as a contrast, "The Absolute."

## Dark Matter

1. As Lyotard says about matter, "Matter is the failure of thought, its inert mass, stupidity." Lyotard, *Inhuman*, 38.

2. Lyotard, *Inhuman*, 140.

3. Lyotard, "Les Immatériaux," 162.

4. See Levinas, *Existence and Existents*, 58–59.

## Matter

1. Plato, *Republic*, 507b–509c.

2. On the "there is," see, among others, Levinas, *On Escape*.

3. In this context, I can only recall here what Heidegger says about being: "The human being is, in one word, *to deinotaton*, the uncanniest. . . . The Greek word *deinon* and our translation call for an advance *explication* here. . . . *deinon* means the violent in the sense of one who needs to use violence—and does not just have violence at his disposal but is violence-doing, insofar as using violence is the basic trait not just of his doing but of his *Dasein*." Heidegger, *Introduction to Metaphysics*, 159–60.

4. Spinoza, *Ethics*, part 1, proposition 15, scholium. Although the quotation given here clearly references Spinoza's modes, the wording used in this chapter with regards to matter references no modes as such. The belief is that expression and reexpression can suffer no reductive modalities, not even, for example, in Spinoza's taxonomy, that of "motion and rest" (*Ethics*, part 1, proposition 32, corollary 2) and/or "will and intellect" (*Ethics*, part 1, proposition 30). As will become clear, matter can be multivocal without necessarily being modal.

5. Spinoza, *Ethics*, part 1, proposition 15, scholium. I obviously omit here Spinoza's crucial characterization of matter as both "corporeal substance" and "eternal." He indeed adds in the same scholium: "Furthermore, water qua water, comes into existence and goes out of existence; but qua substance it does not come into existence nor go out of existence *[corrumpitur]*." Unlike for Spinoza, eternity only occurs here in the madness of hyper-chaos (cf. "The Absolute") and in the play of the event of strife (cf. "Intuiting") without at the same time constituting an eternal substance.

6. For the opposite argument—existence depending on insistence—see Caputo, *Insistence of God*.

7. I use here Levinas's famous characterization of *Autrui* as distinguished from *l'autre*. See Levinas, *Entre Nous*, 94.

8. On this split word, see Derrida, *Writing and Difference*, 97–192.

9. Deleuze, *Expressionism in Philosophy*, 100. Being radically heterogeneous, the sufficient reason for reexpression never manages to settle into a recognizable and reasoned principle; cf. "Law."

10. On this expression, see "Strife."

11. Spinoza, *Ethics*, part 3, proposition 2, scholium.

## Law

1. I deliberately—and perhaps to some too casually—draw no difference between expression/reexpression and composition/decomposition. The reason is

simple. Spinoza, and Deleuze after him, are obviously counteracting arguments that no matter what, death interrupts the seamlessness of immanence. Whether death, decomposition, or reexpression is of the essence matters little. What matters in Deleuze's reading of Spinoza is that there is a truth to the relation involved, whether it be expression and reexpression, composition and decomposition, living and dying. This necessarily unfathomable truth is that immanence is structured by a law that makes it what it is: insistent in expressing reexpression and resistant to any form of destruction or decomposition, including, as we will see, death.

2. Deleuze, *Expressionism in Philosophy*, 236 (my emphasis).

3. This is Spinoza's expression, which reads in its entirety as *facies totius universi*, referring to what he calls a mediate infinite mode and stands for "the figure of the entire universe." There is no space here to analyze the difference he draws between this and other modes or attributes. The important thing for us here is the fact that it stands for an intelligible, unbreakable immanence that knows no rest. See Spinoza, *Ethics*, part 2, proposition 13, axiom and lemma, as well as letter 64. For a commentary, see Bouchilloux, "Les Modes infinis de la pensée"; Badiou, *Being and Event*, 118–19.

4. My insistence in seeing a law at the heart of matter's expression and re-expression is a way to evade a common problem in posthumanist materialist accounts on this issue. Karen Barad, for example, defines matter as an intra-active agential process of materialization that is "radically open to the future." However, Barad never explains how this openness to the future remains either "inherent in the nature of intra-activity" or "as an enfolded participant in matter's iterative becoming" (Barad, *Meeting the Universe Halfway*, 234, 235). Any interpretation of matter that uses expressions such as "inherent" and "enfolded" necessarily implies a principle of sufficient reason at the heart of matter that invalidates the claim of radical openness to the future. Without a hyper-chaos potentially destroying for no reason such principle, Barad's interpretation of matter remains not only an unwarranted universalization, it also stays fastened to a human-centric vision (because rational) of how matter takes place across the universe.

5. In his poem, "A Dice Throw, at Any Time, Will Abolish Chance," in Mallarmé, *Collected Poems*, 67–89. For the most materialist reading of Mallarmé's *hasard*, see Meillassoux, *A Number and the Siren*.

6. Spinoza, *Ethics*, part 2, proposition 29, scholium. There is no space here to analyze how expression/reexpression constitute, in Spinoza's vocabulary, an order. See Spinoza, *Ethics*, part 2, proposition 7.

7. Deleuze, *Spinoza*, 94.

8. Deleuze, *Expressionism in Philosophy*, 237.

9. Deleuze, *Spinoza*, 46. I deliberately eschew here Deleuze's differentiation

between beings and Being. The focus here is matter—that is, a concept that is indeed coextensive with Being, not because it covers the same area but because it extends at the same time. I can only push to another time the elaboration of such a coextensiveness.

10. I explore this "absolute heterogeneity" in Martinon, *End of Man.*

11. This is a classic Levinasian argument, which Tina Chanter summarizes perfectly when addressing the impossibility of distinguishing the Saying from the Said: "In raising [the difference between the saying and the said] to the level of a logical distinction we have already lost sight of the way in which the saying calls for the said out of the very same necessity whereby the saying refuses to be contained by it. Perhaps what should be said is not that this is an organizing distinction, but that it is one that governs by undoing itself: it is an impossible distinction, and it thereby functions not as an organizing thematic, but precisely as a disordering, disruptive force." Chanter, *Time, Death, and the Feminine*, 146.

12. Levinas, *Proper Names*, 59.

## Mortals

1. Heidegger, *History of the Concept of Time*, 316.

2. Heidegger, *History of the Concept of Time*, 316–17.

3. Heidegger, *Poetry, Language, Thought*, 178–79.

4. Derrida, *Animal That Therefore I Am*, esp. 154–60.

5. I realize here that the original sentence says, "Rational living beings must first become mortals." Truncating "rational" is not intended to distort Heidegger's thought, only to emphasize Derrida's point after Heidegger. Heidegger, *Poetry, Language, Thought*, 179.

6. Schürmann, *Heidegger on Being and Acting*, 225. I realize that Schürmann is also referencing here the impossibility of disclosure in relation to the other three components of the fourfold. I have left this aside in order to better flesh out how we become mortal.

7. Schürmann, *Heidegger on Being and Acting*, 225.

8. I obviously do not intend here to either reduce mortals to things or instrumentalize them. What I take from Heidegger's famous analysis of the jug as a thing is not the fact that it is a man-made object but rather the fact that it has existential characteristics that expose the mirror play of the fourfold. Mortals are not vessels, properly speaking, but they hold the void (or the desert, as we will see in "Names") as they are gathered in the giving. This outpouring can only be made to the gods that they are. For a less unruly analysis of this jug, see, e.g., Halliburton, *Poetic Thinking.*

9. Heidegger, *Poetry, Language, Thought*, 172.

10. "Face to face with the other within a glance and a speech which both maintain distance and interrupt all totalities, this being together as separation *[cet être ensemble comme séparation]* precedes or exceeds society, collectivity, community." Derrida, *Writing and Difference,* 119.

## God

1. The word *God* is used here with capitalization in order to differentiate it from gods (cf. "Gods"), which in all cases signify mortals.

2. I use here the masculine gender only to exaggerate and to some extent ridicule the problematic connotation of the word *omnipresent* and its obviously detrimental and prejudicial patriarchal history. On this topic, see Martinon, *End of Man.*

3. Power refers, as Hannah Arendt says, to an ability to act in concert. As such, power is not a hold but rather a concerted effort to act together. Arendt writes: "Power corresponds to the human ability not just to act but to act in concert. Power is never the property of an individual; it belongs to a group and remains in existence only so long as the group keeps together." Arendt, *On Violence,* 43.

4. Spinoza, *Ethics,* part 1, proposition 34.

5. Spinoza, *Opera quae supersunt onmia,* part 1, proposition 34.

6. Spinoza, *Ethics,* part 2, proposition 3.

7. Spinoza, *Opera quae supersunt onmia,* part 2, proposition 3.

8. Spinoza, *Ethics,* part 2, proposition 3, scholium (my emphasis).

9. Deleuze, *Spinoza,* 97.

10. Deleuze, *Spinoza: Practical Philosophy,* 98.

11. Spinoza, *Ethics,* letter 40.

12. Deleuze, *Expressionism in Philosophy,* 87–88.

13. As exemplified in his Third Meditation; Descartes, *Meditations on First Philosophy,* 25–37.

14. Technically, within Spinoza's vocabulary, a proper name such as "God," would fall under the category of a mediate finite mode under the attribute of thought. This crucial distinction, which Deleuze does not do, would require lengthy analyses that cannot take place here. See Spinoza's definition of *Intellectus actu,* in *Ethics,* part 1, proposition 31, and part 1, proposition 9, corollary, demonstration.

15. Deleuze, *Expressionism in Philosophy,* 45.

16. Levinas, *Beyond the Verse,* 118.

17. I am aware that Levinas's interpretation of Maimonides is often seen as a misreading. I will not dispute this. My aim is only to emphasize the importance of words (as name or expression) in the context of any reflection on God. For

the quotation, see Levinas, *Beyond the Verse*, 118. For criticisms of Levinas, see, among others, Fagenblat, *Covenant of Creatures*, esp. 128–29.

18. To use Spinoza's famous example, which Deleuze analyzes in *Expressionism in Philosophy*, 47.

19. I omit here the whole discussion of the use of consonantal semivowels in the tetragrammaton. Suffice to say that the impossibility of pronouncing God's name reinforces the argument I put forward.

20. As is well known, Spinoza equates God with Nature, which he famously writes down as "*Deus sive Natura*—God or Nature." On this topic, see Balibar, "Spinoza's Three Gods." See also Objects.

21. Levinas, *Beyond the Verse*, 118.

22. As I have done in my previous books, *End of Man* and *After "Rwanda,"* I make a distinction between an immemorial Past (with a capital letter) and a memorable past (without capitalization). The latter refers to all forms of memorization and historical narration. The former refers to the radical unhinging of ontic space-time, to what breaks apart all memories and histories—as far as language permits us to hear it. Because it is not possible to account here for the numerous books that articulate such a divide (by Levinas and Derrida, among many others), I can only point to the bibliography included in my first book: Martinon, *On Futurity*.

23. Levinas, *Beyond the Verse*, 119.

24. As with the Past, I make a distinction between the radically unpredictable Future (with a capital letter) and the future (without capitalization) understood as futurity—that is, as projection, prediction, prophecy. The latter refers to a measurable future. The former refers to the radical unhinging of ontic space-time—as far as language permits us to hear it. See Martinon, *On Futurity*.

## Gods

1. The word *god* is used here without capitalization in order to differentiate it from God.

2. For a different reading of this poem—one that attempts to read Heidegger's thought through an ecofeminist perspective—see Claxton, *Heidegger's Gods*, esp. 58–62.

3. Heidegger, *Hölderlin's Hymns*, 143.

4. Heidegger, *Hölderlin's Hymns*, 245.

5. Heidegger, *Hölderlin's Hymns*, 245–46.

6. Heidegger, *Hölderlin's Hymns*, 245–46.

7. Heidegger, *Hölderlin's Hymns*, 246 (translation modified). Unfortunately, I ignore here Heidegger's use of capitalization for the word "other." Suffice to say that mortals in their radicality are here at stake.

8. Heidegger, *Hölderlin's Hymns*, 246.

9. Mortals' Future is obviously not always willed. The gods can open it up in many ways, even in situations in which it heralds the closure of teleological time not with wars or guns, but with slow genetic changes leading to uncontrolled cell growth and tumor formation.

10. Heidegger, *Hölderlin's Hymns*, 247. I disrespectfully alter Heidegger's words here, swapping "need" for "depend on." The close interrelatedness of mortals and gods often make the use of language difficult. The gods need mortals, which means nothing else, of course, than mortals need the gods. Hölderlin in this is clear. However, can such an economic vocabulary be used for the gods? A lack of need cannot quite convert into a need whereby the gods always expect something in return. Having all, the gods exhaust the possibility of need itself, but this does not exonerate them from remaining utterly dependent on mortals, who are chained to always needing economic returns. I hope that this opens up Heidegger from his well-known autism and compensates for my disrespectful "correction" of his Hölderlin.

11. Heidegger, *Hölderlin's Hymns*, 247.

## Beckoning

1. Heidegger, *Being and Time*, 307.

2. I use here the expression "my death" in order to differentiate it from what is commonly understood as death—that is, an external event affecting mortals as if from outside. On this expression, see Derrida, *Aporias*, and for a commentary, see Martinon, *On Futurity*, especially chap. 3.

3. I reverse here an argument made by Derrida about the possible. See Derrida, *Politics of Friendship*, 29.

4. Heidegger, *Poetry, Language, Thought*, 182.

5. Heidegger, *Poetry, Language, Thought*, 147. I realize that in this text Heidegger talks of the gods as "beckoning messengers of the godhead *(die Gottheit)*." Briefly, the godhead stands not for God as such but rather for the Future understood in its radicality—that is, what cannot be anticipated or predicted and yet can only manifest itself through gods as the freeing of possibility (or impossibility). Understood in this way, the godhead is not another monotheistic God beyond the event of being, but the Future of the fourfold. In this, I am following Schürmann's work and in doing so, I am deliberately evading conventional readings of the godhead in Heidegger, such as, for example, Caputo, *Mystical Element in Heidegger's Thought*. For a commentary, see Martinon, "Time Unshackled."

6. Heidegger, *Hölderlin's Hymns*, 31.

7. Heidegger, *Hölderlin's Hymns*, 155–56.

## Obsession

1. Levinas, *God, Death and Time*, 172.
2. Levinas, *God, Death and Time*, 172.
3. Levinas, *God, Death and Time*, 173.
4. Levinas, *God, Death and Time*, 173.
5. Levinas, *God, Death and Time*, 173–74.
6. Levinas, *God, Death and Time*, 174.
7. Levinas, *God, Death and Time*, 174.
8. Levinas, *God, Death and Time*, 174.

## Strife

1. The expression "time-space" refers here alternatively to the time-space of physicists and to Heidegger's *Zeit-Raum*, i.e., to a "making present." When it comes to matter, it is a making present. When it comes to the event, it is the time-space of the physicist—or, here, sundering. In either case, the expression evades giving priority to either time or space. See Heidegger, *On Time and Being*, 14. See also as a contrast to these two time-spaces Meillassoux's understanding of time as hyperchaotic (cf. "The Absolute").

2. Heidegger, *Contributions to Philosophy*, 25 (translation modified in order to emphasize the difference between the sundering and strife; note that Heidegger uses both *sundering* and *strife* for earths/skies).

3. Further proof that this sundering takes place in every kind of event, Heidegger writes immediately afterward and in parentheses, "(beyng and nonbeing)." The former refers to the event of being *(Ereignis)*, i.e., to that which takes place as being; the latter refers to the absence of all event, i.e., the event of absence itself. The event of matter therefore makes no distinction between the event of being (beyng) and its absence (nonbeing). Heidegger, *Contributions to Philosophy*, 25.

4. The plural is mine and is intended to mirror the plural of gods and mortals. Plurality distracts from the literal reading of the physical realities of earth and sky. Justification for this plurality should become apparent in the chapters "Earths" and "Skies," when these are analyzed with reference to specific examples.

5. Here I deliberately replace Heidegger's word "world" with "sky." The reason for such a strange translation is to simply remain faithful to the later Heidegger, who abandoned the expression "world" for "sky." There is no space here to analyze Heidegger's evolution from "world" to "sky." See Mattéi, *Heidegger et Hölderlin*.

6. Heidegger, *Poetry, Language, Thought*, 47–48 (translation corrected because *Streit* does not mean "striving").

7. "Spacing (which is temporizing)—temporizing (which is spacing) (cf. the

conflict of the sundering) as the most proximate configuring domain for the truth of beyng, but not a relapse to the common, formal concepts of space and time (!); instead, resumption into the strife, [sky] and earth—event." Heidegger, *Contributions to Philosophy*, 205 (translation modified: temporizing instead of temporalizing, spacing instead of spatializing. For a justification for this modification, see the introduction to Martinon, *On Futurity*).

8. On this, see Schürmann, *Heidegger on Being and Acting*, 224.

9. As Heidegger writes: "The earth cannot dispense with the Open of the [sky] if it itself is to appear as earth in the liberated surge of its self-seclusion. The [sky], again, cannot soar out of the earth's sight if, as the governing breadth and path of all essential destiny, it is to ground itself on a resolute foundation." Heidegger, *Poetry, Language, Thought*, 47–48 (translation modified).

10. Heidegger, *Elucidations of Hölderlin's Poetry*, 188.

11. Heidegger, *Poetry, Language, Thought*, 48 (translation modified).

12. Heidegger, *Poetry, Language, Thought*, 48 (translation modified).

13. Inasmuch as toil would then be the only way forward for the strife earths/skies. However, as intimated earlier, work brings together utilitarian and nonutilitarian aims. The struggle implied in the work of strife thus also includes a lazy slumbering on a warm summer afternoon.

14. Heidegger, *Contributions to Philosophy*, 66.

## The Absolute

1. Meillassoux, "Contingency and the Absolutization of the One," 13.

2. Meillassoux, "Contingency and the Absolutization of the One," 13.

3. Meillassoux, "Iteration, Reiteration, Repetition," 11n5.

4. This would require a lengthy analysis. Returning to the Greek prefix implies returning to reason, thus invalidating Meillassoux's claim that hyper-chaos is unreasoned. The barbarism might perhaps have then been preferable. However, because hyper-chaos is the truth of things, it therefore makes sense that it should be placed at this fictional heart of Western reason, just to unseat it one more time.

5. Meillassoux, "Contingency and the Absolutization of the One," 13.

6. Meillassoux, "Contingency and the Absolutization of the One," 13.

7. Although Meillassoux limits himself to ontic times, I would also include ontological apperceptions of time, including those considered here under the aegis of Heidegger's fourfold.

8. Meillassoux, "Iteration, Reiteration, Repetition," 16 (translation modified).

9. Meillassoux, "Iteration, Reiteration, Repetition," 16 (translation modified).

10. Meillassoux, "Potentiality and Virtuality," 72.
11. Meillassoux, "Temps et surgissement ex-nihilo" (my translation).
12. Meillassoux, *After Finitude*, 64.
13. Meillassoux, *After Finitude*, 64.
14. Meillassoux, "Contingency and the Absolutization of the One," 12.
15. Meillassoux, "Immanence of the World Beyond," 446.
16. Meillassoux, "Immanence of the World Beyond," 446.
17. For a counterargument, see Bitbol, *Maintenant la finitude.*
18. Meillassoux, "Iteration, Reiteration, Repetition," 10.
19. Meillassoux, "Contingency and the Absolutization of the One," 13.

## Earths

1. For a less unruly and faithful reading of the topic of earth in Heidegger's work, see Michel Haar's remarkable analysis of the ground of being, *Song of the Earth*, esp. 47–64.
2. Heidegger, *Poetry, Language, Thought*, 45–46 (translation modified).
3. Heidegger, *Poetry, Language, Thought*, 53–54.
4. Heidegger, *Poetry, Language, Thought*, 147.
5. Heidegger, *Poetry, Language, Thought*, 176.
6. Heidegger, *Poetry, Language, Thought*, 45.
7. On this variety, see Heidegger, *Poetry, Language, Thought*, 46.
8. Lorca, *Poet in New York*, 7.
9. Lorca, *Poet in New York*, 11.
10. Lorca, *Poet in New York*, 185.
11. Lorca, *Poet in New York*, 197.
12. Lorca, *Poet in New York*, 189.
13. Lorca, *Poet in New York*, 135.
14. Lorca, *Poet in New York*, 210.
15. Heidegger, *Poetry, Language, Thought*, 41.
16. I use here the expression "the curatorial" in the way I defined it in *Curatorial.* In a nutshell, the curatorial is the event of knowledge incurred by an exhibition, whereas curating is the activity of putting on an exhibition. As an event of matter ("Strife"), the curatorial can obviously never be constricted or properly defined. The curatorial seeps and bleeds into many different fields and practices, making it quintessentially of our time, and thus inevitably impossible to define. As such, the curatorial is understood to be taking place irrespective of any specific historical narratives telling us what art is and how it has been "best" exhibited. For those who prefer historical contextualization of this practice, I refer them to the following: Smith, *Thinking Contemporary Curating*; O'Neill, ed., *Culture of Curating*; O'Neill, *Curating Subjects.*

## Skies

1. Heidegger, *Poetry, Language, Thought*, 217.
2. Heidegger, *Poetry, Language, Thought*, 220–21.
3. Heidegger, *Poetry, Language, Thought*, 223.
4. Heidegger, *Poetry, Language, Thought*, 223.
5. Heidegger, *Poetry, Language, Thought*, 224.
6. Balzac, *Wild Ass's Skin*, 32.
7. Balzac, *Wild Ass's Skin*, 33.
8. Balzac, *Wild Ass's Skin*, 34.
9. Balzac, *Wild Ass's Skin*, 34.
10. Balzac, *Wild Ass's Skin*, 35.
11. Balzac, *Wild Ass's Skin*, 37.
12. Balzac, *Wild Ass's Skin*, 37.
13. Balzac, *Wild Ass's Skin*, 39.
14. Balzac, *Wild Ass's Skin*, 40.
15. Balzac, *Wild Ass's Skin*, 42.
16. Balzac, *Wild Ass's Skin*, 37.
17. Balzac, *Wild Ass's Skin*, 38.

## Objects

1. Kandinsky, *On the Spiritual in Art*, 16.
2. Kandinsky, *On the Spiritual in Art*, 15–16, 17.
3. Spinoza, *Theological-Political Treatise*, 13.
4. Spinoza, *Theological-Political Treatise*, 13.
5. Spinoza, *Theological-Political Treatise*, 45. A small portion of this quotation has been omitted because it references God as "truth and necessity." Two reasons justify such an omission. First, in this book, I have chosen to understand God as a nomination with a lost referent (cf. "God"). It is therefore understood without a truth or necessity principle attached to it. Second, even if this nomination were a necessary attribute, to follow Spinoza's vocabulary, hyperchaos would nonetheless relegate God to a parochial event (cf. "The Absolute"). In this way, God cannot be here understood either as truth or obeying a necessity according to which everything must be so by virtue of logic or natural law, even if this necessity is self-constitutive. I therefore thought it essential to omit this crucial Spinozist argument not in order to annoyingly betray or distort his remarkable thought, but in order to remain faithful to the nonnecessitarian arguments of this book.
6. I deliberately omit here Spinoza's important distinction between *natura naturans* and *natura naturata*. The reason for brazenly omitting *natura naturata* is because it unnecessarily creates a split between what actively is

God *(natura naturans)* and what passively follows from God *(natura naturata)*. While *natura naturata* explains how (in)finite modes follow from (in)finite attributes, the split nonetheless divides God. He is self-caused *(natura naturans)* and/or a modification of His own causality *(natura naturata)*. Because all that is conceived under the formulation of the fourfold evades this type of pantheism for which causality needs to be doubled (self-caused/caused by), it follows that such a distinction cannot operate here simply because self-causality can never be properly distinguished from external causality. Is conception, for example, purely one or the other? I cannot say, however much my parents made me mortal. Active self-causality takes place here in this time-space that passively proceeds causally. For a clear exposition of Spinoza's distinction see, e.g., Melamed, *Spinoza's Metaphysics*, especially part 1.

7. Spinoza, *Ethics*, part 1, proposition 29, scholium.

8. A point of clarification is perhaps here in order. Free causality, or what knows no cause other than itself, is necessarily an immanent causality and not a transitive causality. This means that its efficiency and its effects are included in its causation and not outside of it.

9. See, among others, Alberro and Zimmerman, *Lawrence Weiner*; Phillpot, "Words and Word Works"; Rorimer, "Sculpture"; Poinsot, "Nombreux objets colorés."

10. Further analysis of this work could include, for example, Weiner's alternative use of color in typography.

## Angels

1. Oil on canvas, Uffizi Gallery, Florence, Italy.

2. Kierkegaard, *Fear and Trembling*.

3. Levinas, *Proper Names*, 74 (translation modified).

4. Levinas, *Proper Names*, 73.

5. On this topic, see the insightful work of Chalier, especially "Exteriority of the Feminine," "Ethics and the Feminine," and *Figures du feminin*.

6. See, e.g., the position of the angel in Benjamin, *Illuminations*, 245–46.

7. Derrida, *Gift of Death*, 59.

8. Derrida, *Gift of Death*, 76.

9. Derrida, *Gift of Death*, 61.

10. See, e.g., Lucas Cranach the Elder, *The Sacrifice of Isaac* (1530), Paolo Veronese, *The Sacrifice of Isaac* (c. 1586), David Teniers the Younger, *Abraham's Sacrifice of Isaac* (c. 1655), Rembrandt van Rijn, *Abraham and Isaac* (1634), or, in a time closer to us, Marc Chagall, *Sacrifice of Isaac* (1966).

## Words

1. Eleey, "What About Responsibility?" 113.

2. On the fact that exhibitions are utterances, see Bal, *Double Exposure.*

3. Kunsthalle, Bern, March 22–April 27, 1969.

4. Lyotard and Thébaud, *Just Gaming,* 31.

5. Lyotard and Thébaud, *Just Gaming,* 35.

6. Lyotard and Thébaud, *Just Gaming,* 35.

7. Lyotard and Thébaud, *Just Gaming,* 42 (translation modified).

8. Lyotard and Thébaud, *Just Gaming,* 36.

9. Lyotard and Thébaud, *Just Gaming,* 45.

10. Lyotard and Thébaud, *Just Gaming,* 52.

11. Lyotard and Thébaud, *Just Gaming,* 66.

12. Lyotard and Thébaud, *Just Gaming,* 66 (translation modified).

13. Lyotard and Thébaud, *Just Gaming,* 72.

14. Lyotard and Thébaud, *Just Gaming,* 111.

## Ghosts

1. Mayer et al., eds., *Code of Ethics,* 4.

2. I read and receive inspiration from Nancy's essay, "Kategorien of Excess," as the introductory remarks about the sovereignty of curators' principle testifies.

3. Nancy, "Kategorien of Excess," 145.

4. Nancy, "Kategorien of Excess," 145–46.

5. Nancy, "Kategorien of Excess," 147.

6. Nancy, "Kategorien of Excess," 147.

7. Nancy, "Kategorien of Excess," 139.

8. Nancy, "Kategorien of Excess," 147.

## Images

1. On this topic, see Levinas, "Revelation in the Jewish Tradition," 202.

2. Another version of this painting, with the figures arranged differently, is in Petworth House in the United Kingdom.

3. Teniers, *Theatrvm Pictorium.*

4. In this description of Teniers's display, I deliberately omit a landscape by an unknown artist. Such omission only reinforces the arbitrariness of any formalist reading, including mine.

5. Claudel, *Art Poétique,* 50 (my translation).

6. Lyotard, *Discourse, Figure,* 3–4.

7. Lyotard, *Discourse, Figure,* 4.

8. Lyotard, *Discourse, Figure,* 7.

9. Lyotard, *Discourse, Figure*, 7.
10. Lyotard, *Differend*, 79.
11. Lyotard, *Discourse, Figure*, 5.
12. Lyotard, *Libidinal Economy*, 11.

## Gnoses

1. Lévi-Strauss, "Rousseau," 13 (translation modified).
2. Lévi-Strauss, "Rousseau," 12.
3. Lévi-Strauss, "Rousseau," 12.
4. Lévi-Strauss, "Rousseau," 12–13.
5. Lévi-Strauss, "Rousseau," 13.
6. Mudimbe, *Invention of Africa*, xi. For a further reflection on this issue, see Mudimbe, *Parables and Fables*, ix–xxii. For a commentary on this approach to Mudimbe's confessional work, see Martinon, "Valentin Mudimbe."
7. See Aristotle, *Posterior Analytic*, especially part 2, 99b–100b.
8. Mudimbe, *Invention of Africa*, ix.
9. Levinas, *Existence and Existents*, 89.
10. Mudimbe, *Invention of Africa*, 186.
11. For more information on this project, see Haha, "Flood"; Jacob, Paler, and Ploof, eds., *With Love from Haha*; Davis, "Growing Collectives."

## Contents

1. On this topic, see Byrne, "Great Curator."
2. I will not be interpreting hyperlinks and hypertexts as new forms of texts. My focus is exclusively the performative and temporal dimensions of hyperlinks or hyphens in curatorial contexts. For the former, see, e.g., Landow, *Hypertext 3.0.*
3. Lyotard and Gruber, *Hyphen*, 29.
4. Lyotard and Gruber, *Hyphen*, 29.
5. See Lyotard and Gruber, *Hyphen*, 69.
6. On this frenetic standstill, see Martinon, "Time Unshackled."
7. Lyotard and Gruber, *Hyphen*, 32.
8. Lyotard and Gruber, *Hyphen*, 5.
9. Lyotard and Gruber, *Hyphen*, 31.

## Names

1. I am aware that some societies and cultures do not have family names that are repeated over centuries, thus making them into properties/improprieties. I am thinking here of Rwandese names inasmuch as they are often composites of expressions that bear no relation to parents or ascendants. For

example, a man was known as Ukurikirayezu, "He who follows Jesus." For how names are given to children in Rwanda, see Kimenyi, *Kinyarwanda and Kirundi Names*.

2. Derrida, *On the Name*, 61 (translation modified).

3. Derrida, *On the Name*, 58.

4. Derrida, *On the Name*, 57.

5. Derrida, *On the Name*, 65.

6. Derrida, *On the Name*, 84–85.

7. Derrida, *On the Name*, 65.

8. Derrida, *On the Name*, 66.

9. Even if such mutual giveness take different directions—a topic I cannot explore here. As Derrida rightly explains, "[The fracture] extends its crack into the analogy between God and me, creator and creature. This time the analogy does not repair, nor reconcile, but aggravates the dissociation." Derrida, *On the Name*, 66.

## Saving

1. For more than 110 years, the UK National Art Collections Fund has supported British museums and galleries by helping them acquire and display art as well as running public appeals when particular works of art are under threat of leaving the country; see http://www.artfund.org/.

2. De Quincy, *Considérations morales*.

3. Heidegger, *Poetry, Language, Thought*, 145.

4. Heidegger, *Poetry, Language, Thought*, 145.

5. Heidegger, *Poetry, Language, Thought*, 146–47.

6. Heidegger, *Poetry, Language, Thought*, 147–48.

7. Heidegger, *Poetry, Language, Thought*, 147–48.

8. Heidegger, *Poetry, Language, Thought*, 148–49.

9. Heidegger, *Poetry, Language, Thought*, 148.

10. What is "unhoped for" cannot be understood as (or compared to) a kind of inverted hope that can be conceptualized—the "unlooked for" or the "unplanned," for example. As such, it cannot enter the framework of concepts, whether those, for example, of Ernst Bloch in *The Principle of Hope* or Richard Rorty in *Philosophy and Social Hope*.

11. This would require a lengthy commentary inasmuch as the process of mummification (I am thinking here of Jeremy Bentham's *Auto-Icon* at UCL in London) and cryonics (the belief that a person's body can be stored in a cryogenic vessel and later brought back to life) might debunk this argument. Suffice it to say that the issue of dwelling does not go away, however complex the survival or afterlife amid earths and skies; cf. "Matter."

12. As is well known, an auction house sold Leonardo da Vinci's rediscovered portrait of Jesus Christ, *Salvator Mundi* (Savior of the world), for $450.3 million, making it, as of 2017, the most expensive work of art ever sold.

## Caring

1. If this study did not focus so assiduously, for good or bad, on turning Heidegger's fourfold into a potential ethical midwifery, then it would no doubt need to address the many approaches to ethics that exploit these gestures, feelings, and acts, now institutionally grouped under the denomination "ethics of care." These approaches are not treated here because they rely on two seemingly self-evident truths: first, that an intuitive ethics is predominantly feminine; and second, that such an ethics is mostly conscious and therefore reasoned or reasonable. These two truths are based on a monological understanding of subjectivity and ethics—one feminine subject, for example, aspiring to change the world for the better through intuitive/reasoned gestures that male subjects are not always able to perform. While I am not fundamentally disputing the goodness of these proposals, I cannot here articulate counterarguments for the problems they entail. I can only point in the direction of a previous work that dismantles these monological apperceptions of sex and gender (see Martinon, *End of Man*) and in the direction of some of the best work in the field: Ruddick, *Maternal Thinking*; Tronto, *Moral Boundaries*; Held, *Ethics of Care*; Noddings, *Caring.*

2. Quoted in McClellan, *Inventing the Louvre*, 107.

3. Szeemann, "Does Art Need Directors?," 167.

4. Huberman, "Take Care," 9–17. For a more comprehensive history of the way contemporary curating addresses care, see, among others, Fowle, "Who Cares?"; Reckitt, "Support Acts."

5. With one notable exception: Michel Foucault's famous study of *epimeleia heautou*, or care of self. The reason I evade addressing Foucault's take on this topic is simple. His understanding of the subject is still riveted to the twins *ipse/idem*, and his aim—at least in the last volume of his *History of Sexuality*—is the development of an ethics defining how these twins can develop (through modes of self-care) as a counterpoint to the hegemonic "know-thyself." I cannot address this approach because it is in radical contrast to the fractured dimensions of mortals/gods and earths/skies explored here. For Foucault's breathtaking analyses, see Foucault, *Hermeneutics of the Subject* and *Care of the Self.*

6. Virgil, *Aeneid*, 551–53.

7. In antiquity, wine, for example, was called the downer of Cares in the sense that its properties were deemed to ease the pains and sorrows of life. Müller, *History of the Literature of Ancient Greece*, 169.

8. Seneca, *Epistulae Morales*, 443–45.

9. On this fable, see Nowotny, "The Curator Crosses the River: A Fabulation," in Martinon, ed., *Curatorial*, 59–64.

10. Hyginus, *Fables*, 34.

11. Herder, *Volkslieder*, 743–44 (my translation).

12. Goethe, *Faust*, 218–19 (part 2, act 5, verses 11418–32).

13. Heidegger, *History of the Concept of Time*, 295.

14. Heidegger, *History of the Concept of Time*, 298.

15. I use this expression following Derrida in "The Ends of Man," in Derrida, *Margins of Philosophy*, 109–36.

## Preparing

1. For a detailed analysis of d'Angiviller's aborted dream and the way it was recuperated first by the French Revolution and later by Napoleon, see McClellan, *Inventing the Louvre*.

2. It is violent inasmuch as it does not follow Foucault's line of argumentation but reinterprets one term only. As such, there will be no analysis here of this word in relation to this other term Foucault analyzes, namely *ascesis*, which refers to the exercise of self on self. Detached from this term, and in line with the argumentation of this book, the present analysis will not seek to develop an ethics of care for self (cf. "Caring"). Contrary to Foucault, the interpretation of *paraskeue* will be made in order to emphasize an inductive scheme of action, the preparedness to whatever comes to be without prior or accompanying *ascesis*. As such, *paraskeue* cannot be confused—as Foucault often does in his unusual cross-reading of Greek and Latin texts—with particular Stoic forms of *ascesis*, especially Seneca's famous *praemeditatio malorum*, imagining future misfortunes (recuperated today in CBT practices as negative visualization). It is by distinguishing it from these later eidetic temporal reductions that the separate and distinctive meaning of *paraskeue* can emerge. For Foucault's continued use of *paraskeue* as *askesis*, see Foucault, *Ethics*, esp. 238–42.

3. In a military sense: "The day, however, was too far spent for them to begin the battle, since night already approached: so they prepared to engage upon the morrow." Herodotus, *Histories*, 572.

4. Foucault, *Hermeneutics of the Subject*, chap. 12, 240.

5. Foucault, *Hermeneutics of the Subject*, chap. 16, 320–21.

6. Foucault, *Hermeneutics of the Subject*, chap. 16, 321.

7. Foucault, *Hermeneutics of the Subject*, chap. 16, 321.

8. Foucault, *Hermeneutics of the Subject*, chap. 16, 322.

9. Foucault, *Hermeneutics of the Subject*, chap. 16, 323.

10. Foucault, *Hermeneutics of the Subject*, chap. 16, 323.

11. Foucault, *Hermeneutics of the Subject*, chap. 16, 323.

12. Foucault, *Hermeneutics of the Subject,* chap. 16, 323.

13. Foucault, *Hermeneutics of the Subject,* chap. 16, 324.

14. Foucault, *Hermeneutics of the Subject,* chap. 16, 327.

15. Levinas, *Entre Nous*, 129.

16. To say nothing of time as absolute contingency; cf. "The Absolute."

17. Namely Herodotus, Aeschylus, Sophocles, Euripides, Aristophanes, Cratinus, Xenophon, Antiphon, Andocides, Lysias, Lycurgus, Dinarchus, Plato, Democritus, and Pythagoras.

18. Allison, *Power and Preparedness in Thucydides*, 87.

19. Allison, *Power and Preparedness in Thucydides*, 101.

## Irritating

1. Not one particular project will be given here to exemplify this. From biennales to Manifestas, from Documentas to small local shows, and from Web projects to social media campaigns, the specter of the partisan is pervasive enough.

2. See Clausewitz, *On War*; Lenin, "Guerrilla Warfare"; Ewald, *Treatise on Partisan Warfare*; Schroers, *Partisan*; Zedong, *On Guerrilla Warfare*, part 2; Guevara, *Guerrilla Warfare*.

3. Schmitt, *Theory of the Partisan*, 77.

4. This does not mean that exhibitions or curatorial projects have no impact. Curating's socioeconomic and political effectiveness is here not on trial. The aim is simply to take a wider perspective and reflect on the effects of contemporary forms of partisanship among curators and their projects.

5. Derrida, *Politics of Friendship*, 142. Derrida goes further when he rightly says that the telluric character of the classical partisan is already a teletechnological response to a question of place. I unfortunately cannot explore this further argument in enough depth for lack of space.

6. Schmitt, *Theory of the Partisan*, 14–22.

7. Schmitt, *Nomos of the Earth*, 42.

8. Schmitt, *Nomos of the Earth*, 42.

9. Schmitt, *Theory of the Partisan*, 69.

10. Schmitt, *Theory of the Partisan*, 71.

11. Schmitt, *Theory of the Partisan*, 77.

12. On the need of letting go of the imperative for calculation and measurement with regards to clock time, I refer the reader to Martinon, "Time Unshackled."

13. This argument is obviously close to the one Heidegger puts forward in his late work. The fourfold is indeed often seen as a way of articulating a nontechnological form of poetic dwelling that would save us from the dangers of technology. The reason I do not explore this issue through the prism of Heidegger

is because I want to infuse the fourfold with a radically different vocabulary, thus provoking different readings and perspectives—namely the political potential of the partisan. For a faithful and exemplary analysis of the issue of technology in relation to Heidegger's fourfold, see Wrathall, "Between the Earth and the Sky."

## Fraternizing

1. This does not mean that curators do not also get along nicely with everybody. Curators, whether online or in art institutions, are not on trial. The point is simply that curators, like anyone involved in any form of business, are violent not in the sense of having violence at their disposal—although some, no doubt, do—but in being structured as violence, as strife. Violence (and therefore war) is mortals' basic trait—not just of their doing but of their very being. There would be no engagement in any sphere of work without this fundamental trait (cf. "Matter" and "Mortals").

2. There is no space here to justify that any discursive attempt to eradicate war is futile. For a lengthy analysis of this topic with regards to one of the worst wars in history, the Rwandan genocide, see Martinon, *After "Rwanda."*

3. Baudelaire, *Flowers of Evil*, 7.

4. Chalier, *Fraternité*, 123 (all translations are my own).

5. Chalier, *Fraternité*, 124.

6. Chalier, *Fraternité*, 126.

7. Chalier, *Fraternité*, 132.

8. Chalier, *Fraternité*, 132–33.

9. Chalier, *Fraternité*, 133.

10. Chalier, *Fraternité*, 137–38.

11. Chalier, *Fraternité*, 148.

12. Chalier, *Fraternité*, 149–50.

13. Chalier, *Fraternité*, 151–52.

14. See also, among others, Levinas, *Otherwise Than Being*, 142; Derrida, "At This Very Moment."

15. As Chalier says elsewhere, "There can be no witness of the immemorial appeal, whether consciously or willingly." Chalier, *Transmettre de génération en generation*, 261 (my translation).

16. Chalier, *Fraternité*, 153–54.

17. Chalier, *Fraternité*, 153–54.

## Communing

1. See Hoffmann and McDowell, "Reflection"; Páldi, "Notes on the Paracuratorial."

2. Hoffmann and McDowell, "Reflection."

3. In Schürmann, *Wandering Joy*, 135.

4. Schürmann, *Wandering Joy*, 136.

5. To this idea, Eckhart adds that although man never ceases to be one with God, he also needs to make an effort—through apprenticeship—to become more godly. There is no space here to expose this apparent contradiction or the way Eckhart sees such an ethical transformation.

6. Schürmann, *Wandering Joy*, 138.

7. Schürmann, *Wandering Joy*, 138.

8. John 1:14.

9. Schürmann, *Wandering Joy*, 29.

10. In Schürmann, *Wandering Joy*, 158.

11. Schürmann, *Wandering Joy*, 159.

12. Schürmann, *Wandering Joy*, 161.

## Dignifying

1. A revealing instance of this type of problematic and dangerous ranking is the contrast drawn, for example, by the curators of the 9/11 memorial museum at the World Trade Center in New York: "The museum attests to the triumph of human dignity over human depravity and affirms an unwavering commitment to the fundamental value of human life." 9/11 Memorial Museum Map, 2016.

2. Nancy, "Our Probity!," 68.

3. Nancy, "Our Probity!," 69.

4. Nancy, "Our Probity!," 69.

5. See Nietzsche, "§335" in *Gay Science*, 187–89.

6. Nancy, "Our Probity!," 77 (translation modified).

7. Nancy, "Our Probity!," 78.

8. Nancy, "Our Probity!," 78.

9. Nancy, "Our Probity!," 78.

10. Nancy, "Our Probity!," 84.

11. Nancy, "Our Probity!," 84. I deliberately swap Nancy's "imperative" for "necessity" in order to retain the same vocabulary throughout.

12. Nancy, "Our Probity!," 84–85.

13. Nancy, "Our Probity!," 85.

14. Kant, *Groundwork*, 71.

## Midwifing

1. Martinon, "Theses in the Philosophy of Curating," in Martinon, ed., *Curatorial*, 31.

2. As is well known, *techne* is a Greek term (*τέχνη*) that is often translated as "craft" or "art." Although some major implications can be drawn between these two translations, I will retain the broader meaning of "practice." The im-

portant thing here is to remember that a practice is always concrete, variable, and context dependent, and the knowledge it produces is intended to be practically or aesthetically applied. As such, it is contrasted with a type of work *(theoria)* that often operates in a disinterested way and the knowledge it produces is only intended to be theoretically or scientifically applied. The present chapter intends to challenge this facile distinction.

3. Kofman, *Comment s'en sortir?*, 13–14 (all translations are my own).
4. Kofman, *Comment s'en sortir?*, 13–14.
5. Kofman, *Comment s'en sortir?*, 83–84.
6. Kofman, *Comment s'en sortir?*, 84.
7. Kofman, *Comment s'en sortir?*, 90.
8. Kofman, *Comment s'en sortir?*, 90.
9. Kofman, *Comment s'en sortir?*, 92.
10. Kofman, *Comment s'en sortir?*, 92–93.
11. Kofman, *Comment s'en sortir?*, 93.
12. Kofman, *Comment s'en sortir?*, 54–55.
13. Kofman, *Comment s'en sortir?*, 55.
14. Kofman, *Comment s'en sortir?*, 55.
15. Kofman, *Comment s'en sortir?*, 56.

## Intuiting

1. Pan and Luyckx, "Face to Face."
2. Bell Farrell, "Curating as a Divining Process," 240.
3. For lack of space, I deliberately leave aside the thorny issue of justifying the curious parallel drawn here between Spinoza's eternity and the immemorial or the unhoped for. Suffice to say for clarity that Spinoza does allude to the immemorial when, for example, he remarks that "it is not possible that we should remember existing before our body" (*Ethics*, part 5, proposition 23, scholium), thus clearly hinting at what cannot be remembered from a finite perspective. This lack of memory of any preexistence is precisely what prompts this desire to intuitively shift to an eternal perspective, one for which memory and the imagination no longer play a role. I'm aware that such a parallel would of course necessitate further close readings of Spinoza's *Ethics*, and specifically of the many instances in which the past and the future are described in relation to finite and infinite modes.
4. Jacquet, *Sub specie aeternitatis*, 127 (all translation are my own).
5. Jacquet, *Sub specie aeternitatis*, 128.
6. Spinoza, *Ethics*, part 2, proposition 8, scholium.
7. Jacquet, *Sub specie aeternitatis*, 135.
8. See Spinoza, *Ethics*, part 2, proposition 40, scholium 2.
9. Spinoza, *Ethics*, part 2, proposition 40, scholium 2.

10. Jacquet, *Sub specie aeternitatis*, 135.
11. Jacquet, *Sub specie aeternitatis*, 136.
12. Jacquet, *Sub specie aeternitatis*, 136.
13. Jacquet, *Sub specie aeternitatis*, 137.
14. See Spinoza, "Letter 12 to Ludwig Meyer," in *Ethics*, 269.

## Dispensing

1. I realize that within the context of an ethics, this example is a little lame in comparison to serious crimes such as pedophilia or mass murder. The premise for such a seemingly necessary comparison is that a book on ethics invariably needs testing with extreme examples in order to validate the claims made. The reason I want to evade this kind of normative comparative hierarchy is simple. As I explored in depth in *After "Rwanda"* and tangentially in the preceding pages, mortals not only have violence at their disposal but are also violence doing. As Heidegger says, "The human being is, in one word, *to deinotaton*, the uncanniest. . . . The Greek word *deinon* and our translation call for an advance explication here . . . *deinon* means the violent in the sense of one who needs to use violence—and does not just have violence at his disposal but is violence-doing, insofar as using violence is the basic trait not just of his doing but of his Dasein." Heidegger, *Introduction to Metaphysics*, 159–60. In this way, there is no possibility of evading the fact that mortals equal violence both as a basic trait and at their disposal and this, whether they are saints or criminals. Once again, such equivalence does not invalidate normative attempts to curb one form of violence or another (inasmuch as everybody is violent and not much can therefore be done to address it). Normative ethics can only flourish with the same degree of inventiveness as that exposed by criminals. But such equivalence also calls for the recognition of what is truly at stake in this violence-doing and violence-having, namely that all mortals are givers of time, the great dispenser, and this even if they dispense, through criminal acts, the end of time to their victims. The question then is to go right at the core of this violence doing/having, a core whose temporal dimension alone (mortals, these gods being always violent) is always insufficient outside of or in abstraction from the way the three other folds operate together (cf. "Conclusion").

2. The most remarkable of which was Roma, *Unavowable Community*.

3. To name just the most popular ones: Bataille, *Accursed Share*; Nancy, *Inoperative Community*; Hardt, "Production and Distribution of the Common"; Hardt and Negri, *Commonwealth*; Harney and Moten, *Undercommons*.

4. Blanchot, *Unavowable Community*, 3.

5. Blanchot, *Unavowable Community*, 9.

6. Blanchot, *Unavowable Community*, 10 (translation modified).

7. Blanchot, *Unavowable Community*, 10–11.

8. Blanchot, *Unavowable Community*, 11.

9. Blanchot, *Unavowable Community*, 15.

10. I'm thinking here specifically of Nancy's various treatments of Blanchot's work. For an example, see Nancy, *Disavowed Community*.

11. Blanchot, *Unavowable Community*, 11.

12. Blanchot, *Unavowable Community*, 19.

13. Blanchot, *Unavowable Community*, 25.

14. Hegel, *Phenomenology of Spirit*, 19.

## Conclusion

1. In what follows, I deliberately distance myself from a number of interpretations of irony, such as Socratic irony, which is an economic technique aimed at revealing the other's lack of knowledge in order to (supposedly) advance knowledge. (See Kofman, *Socrates*). The same goes with German Romantics' version of it because their irony ultimately attempts to seek out truth. Not unlike Socrates, their technique aims to create a form of irony that posits the absolute identity of the creative self in order to unveil the absolute (see de Man, *Aesthetic Ideology*, 169). Close to the German Romantics is Kierkegaard, who equally understands irony as a technique of the subject, one that allows the poet to reveal his or her truth: the infinite amid finitude (see Kierkegaard, *Writings*, vol. 2, particularly 262). This is also the case of Walter Benjamin, for whom irony is again a technique whereby the deliberate destruction of works of art reveal not truth but rather the infinite form of its own limits (see Benjamin, "Concept of Criticism"). As this far too quick and incomplete survey shows, irony is always a technique or device. By contrast, time's irony—that is, the irony of the fourfold—cannot be understood as a revealing technique. If it were, it would be like holding "the technique of life" itself, which would be absurd because as a technique it would end up undermining itself. For a good analysis of irony as technique, see Newmark, *Irony on Occasion*.

2. As is well known—being the current mind-set of our epoch—cynicism rests on a previous belief in truth in a situation where there is no longer faith in truth. Irony, by contrast, never rests on truth, past, present, or future. On cynicism, see Sloterdijk, *Critique of Cynical Reason*.

3. For a justification for this masculine embodiment, see Mooij, *Time and Mind*, esp. 1–11.

4. On this topic, see Conche, *Pyrrhon ou l'apparence*, esp. 114–17.

5. On the fact that causality is always related to a fall, see Heidegger, *Question Concerning Technology*, 7.

6. I deliberately swap Levinas's "fecundity" with "progeny" in order to

maintain a seamlessness in the argument. I do not dispute that the difference between the two is crucial, but such a difference only makes sense within the context of a reading of Levinas's work that would go from his blistering attack on Being, to eros, and then to fecundity, without mentioning the controversies surrounding his choice of father/son relationship. Outside of this trajectory of thought, my aim is simply to focus on what time "does" over and beyond a critique of the autism of Being.

7. Levinas, *Totality and Infinity*, 268.

8. Levinas, *Totality and Infinity*, 269.

9. "The future does not come to me from a swarming of indistinguishable possibles which would flow towards my present and which I would grasp." Levinas, *Totality and Infinity*, 283.

10. Levinas, *Totality and Infinity*, 282.

11. As previously explored (cf. "Dignifying"), the notion of "life" is understood here in a Nietzschean sense: necessity imparted by physics. However, this can also be understood in a Derridean sense, as the "living present," thus giving it a stronger temporal dimension. As Derrida writes: "There is no experience which can be lived other than in the present. The absolute impossibility of living other than in the present, this eternal impossibility, defines the unthinkable as the limit of reason. . . . In the living present . . . all temporal alterity can be constituted and appear as such: as other past present, other future present, other absolute origins relived in intentional modification, in the unity and actuality of my living present. Only the actual unity of my living present permits other presents (other absolute origins) from appearing as such, in what is called memory or anticipation. . . . But only the alterity of past and future presents permits the absolute identity of the living present as the self-identity of non-self identity." The Nietzschean necessity imparted by physics is all included in this self-identity of non-self identity, that is, what knows no repose, plenitude, or presence, the "life" of the fourfold. See Derrida, *Writing and Difference*, 165.

12. Once again, this does not invalidate extrinsic values. This only highlights the necessity to always rethink and reinvent these values as part of the fourfold, in the taking place of earths and skies and not simply for the benefit of mortals, these supposed sovereign regents of Earth.

# BIBLIOGRAPHY


Alberro, Alexander, and Alice Zimmerman. *Lawrence Weiner*. London: Phaidon, 1998.

Allison, June W. *Power and Preparedness in Thucydides*. Baltimore, Md.: Johns Hopkins University Press, 1989.

Arendt, Hannah. *On Violence*. Orlando: Harcourt Brace, 1970.

Aristotle. *Posterior Analytic*. Translated by Hugh Tredennick and E. S. Forster. London: Loeb Classical Library, 1960.

Badiou, Alain. *Being and Event*. Translated by Oliver Feltham. London: Continuum, 2006.

Badiou, Alain. *Ethics*. Translated by Peter Hallward. London: Verso, 2001.

Bal, Mieke. *Double Exposure: The Subject of Cultural Analysis*. London: Routledge, 1996.

Balibar, Etienne. "Spinoza's Three Gods and the Modes of Communication." *European Journal of Philosophy* 20, no. 1 (2012): 26–49.

Balzac, Honoré de. *The Wild Ass's Skin*. Translated by Herbert J. Hunt. London: Penguin, 1977.

Balzer, David. *Curationism: How Curating Took Over the Art World and Everything Else*. Toronto: Coach House Books, 2014.

Barad, Karen. *Meeting the Universe Halfway: Quantum Physics and the Entanglement of Matter and Meaning*. Durham, N.C.: Duke University Press, 2007.

Bataille, Georges. *The Accursed Share*. Vol. 1. Translated by Robert Hurley. Cambridge, Mass.: MIT Press, 1991.

Baudelaire, Charles. *The Flowers of Evil*. Translated by James McGowan. Oxford: Oxford University Press, 1993.

Bell Farrell, Carolyn. "Curating as a Divining Process." In *Technologies of Intuition*, edited by Jennifer Fisher, 220–42. Toronto: Yyz Books, 2007.

Benjamin, Walter. "The Concept of Criticism in German Romanticism." Translated by Rodney Livingstone. In *Selected Writings, Vol. 1: 1919–1926*, edited by Marcus Bullock and Michael Jennings, 116–200. Cambridge, Mass.: Harvard University Press, 1996.

Benjamin, Walter. *Illuminations*. Translated by Harry Zorn. London: Pimlico, 1973.

Beshty, Walead, ed. *Ethics: Documents of Contemporary Art*. Cambridge, Mass.: MIT Press, 2015.

Bhaskar, Michael. *Curation: The Power of Selection in a World of Excess*. London: Piatkus, 2016.

Bitbol, Michel. *Maintenant la finitude, Peut-on penser l'absolu?* Paris: Flammarion, 2019.

Blanchot, Maurice. *The Unavowable Community*. Translated by Pierre Joris. New York: Station Hill Press, 1988.

Bloch, Ernst. *The Principle of Hope*. 3 vols. Translated by Neville Plaice, Stephen Plaice, and Paul Knight. Cambridge, Mass.: MIT Press, 1995.

Bouchilloux, Hélène. "Les Modes infinis de la pensée: Un défi pour la pensée." *Revue philosophique de la France et de l'étranger* 2, no. 137 (2012): 163–85. https://doi.org/10.3917/rphi.122.0163.

Bradley, Arthur. "God *sans* Being: Derrida, Marion and 'A Paradoxical Writing of the Word Without.'" *Literature and Theology* 14, no. 3 (2000): 299–312.

Byrne, David. "A Great Curator Beats Any Big Company's Algorithm." *New Statesman*, May 27, 2015, 7.

Caputo, John D. *Against Ethics*. Bloomington: Indiana University Press, 1993.

Caputo, John D. *The Insistence of God: Theology of Perhaps*. Bloomington: Indiana University Press, 2013.

Caputo, John D. *The Mystical Element in Heidegger's Thought*. New York: Fordham University Press, 1986.

Caputo, John D., and Michael J. Scanlon, eds. *God, the Gift, and Postmodernism*. Bloomington: Indiana University Press, 1999.

Cgercgu Usai, Paolo. "A Charter of Curatorial Values." *NFSA Journal* 1, no. 1 (2006): 1–10.

Chalier, Catherine. "Ethics and the Feminine." In *Re-reading Levinas*, edited by Robert Bernasconi and Simon Critchley, 11–47. London: Athlone Press, 1991.

Chalier, Catherine. "The Exteriority of the Feminine." Translated by Bettina Bergo. In *Feminist Interpretations of Emmanuel Levinas*, edited by Tina Chanter, 171–80. University Park: Pennsylvania State University Press, 2001.

Chalier, Catherine. *Figures du feminin*. Paris: Des Femmes: Antoinette Fouque, 2006.

Chalier, Catherine. *La Fraternité, un espoir en clair-obscur*. Paris: Buchet Chastel, 2003.

Chalier, Catherine. *Transmettre de génération en generation*. Paris: Buchet Chastel, 2008.

Chanter, Tina. *Time, Death, and the Feminine.* Stanford, Calif.: Stanford University Press, 2001.

Claudel, Paul. *Art Poétique.* Paris: Mercure de France, 1913.

Clausewitz, Carl von. *On War.* Translated by Michael Howard and Peter Paret. Princeton, N.J.: Princeton University Press, 1976.

Claxton, Susanne. *Heidegger's Gods: An Ecofeminist Perspective.* Lanham, Md.: Rowman and Littlefield, 2017.

Conche, Marcel. *Pyrrhon ou l'apparence.* Paris: Presses universitaires de France, 1994.

Crownfield, David. "The Last God." In *Companion to Heidegger's Contributions to Philosophy,* edited by Charles E. Scott, Susan Schoenbohm, Daniela Vallega-Neu, and Alejandro Vallega, 213–27. Bloomington: Indiana University Press, 2001.

Darwiche, Frank. *Heidegger, Le Divin et le Quadriparti.* Nice: Les Editions Ovadia, 2013.

Davis, Heather. "Growing Collectives: Haha + Flood." *Public* 41 (2010): 36–47.

de Man, Paul. *Aesthetic Ideology.* Minneapolis: University of Minnesota Press, 1996.

de Quincy, Antoine Quatremère. *Considérations morales sur la destination des ouvrages de l'art.* Paris: Arthème Fayard, 1989.

Deleuze, Gilles. *Expressionism in Philosophy: Spinoza.* Translated by Martin Joughin. New York: Zone Books, 1990.

Deleuze, Gilles. *Negotiations.* Translated by Martin Joughin. New York: Columbia University Press, 1995.

Deleuze, Gilles. *Spinoza: Practical Philosophy.* Translated by Robert Hurley. San Francisco: City Lights Books, 1988.

Derrida, Jacques. *The Animal That Therefore I Am.* Translated by David Wills. New York: Fordham University Press, 2008.

Derrida, Jacques. *Aporias: Dying—Awaiting (One Another at) the "Limits of Truth."* Translated by Thomas Dutoit. Stanford, Calif.: Stanford University Press, 1993.

Derrida, Jacques. "At This Very Moment in This Work, Here I Am." Translated by Ruben Berezdivin. In *Re-reading Levinas,* edited by Robert Bernasconi and Simon Critchley, 11–48. London: Athlone Press, 1991.

Derrida, Jacques. *The Gift of Death.* Translated by David Wills. Chicago, Ill.: University of Chicago Press, 1996.

Derrida, Jacques. *Margins of Philosophy.* Translated by Alan Bass. Chicago, Ill.: University of Chicago Press, 1982.

Derrida, Jacques. *On the Name.* Translated by Charles Dutoit. Stanford, Calif.: Stanford University Press, 1995.

Derrida, Jacques. *Politics of Friendship.* Translated by George Collins. London: Verso, 1997.

Derrida, Jacques. *Writing and Difference.* Translated by Alan Bass. London: Routledge, 2001.

Descartes, René. *Meditations on First Philosophy.* Translated by Michael Moriatri. Oxford: Oxford University Press, 2008.

Edwards, James C. "The Thinging of the Thing: The Ethic of Conditionality in Heidegger's Later Work." In *A Companion to Heidegger*, edited by Hubert L. Dreyfus and Mark A. Wrathall, 456–67. London: Blackwell, 2005.

Eleey, Peter. "What About Responsibility?" In *Ten Fundamental Questions of Curating*, edited by Jen Hoffmann, 113–19. Milan: Mousse, 2013.

Ewald, Johan. *Treatise on Partisan Warfare.* Translated by Robert Selig and David Skaggs. New York: Greenwood Press, 1991.

Fagenblat, Michael. *A Covenant of Creatures: Levinas's Philosophy of Judaism.* Stanford, Calif.: Stanford University Press, 2010.

Faye, Emmanuel. *Heidegger, l'introduction du nazisme dans la philosophie: Autour des séminaires inédits de 1933–1935.* Paris: Albin Michel, 2005.

Fisher, Jennifer. "Curators and Instagram: Affect, Relationality and Keeping in Touch." *Journal of Curatorial Studies* 5, no. 1 (2016): 100–123.

Foucault, Michel. *The Care of the Self.* Vol. 3 of *The History of Sexuality.* Translated by Robert Hurley. New York: Pantheon Books, 1986.

Foucault, Michel. *Ethics: Subjectivity and Truth.* Translated by Robert Hurley. New York: New Press, 1994.

Foucault, Michel. *The Hermeneutics of the Subject: Lectures at the Collège de France, 1981–2.* Translated by Graham Burchell. London: Palgrave Macmillan, 2001.

Fowle, Kate. "Who Cares? Understanding the Role of the Curator Today." In *Cautionary Tales: Critical Curating*, edited by Stephen Rand and Heather Kouris, 10–19. New York: apexart, 2007.

Goethe, J. W. von. *Faust.* Translated by David Luke. Oxford: Oxford University Press, 2008.

Guevara, Che. *Guerrilla Warfare.* Translated by Brian Loveman. Lincoln: University of Nebraska Press, 1985.

Haar, Michel. *The Song of the Earth: Heidegger and the Ground of the History of Being.* Translated by Reginald Lilly. Bloomington: Indiana University Press, 1993.

Haha. "Flood." In *Culture in Action: A Public Art Program of Sculpture Chicago*, edited by Mary-Jane Jacob, Michael Brenson, and Eva M. Olson, 88–97. Seattle: Bay Press, 1995.

Halliburton, David. *Poetic Thinking: An Approach to Heidegger.* Chicago, Ill.: University of Chicago Press, 1981.

Hardt, Michael. "Production and Distribution of the Common: A Few Questions for the Artist." *Open! Platform for Art, Culture and the Public Domain*, February 6, 2006. https://www.onlineopen.org/production-and-distribution-of-the-common.

Hardt, Michael, and Antonio Negri. *Commonwealth*. Cambridge, Mass.: Harvard University Press, 2009.

Harney, Stefano, and Fred Moten. *The Undercommons: Fugitive Planning and Black Study*. Wivenhoe: Minor Compositions, 2013.

Hatab, Lawrence J. *Ethics and Finitude: Heideggerian Contributions to Moral Philosophy*. Lanham, Md.: Rowman & Littlefield, 2000.

Hegel, G. W. F. *Phenomenology of Spirit*. Translated by A. V. Miller. Oxford: Oxford University Press, 1977.

Heidegger, Martin. *Being and Time*. Translated by John Macquarrie and Edward Robinson. New York: Harper Collins, 1962.

Heidegger, Martin. *Bremen and Freiburg Lectures (Insight into That Which Is and Basic Principles of Thinking)*. Translated by Andrew J. Mitchell. Bloomington: Indiana University Press, 2012.

Heidegger, Martin. *Contributions to Philosophy (Of the Event)*. Translated by Richard Rojcewicz and Daniela Vallega-Neu. Bloomington: Indiana University Press, 2012.

Heidegger, Martin. *Elucidations of Hölderlin's Poetry*. Translated by Keith Hoeller. Amherst, Mass.: Humanity Books, 2000.

Heidegger, Martin. *Four Seminars*. Edited by Andrew J. Mitchell and François Raffoul. Bloomington: Indiana University Press, 2012.

Heidegger, Martin. *History of the Concept of Time—Prolegomena*. Translated by Theodore Kisiel. Bloomington: Indiana University Press, 1985.

Heidegger, Martin. *Hölderlin's Hymns, "Germania" and "The Rhine."* Translated by William McNeill and Julia Ireland. Bloomington: Indiana University Press, 2014.

Heidegger, Martin. *Introduction to Metaphysics*. Translated by Gregory Fried and Richard Polt. New Haven, Conn.: Yale University Press, 2000.

Heidegger, Martin. *Mindfulness*. Translated by Parvis Emad and Thomas Kalary. London: Continuum, 2006.

Heidegger, Martin. *On Time and Being*. Translated by Joan Stambaugh. New York: Harper, 1972.

Heidegger, Martin. *Poetry, Language, Thought*. Translated by Albert Hofstadter. New York: Harper Perennial, 1975.

Heidegger, Martin. *The Question Concerning Technology and Other Essays*. Translated by William Lovitt. New York: Harper and Row, 1977.

Held, Virginia. *The Ethics of Care: Personal, Political, and Global*. Oxford: Oxford University Press, 2007.

Herder, Johann Gottfried. *Volkslieder, Übertragungen, Dichtungen*. Edited by Martin Bollacher. Frankfurt: Deutscher Klassiker Verlag, 1990.

Herodotus. *The Histories*. Translated by John M. Marincola. London: Penguin Classic, 2003.

Hodge, Joanna. *Heidegger and Ethics*. London: Routledge, 1995.

Hoffmann, Jens, and Tara McDowell. "Reflection." *Exhibitionist* 4 (2011): 2–5.

Huberman, Anthony. "Take Care." In *Circular Facts*, edited by Mai Abu ElDahab et al., 9–17. Berlin: Sternberg Press, 2011.

Hyginus, Gaius Julius. *Fables*. Translated by Mary Grant. Lawrence: University of Kansas Press, 1960.

Jacob, Wendy, Laurie Paler, and John Ploof, eds. *With Love from Haha: Essays and Notes on a Collective Practice*. Chicago, Ill.: University of Chicago Press, 2008.

Jacquet, Chantal. *Sub specie aeternitatis: Étude des concepts de temps, durée, et éternité chez Spinoza*. Paris: Classiques Garnier, 2015.

Kandinsky, Wassily. *On the Spiritual in Art*. Translated by Michael T. H. Sadler. New York: Solomon R. Guggenheim Foundation, 1946.

Kant, Immanuel. *Groundwork for the Metaphysics of Morals*. Translated by Allen W. Wood. New Haven, Conn.: Yale University Press, 2002.

Kearney, Richard, and Jens Zimmermann, eds. *Reimagining the Sacred: Richard Kearney Debates God*. New York: Columbia University Press, 2015.

Kierkegaard, Søren. *Fear and Trembling*. Translated by Alastair Hannay. London: Penguin Classics, 1985.

Kierkegaard, Søren. *Writings*. Vol. 2, *The Concept of Irony, with Continual Reference to Socrates*. Translated by Howard V. Hong and Edna H. Hong. Princeton, N.J.: Princeton University Press, 2013.

Kimenyi, Alexandre. *Kinyarwanda and Kirundi Names: A Semio-Linguistic Analysis of Bantu Onomastics*. Lewiston, N.Y.: Edwin Mellen, 1989.

King, Elaine A., and Gail Levin. *Ethics and the Visual Arts*. New York: Allworth, 2006.

Kofman, Sarah. *Comment s'en sortir?* Paris: Éditions Galilée, 1983.

Kofman, Sarah. *Socrates*. Translated by Catherine Porter. Ithaca, N.Y.: Cornell University Press, 1998.

Krysa, Joasia, ed. *Curating Immateriality: The Work of the Curator in the Age of Network Systems*. New York: Autonomedia, 2006.

Lacoue-Labarthe, Philippe, and Jean-Luc Nancy. *The Literary Absolute: The Theory of Literature in German Romanticism*. Translated by Philip Barnard and Cheryl Lester. New York: State of New York University Press, 1988.

Landow, George P. *Hypertext 3.0: Critical Theory and New Media in an Era of Globalization*. Baltimore, Md.: Johns Hopkins University Press, 2006.

Lenin, Vladimir. "Guerrilla Warfare," In *Collected Works*, Vol. 11, *June 1906–January 1907.* Translated by Clemens Dutt, 213–23. Moscow: Progress, 1965.

Levinas, Emmanuel. *Beyond the Verse.* Translated by Gary D. Mole. London: Continuum, 2007.

Levinas, Emmanuel. *Entre Nous.* Translated by Michael B. Smith and Barbara Harshav. London: Continuum, 2006.

Levinas, Emmanuel. *Existence and Existents.* Translated by Alphonso Lingis. Pittsburgh, Pa.: Duquenes University Press, 2001.

Levinas, Emmanuel. *God, Death and Time.* Translated by Bettina Bergo. Stanford, Calif.: Stanford University Press, 2000.

Levinas, Emmanuel. *On Escape.* Translated by Bettina Bergo. Stanford, Calif.: Stanford University Press, 2003.

Levinas, Emmanuel. *Otherwise Than Being or Beyond Essence.* Translated by Alphonso Lingis. Pittsburgh, Pa.: Duquesne University Press, 2004.

Levinas, Emmanuel. *Proper Names.* Translated by M. B. Smith. Stanford, Calif.: Stanford University Press, 1996.

Levinas, Emmanuel. "Revelation in the Jewish Tradition." In *The Levinas Reader*, edited by Sean Hand, 190–210. London: Blackwell, 1989.

Levinas, Emmanuel. *Totality and Infinity.* Translated by Alphonso Lingis. Pittsburgh, Pa.: Duquesne University Press, 2005.

Lévi-Strauss, Claude. "Rousseau: Founder of Anthropology." Translated by M. Layton. *UNESCO Courier*, March 1963, 13–17.

Lewis, Michael. *Heidegger and Place of Ethics.* London: Continuum, 2005.

Lorca, Federico García. *Poet in New York.* Translated by Greg Simon and Steven F. White. London: Penguin, 1988.

Lyotard, Jean-François. *The Differend: Phrases in Dispute.* Translated by Georges Van Den Abbeele. Minneapolis: University of Minnesota Press, 2002.

Lyotard, Jean-François. *Discourse, Figure.* Translated by Anthony Hudek and Mary Lyndon. Minneapolis: University of Minnesota Press, 2011.

Lyotard, Jean-François. "Les Immatériaux." In *Thinking About Exhibitions*, edited by Reesa Greenberg, Bruce W. Ferguson, and Sandy Nairne, 159–73. London: Routledge, 1996.

Lyotard, Jean-François. *The Inhuman.* Translated by Geoffrey Bennington and Rachel Bowlby. Stanford, Calif.: Stanford University Press, 1991.

Lyotard, Jean-François. *Libidinal Economy.* Translated by lain Hamilton Grant. Bloomington: Indiana University Press, 1993.

Lyotard, Jean-François, and Eberhard Gruber. *The Hyphen: Between Judaism and Christianity.* Translated by P.-A. Brault and Michael Naas. New York: Humanities Book, 1999.

Lyotard, Jean-François, and Jean-Loup Thébaud. *Just Gaming*. Translated by Wlad Godzich. Minneapolis: University of Minneapolis Press, 2008.

Mallarmé, Stephane. *Collected Poems*. Translated by E. H. and A. M. Blackmore. Oxford: Oxford University Press, 2006.

Martinon, Jean-Paul. *After "Rwanda": In Search of a New Ethics*. Amsterdam: Rodopi, 2013.

Martinon, Jean-Paul. "Between Earth and Sky." *Journal of Francophone Philosophy* 24, no. 1 (2016): 25–44.

Martinon, Jean-Paul. "Edging Disciplines." *Journal of Curatorial Studies* 6, no. 2 (2017): 221–29.

Martinon, Jean-Paul. *The End of Man*. New York: Punctum Books, 2013.

Martinon, Jean-Paul. "Im-mundus, or Nancy's Globalizing-World-Formation." In *Nancy and the Political*, edited by Sanja Dejanovic, 219–44. Edinburgh: Edinburgh University Press, 2015.

Martinon, Jean-Paul. *On Futurity: Malabou, Nancy, and Derrida*. London: Palgrave, 2007.

Martinon, Jean-Paul. "Time Unshackled." *New Formations* 89 (2017): 11–24.

Martinon, Jean-Paul. "Valentin Mudimbe or the Work of Invention." *Darkmatter* 8 (2012). http://www.darkmatter101.org/site/2012/05/18/valentin-mudimbe-or-the-work-of-invention/.

Martinon, Jean-Paul, ed. *The Curatorial: A Philosophy of Curating*. London: Bloomsbury, 2013.

Marx, Karl. *Capital*. Vol. 1. Edited by Friedrich Engels. Translated by S. Moore and E. Aveling. New York: Lawrence & Wishart, 2003.

Mattéi, Jean-François. "Emmanuel Faye, l'introduction du fantasme dans la philosophie." *Portique* 18 (2006). http://journals.openedition.org/leportique/815.

Mattéi, Jean-François. *Heidegger et Hölderlin: Le Quadriparti*. Paris: Presses Universitaires de France, 2001.

Mayer, John, James Burns, Stephanie Gaub, Brian H. Peterson, James A. Michener, and John Russick, eds. *A Code of Ethics for Curators*. Washington, D.C.: American Alliance of Museums/American Association of Museums Curators Committee, 2009.

McClellan, Andrew. *Inventing the Louvre: Art, Politics, and the Origins of the Modern Museum in Eighteenth-Century Paris*. Berkeley: University of California Press, 1999.

McNeill, William. *The Time of Life: Heidegger and Ethos*. New York: State University of New York Press, 2006.

Meillassoux, Quentin. *After Finitude: An Essay on the Necessity of Contingency*. Translated by Ray Brassier. London: Continuum, 2008.

Meillassoux, Quentin. "Contingency and the Absolutization of the One."

Translated by Benjamin James Lozano. Unpublished manuscript, March 13, 2011.

Meillassoux, Quentin. "The Immanence of the World Beyond." Translated by Peter M. Candler Jr., Adrian Pabst, and Aaron Riches. In *The Grandeur de Reason: Religion, Tradition, and Universalism*, edited by Conor Cunningham and Peter M. Candler, 438–46. Norwich: SCM Press, 2010.

Meillassoux, Quentin. "Iteration, Reiteration, Repetition: A Speculative Analysis of the Meaningless Sign." Translated by Robin Mackay. Unpublished manuscript, April 20, 2012.

Meillassoux, Quentin. *A Number and the Siren: A Decipherment of Mallarme's "Coup de dés."* Translated by Robin Mackay. London: Urbanomic, 2011.

Meillassoux, Quentin. "Potentiality and Virtuality." Translated by Robin MacKay. *Collapse* 2 (2002): 65–72.

Meillassoux, Quentin. "Temps et surgissement ex-nihilo." Lecture, Les Lundis de la philosophie. Organized by Francis Wolff. Paris: École Nationale Supérieure, April 24, 2006.

Melamed, Itzhak Y. *Spinoza's Metaphysics: Substance and Thought*. Oxford: Oxford University Press, 2013.

Mitchell, Andrew J. *The Fourfold: Reading the Late Heidegger*. Evanston, Ill.: Northwestern University Press, 2015.

Montmann, Nina, ed. *Scandalous: A Reader on Art and Ethics*. Berlin: Sternberg, 2013.

Mooij, J. J. A. *Time and Mind*. New York: Brill, 2005.

Mudimbe, Valentin Y. *The Invention of Africa: Gnosis, Philosophy, and the Order of Knowledge*. Bloomington: Indiana University Press, 1988.

Mudimbe, Valentin Y. *Parables and Fables: Exegesis, Textuality, and Politics in Central Africa*. Madison: University of Wisconsin Press, 1991.

Müller, Karl Otfried. *History of the Literature of Ancient Greece*. London: Baldwin, 1840.

Nancy, Jean-Luc. *After Fukushima: The Equivalence of Catastrophes*. Translated by Charlotte Mandell. New York: Fordham University Press, 2015.

Nancy, Jean-Luc. *The Disavowed Community*. Translated by Philip Armstrong. New York: Fordham University Press, 2016.

Nancy, Jean-Luc. *Dis-enclosure: The Deconstruction of Christianity*. Translated by Bettina Bergo. New York: Fordham University Press, 2008.

Nancy, Jean-Luc. "Heidegger's 'Originary Ethics.'" In *Heidegger and Practical Philosophy*, edited by François Raffoul and David Pettigrew, 65–85. New York: State University of New York Press, 2002.

Nancy, Jean-Luc. *L'Impératif Catégorique*. Paris: Flammarion, 1983.

Nancy, Jean-Luc. *The Inoperative Community*. Translated by Peter Connor et al. Minneapolis: University of Minnesota Press, 1991.

Nancy, Jean-Luc. "The Kategorien of Excess." In *A Finite Thinking*, edited by Simon Sparks, 133–51. Stanford, Calif.: Stanford University Press, 2003.

Nancy, Jean-Luc. "Our Probity! On Truth in the Moral Sense in Nietzsche." Translated by Peter Connor. In *Looking after Nietzsche*, edited by Laurence A. Rickels, 65–88. New York: State University of New York Press, 1986.

Newmark, Kevin. *Irony on Occasion*. New York: Fordham University Press, 2012.

Nietzsche, Friedrich. *The Gay Science*. Translated by Josephine Nauckhoff. Cambridge: Cambridge University Press, 2001.

Noddings, Nel. *Caring: A Feminine Approach to Ethics and Moral Education*. Berkeley: University of California Press, 2013.

O'Neill, Paul. *Curating Subjects*. London: Open Editions, 2007.

O'Neill, Paul, ed. *The Culture of Curating and the Curating of Culture(s)*. Cambridge, Mass.: MIT Press, 2012.

Páldi, Lívia. "Notes on the Paracuratorial." *Exhibitionist* 6 (2011): 71–76.

Pan, Lara, and Filip Luyckx. "Face to Face: Challenges of Curating Today: A Conversation." *Artpulse* 1, no. 4 (2010): 13–17.

Philbrick, Harry. "Exhibition Ethics." *NEMA*, Fall 2005, 6–7.

Phillpot, Clive. "Words and Word Works." *Art Journal* 42, no. 2 (1982): 120–24.

Plato. *The Republic*. Translated by H. D. P. Lee and Desmond Lee. London: Penguin, 2007.

Poinsot, Jean-Marc. "De Nombreux objets colorés places côte à côte pour former une rangée de nombreux objets colorés." *Artstudio* 15 (1989): 114–22.

Popova, Maria. *Curator's Code for the Internet*. 2012. https://www.brainpickings.org/2012/03/09/curators-code/.

Raffoul, François. *The Origins of Responsibility*. Bloomington: Indiana University Press, 2010.

Reckitt, Helena. "Support Acts: Curating, Caring and Social Reproduction." *Journal of Curatorial Studies* 5, no. 1 (2016): 6–30. https://doi.org/10.1386/jcs.5.1.6_1.

Roma, Valentin. *The Unavowable Community*. Bòlit: Centre d'art Contemporani, Girona, Italy, February 5–April 11, 2010.

Rorimer, Anne. "Sculpture: Figures of Structure. The Work of Lawrence Weiner." In *5 Figures of Structure*. Chicago, Ill.: Arts Club of Chicago, 1987.

Rorty, Richard. *Philosophy and Social Hope*. London: Penguin, 1999.

Ruddick, Sara. *Maternal Thinking: Toward a Politics of Peace*. Boston: Beacon Press, 1989.

Schmitt, Carl. *The Nomos of the Earth, in the International Law of the Jus Publicum Europaeum*. Translated by G. L. Ulmen. Candor, N.Y.: Telos Press Publishing, 2006.

Schmitt, Carl. *Theory of the Partisan, Immediate Commentary on the Concept of the Political.* Translated by G. L. Ulmen. Candor, N.Y.: Telos Press Publishing, 2007.

Schroers, Rolf. *Des Partisan: Ein Beitrag zur politischen Anthropologie.* Cologne: Kiepenheuer & Witsch, 1961.

Schürmann, Reiner. *Broken Hegemonies.* Translated by Reginald Lilly. Bloomington: Indiana University Press, 2003.

Schürmann, Reiner. *Heidegger on Being and Acting: From Principles to Anarchy.* Bloomington: Indiana University Press, 1990.

Schürmann, Reiner. *Wandering Joy: Meister Eckhart's Mystical Philosophy.* Great Barrington, Mass.: Lindisfarne Books, 2001.

Seneca, Lucius Annaeus. *Epistulae Morales to Lucilius.* Vol. 3. Translated by Richard Gummere. London: William Heinemann, 1953.

Shiomitsu, Takeshi. "Curation as a Practice of Negotiating the Ethics of Appropriation." M.A. essay, Goldsmiths College, London, 2016.

Sloterdijk, Peter. *Critique of Cynical Reason.* Translated by Michael Eldred. Minneapolis: University of Minnesota Press, 1987.

Smith, Terry. *Thinking Contemporary Curating.* New York: ICI, 2012.

Spinoza, Benedict de. *Ethics.* Translated by Samuel Shirley. Indianapolis, Ind.: Hackett, 1992.

Spinoza, Benedict de. *Opera quae supersunt onmia.* Edited by Carl Hermann Bruder. Lipsiae [Leipzig]: Tauchnitz, 1843–46.

Spinoza, Benedict de. *Theological-Political Treatise.* Translated by Michael Silverthorne and Jonathan Israel. Cambridge: Cambridge University Press, 2007.

Szeemann, Harald. "Does Art Need Directors?" In *Words of Wisdom: A Curator's Vade Mecum on Contemporary Art,* edited by Carin Kuoni, 160–67. New York: Independent Curators International, 2001.

Teniers, David. *Theatrvm Pictorium.* Antwerp: Apud Iacobum Peeters, 1684.

Trevelyan, Vanessa, ed. *Code of Ethics for Museums: Ethical Principles for All Who Work for or Govern Museums in the U.K.* London: Museums Association, 2008.

Tronto, Joan. *Moral Boundaries: Political Argument for an Ethic of Care.* London: Routledge, 1994.

Virgil. *Aeneid.* Translated by H. R. Fairclough. Harvard: Loeb Classical Library, 1999.

Webb, David. *Heidegger, Ethics and the Practice of Ontology.* London: Bloomsbury, 2011.

Wrathall, Mark A. "Between the Earth and the Sky: Heidegger on Life after the Death of God." In *Religion After Metaphysics,* edited by Mark A. Wrathall, 69–87. Cambridge: Cambridge University Press, 2003.

Zedong, Mao. *On Guerrilla Warfare.* Translated by Samuel F. Griffith. El Paso, Tex.: El Paso Norte Press, 2009.

# INDEX

JEAN-PAUL MARTINON is reader in visual cultures and philosophy at Goldsmiths College, University of London. He is author of *Swelling Grounds: A History of Hackney Workhouse; On Futurity: Malabou, Nancy, and Derrida; The End of Man;* and *After "Rwanda": In Search of a New Ethics.* He is editor of *The Curatorial: A Philosophy of Curating.*

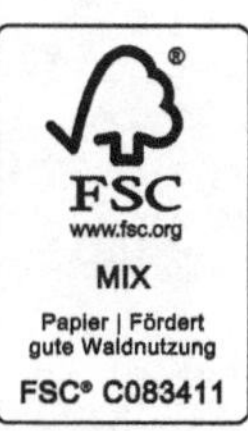


Zeitfracht Medien GmbH
Ferdinand-Jühlke-Straße 7
99095 Erfurt, Deutschland
produktsicherheit@kolibri360.de